That Book about That Girl

D1566341

When Marlo Thomas was a child her mother told her that daisies are a happy smiling flower. She has been crazy about them ever since and that was the inspiration for the name of her company, Daisy Productions.

That Book

about

That Girl

THE UNOFFICIAL COMPANION

Stephen Cole

RENAISSANCE BOOKS

Los Angeles

This book is dedicated to Marlo Thomas
and the memory of Ted Bessell

10 9 8 7 6 5 4 3 2 1

Design by Laurie Young

Published by Renaissance Books
Distributed by St. Martin's Press
Manufactured in the United States of America
First Edition

Contents

My Cast and Crew

That Girl ran for five seasons (1966–71) on ABC-TV and has been in syndication ever since 1971, when it officially shut down production. The series and the character of Ann Marie have become not only icons of the 1960s, but beacon lights for young women all over the world who want an independent life. It all began with a dream and an idea: that television *should* show a single girl living an independent life. This book would not exist without that idea.

I would like to express my deep appreciation and gratitude to the following people and organizations for their help with this, the first book about this seminal television show: Timothy Leetch at ABC-TV who provided me with all the original airdates for the series; Gail Newman, Marlo Thomas's brilliant, personable, and talented personal assistant; Michelle Mayo, who also works with Ms. Thomas at Open Road Productions.

These people have been helpful, cooperative, and delightful: Jonathan Rosenthal and Jane Klain of the Museum of Television and Radio in New York City; Stephen McDonnell, Doris Silverton, Susan L. Dworkin, and Gloria Steinem (the latter two providing me with valuable feminist insights into the series); and Leo Ziffren (Ms. Thomas's attorney and partner in Daisy Productions).

The following libraries and research centers were particularly helpful: the Billy Rose Theater Collection of the New York Public Library, and the Museum of Television and Radio (in both New York and Beverly Hills).

For their time and memories, my eternal gratitude goes to the creators of *That Girl*: Sam Denoff and Bill Persky. What a pair of funny and gentle men! And my hat is off to Ronald Jacobs, the Executive in Charge of Production, Bernie Kopell for his "appreciation" and enthusiasm, and Ann Marie's mom, Rosemary DeCamp, for so graciously taking the time to answer my letter.

And to the woman without whom there would be no *That Girl*, and certainly no *That Book about That Girl: The Unofficial Companion*, Marlo Thomas, what can I say? I love you, Marlo.

Finally, I need to thank my editor and friend, James Robert Parish, for his determination and guidance on this project, which has taken longer than it might have, but also as long as it needed to. Thanks, Jim.

That Girl and Me

It's really important to me if you're going to write a book about That Girl *that the history be accurate.*

—MARLO THOMAS, STAR OF *THAT GIRL*

I am a child of television. Growing up in Brooklyn, New York, my babysitters were Lucy, Margie, Oh Susanna (I not only thought that was her name, I also didn't know that both Margie and Susanna were pert Gale Storm), Susie and Katy (also, seemingly, twin Ann Sotherns), and all those video housewives like Harriet Nelson, Donna Stone, and Margaret Anderson (played, respectively, by Harriet Nelson, Donna Reed, and Jane Wyatt). My fascination with "our ladies of the reruns" who schemed and made me laugh knew no bounds. One day in the mid-1960s, the woman downstairs—the most bohemian person I had ever seen, despite her dark black hair which was teased and lacquered into a perfect flip with bangs—invited me to watch television with her.

"See that girl! That's gonna be me, if I ever get outta Brooklyn," she whined. "I'm young, I'm pretty, I'm an actress too! I am Ann Marie, but Jewish!"

From that day on, we watched *That Girl* together and I watched as my friend changed her hairdos and attempted to dress like Ann, despite her S. Klein taste and Woolworth budget. ("How does she get the money for those clothes, let alone the makeup? Sheesh!") Being a little boy and primarily a *The Beverly Hillbillies* (1962–71) fan, I most enjoyed the *That Girl* episodes where heroine Ann got her toe stuck in a bowling ball or got locked in a backstage elevator causing her to miss her entrance cue on opening night. (Who knew that fictional mishap was to become my recurring actor's nightmare in real life?) My adult neighbor loved what she called the powerful relationships between Ann and Donald and especially between Ann and her stern but loving father, Lou. Neither of us knew that the oncamera Ann was Marlo Thomas whose real father, Danny Thomas, was my beloved Danny Williams on *Make Room for Daddy* (1953–64), which later became *The Danny Thomas Show* (1965–69) and *Make Room for Grandaddy* (1970–71). In those innocent 1960s, who put two and two together? Certainly not me.

How I wanted to be Danny Williams (once again in rerun heaven) and my downstairs friend, of course, wanted to be Ann Marie. This was the magnetic power of television. The shaper of our dreams. Did either of us realize at the time that Ann was the first of those TV ladies to live alone and seek a career in addition to (although not in lieu of) romance? Did we know that this was the beginning of the "single girl on her own" craze on TV? Could we foresee the debt that Mary Richards of *The Mary Tyler Moore Show* (1970–77) would owe to Ann Marie? Or that we would still be enjoying these episodes today on cable's TV Land, in color? (Our own television sets at that time were black-and-white.) Of course not! We just sat back on Thursday nights (until 1970, when it moved to Fridays) and existed vicariously through Ann, That Girl, who lived just over that bridge in Manhattan.

From 1966 through 1968 we watched *Bewitched*, went to get some potato chips, and ran back to our TV sets in time to catch our girl. (In 1969 *Bewitched* and *That Girl* flip-flopped time slots and in 1970 we had to endure *The Partridge Family* first.)

That Girl was a show that seemed as if it couldn't wait to begin each episode. It started even before the opening titles. There was always a prologue in which someone (the guest star preferably) would inform someone else that they wanted *"that girl!"* The camera would swing around and we would see Marlo Thomas as Ann Marie. The music would pick up and the opening credits would begin. Earle Hagen's pizzicato strings, hesitant but determined, began the theme (in the last season there were lyrics too). This music started Ann Marie out on her freewheeling journey to stardom and fame, and swelled into a full orchestral sound signaling that she would be successful in life and love in the big city. We wallowed in the visual images of a young, miniskirted girl taking in the exciting sights of New York City (the landmarks and scenes I would soon come to know and love): Lincoln Center, Broadway, Fifth Avenue stores, shots of Broadway marquees of such then-current hits as *Cabaret* and *Cactus Flower* juxtaposed onscreen with such forgotten plays as Neil Simon's *The Star-Spangled Girl*, scenes of cars and buses and excited people. Ann seemed to embrace it all, even seeing herself as a mannequin in a store window on Fifth Avenue. The show's opening credits would end with Ann/Marlo flying a kite in Central Park as the music, the kite, and her spirits soared high above Manhattan.

After the first commercial, the story would begin from where it left off in the prologue, and we would sit mesmerized in front of the TV for the next half-hour.

I believed in the reality of *That Girl*'s Ann and Donald and Lou and Helen, and had no thought about how the show came to be, how it was made, or how it fit into the history of television. However, watching those shows again, all these years later, I am struck by how innovation and convention mixed together to make such solid entertainment. This book explores how it all came to be and how Ann and her crew forged a place in the hearts of American television viewers. She wasn't Lucy (of *I Love Lucy*) and she wasn't Margie (of *My Little Margie*). She was something new and contemporary. One part Doris Day, two parts Jean Arthur, and all parts Marlo Thomas. She was the bridge to *Murphy Brown* (1988–98) and all other modern women in the sitcoms of today. She was Ann Marie. *That Girl!*

An Appreciation

by Bernie Kopell [*]

How Could You Not Love That Girl?

It was 1968. I'd been doing *That Girl* (as neighbor Jerry Bauman) for two years. At the same time, I was playing Siegfried on *Get Smart*. Some weeks I was Jerry on Tuesday and Thursday, and Siegfried on Monday, Wednesday, and Friday. Miraculously in the five years between 1966 and 1970, there was never a conflict! In part, that was due to getting to know the assistant directors (those who made up the shooting schedules) really well, but mainly it was due to having the confidence of the *Get Smart* producers, and Marlo Thomas and her producers, that I could "deliver" on both with no loss of energy or focus.

But, I'm getting ahead of myself. In the beginning of this cycle I was very excited and grateful. What wonderful present could I get for Marlo for her birthday—a gift that would absolutely delight her and let her know how happy I was to be playing Jerry Bauman on her show? I hadn't a clue. Who would know? Ah ha! I'll ask her father, Danny Thomas.

At that time Danny Thomas, maximizing his success with *Make Room for Daddy* and combining his producing talents with Sheldon Leonard, rented just about all the stages at Desilu-Cahuenga (now

---

[*]Jerry Bauman on *That Girl*, 1966–71

Ren-Mar Studios, on Cahuenga Boulevard between Santa Monica Boulevard and Melrose Avenue in Hollywood). It was a tiny studio, compared with Universal or Twentieth Century-Fox, but it was home to an incredible number of the most successful shows on TV: *I Spy* with Bill Cosby and Robert Culp, *The Dick Van Dyke Show*, *The Andy Griffith Show* (later *Mayberry R.F.D*), *Gomer Pyle U.S.M.C.*, and *Hogan's Heroes*, among others. In fact, the historic *Dick Van Dyke Show* was filmed on Stage 8 from 1960–65. *That Girl* took over that same Stage 8 from 1966–70. In some circles the number eight is the symbol of success and money. It certainly was during those ten years.

After waiting days to get an "audience" with Danny Thomas—he was a very busy man—I was finally ushered into his office. What if he says, "Marlo would like a Ferrari or the Crown Jewels for her birthday?" I'd be committed to getting whatever he suggested. Now I was getting nervous. I explained why I was there and waited for his words of wisdom. He thought about it a minute, then turned to me with his *Make Room for Daddy* smile, held up his hand, and said, "Save your money. There's nothing you could buy for her that would mean as much as your words, expressing what you feel." After I thanked him and was on my way out, he called to me, "And she's crazy about daisies!" So on her birthday in 1968, I sent Marlo a bunch of daisies . . . and a note telling her how happy I was to be a part of *That Girl*.

....

Doing *That Girl* was heaven for me because it was the first time I got to play myself, not a character with a mustache and an accent. I was Don Hollinger's pal at work at the magazine, and my wife, Ruthie, and I lived in the same apartment building as Ann Marie. So, the show had the juxtaposition of the single girl/single couple/married couple.

It was a very happy set, because even with all the inhuman pressure on her to come up with an excellent show week after week, Marlo was amazingly responsive to the humor in every situation and knew intuitively what worked for the characters.

My wife, Catrina, and I saw Marlo at a Museum of Television and Radio Gala in 1997. I ran over to give Marlo a hug and a kiss and to introduce her to Catrina, who was very close to her due date with our son, Adam. Marlo excitedly asked when the baby was due, was it a boy or a girl, and did we have a name picked out. Then, with the same thoroughness and consideration that has marked everything she's done since I first met her, she said, "Bernie, give me your address again just to make sure I have it. I want to send you something for the baby. After all, we are extended family."

The day Adam was born, October 31, 1997 (Halloween), Marlo sent a beautiful baby quilt, hand-worked, with pictures of Noah and the Ark. I look at it every day on the wall next to his crib.

How could you not love that girl?

Flashback: That Seminar

It's thirty years. 1965—thirty-three years. The girls who were watching it were ten. So they're in their forties. But there's a lot of younger girls too, a lot of women who, when they find out that I was involved in That Girl, *[tell me] it was a turning point in their life. Because up until that point there really wasn't a show like that. There was* My Little Margie, *but she was involved with her father. There was never a case of anyone on their own.*

—BILL PERSKY, CO-CREATOR AND
CO-EXECUTIVE PRODUCER OF *THAT GIRL*

Los Angeles, October 11, 1996. The Directors Guild of America—In September 1966, ABC-TV ran its first episode of a situation comedy that would from then on change the way viewers thought of sitcom women. This October night—thirty years later—the auditorium is packed for a seminar sponsored by the Museum of Television and Radio in Beverly Hills. Everyone in the house feels the mixture of jubilation, celebration, and great sadness in the air. Everyone who helped create *That Girl* is present: Sam Denoff and Bill Persky (the creators and executive producers), Ronald Jacobs (the executive in charge of production), Edgar Scherick (the vice president in charge of programming at ABC-TV at the time), Hal Cooper (director of twenty-three of the series' 136 half-hour episodes), Alice Borden (one of the two Ruth Baumans, a sidekick on the show), Bernie Kopell (Jerry Bauman), and, of course, *That Girl* herself, Marlo Thomas.

In the audience are Tom Case (makeup man), Lynn Masters (hairstylist), Marilyn Lewis, known as Cardinelli (clothes), Eddie Foy III (associate producer/casting), Lew Gallo (another associate producer) . . . everyone one would expect, except for "That Guy," Ted Bessell.

Just five days earlier, on October 6, 1996, Ted Bessell had died of a heart attack. Rather than cancel the *That Girl* event, Marlo Thomas, along with the Bessell family, had agreed to go on with the show and make the evening a tribute to the actor as well as a celebration of the landmark TV series.

Hosting the panel is Ron Simon, curator of the Museum. He terms *That Girl* a "very influential" television show and introduces its two creators, Sam Denoff and Bill Persky, who, using the device that started every one of the 136 episodes, introduce their star, Marlo Thomas, as "That Girl!"

After a huge ovation, Marlo's warmth and sincerity fills the room. She thanks the audience and begins to talk about her late costar, calling their working relationship "intimate and irreplaceable. To this day, people stop me on the street and say, 'How's Donald?'"

Marlo goes on to state emphatically that "our show was called *That Girl*, but we all knew that *that guy* was half of its success. I worked with Teddy every day. Fourteen long hours a day for five years. He not only made them bearable, he made them hilarious. When you work with someone for that many hours and that many years, you either end up adoring them or never wanting to see them again. With Teddy and me, it was a match made in heaven."

She proceeds to tell funny stories about Teddy (as those who were close to the actor called him). How Teddy and Tom Case (Marlo's makeup man) played a practical joke on Marlo's newly hired and totally inexperienced secretary. She smiles as she recalls how the two men told the youngster to yell "cut!" whenever she wanted Marlo. The unsuspecting secretary did just that, to everyone but Ted and Tom's consternation. Marlo and the audience laugh as she introduces a compilation of TV clips from Ted Bessell's career.

"I loved him," says a visibly choked-up Marlo, "and I will miss him for the rest of my life."

On come the video clips. Myriad images light up the screen. We see Marlo and Ted at the fiftieth anniversary of the Emmy Awards. Fade in on Bessell doing scenes from *It's a Man's World* (1962–63), and sharing the screen with Anita Gillette and a monkey on *Me and the Chimp* (1972). Bleed through to Bessell doing guest shots on both *Marcus Welby, M.D.* (1969–76) and *The Greatest Show on Earth* (1963–64). Jump-cut to him playing opposite Patty Duke in *Hail to the Chief* (1985) and Mary Tyler Moore on *The Mary Tyler Moore Show.* Segue to Ted in the pilot of *Bobby Parker and Company,* in the 1981 TV movie *The Acorn People,* and finally directing Tracey Ullman on her award-winning television show.

When the lights come up, Marlo presents to the Beverly Hills branch of the Museum of Television and Radio a newly commissioned caricature of Don Hollinger by noted artist Al Hirshchfeld. It will hang alongside drawings of Ralph Kramden, Archie Bunker, and Lucy and Ethel and Fred and Ricky. And then Ms. Thomas introduces someone from the audience who also loved and worked with Bessell: Penny Marshall. After Penny lets the crowd in on the fact that she appeared on a couple of *That Girl*s as an actress ("I said, 'Who?' and they said, 'That girl'"), she begins to speak about Ted and the *Bewitched* feature film on which they were working, she as producer and he as director. A project that is not to be. "My heart's not in it," says Marshall, "if Teddy's not in it."

The seminar is divided into two parts. The first half of the evening is to be a viewing of pristine prints of two of Marlo Thomas's favorite *That Girl* episodes. When Bessell died, the original choice of segments was replaced by two of his best performances on the series, and these are shown instead. The first offering is the very first installment of the series: the show in which Ann and Donald meet, entitled "Don't Just Stand There, Do Something!" An enthusiastic house watches and laughs as Ann acts the role of a woman in distress for a TV commercial and Donald (also known on this episode as Captain Dum Dum), thinking the abduction is real, tries to save her. It is as if the audience has never seen the installment and time itself has turned back. The second offering, entitled "Anatomy of a Blunder" (episode #5), is received even more enthusiastically. The audience is enraptured as everything bad that could happen to a man on his way to meet his girlfriend's parents does occur. The expert comic timing of this farce-like episode showcases not only Bessell, but Thomas as well. It is one of the best from the long-running series and the house applauds wildly at its conclusion.

As the lights come up again in the auditorium and the screen goes blank, the panelists take their seats for the discussion and question-and-answer period. Thomas is flanked by Denoff, Persky, and Scherick. They are joined by Cooper, Borden, Kopell, and Jacobs. The memories emerge and sometimes diverge. The story of how the show began takes the form of overlapping sound bites:

Edgar was interested in doing something with Marlo. I think they did a pilot called Two's Company *first at ABC that didn't fly.*

—BILL PERSKY

ABC had no star power. So I made a commitment to Sam and Bill and Marlo.

—EDGAR SCHERICK

I saw Marlo in Barefoot in the Park *with Daniel Massey in London. She was brilliant.*

—SAM DENOFF

We wanted to call the show Miss Independence, *but Edgar said it sounded like the title of a 1935 Irving Berlin musical.*

—MARLO THOMAS

We had a meeting at the Beverly Hills Hotel.

—BILL PERSKY

It was not a fall-down funny show. It was a relationship show.

—MARLO THOMAS

TV was different then.

—BILL PERSKY

Ruth Brooks Flippen came on board when Danny Arnold hired her as story editor. It was great because now I wasn't the only one saying "a girl wouldn't say that."

—Marlo Thomas

Now TV is in the eleventh generation of cousins marrying cousins.

—Bill Persky

We had a really good time.

—Marlo Thomas

But let's not get ahead of ourselves. To really understand the impact that *That Girl* made, we need to know what came before, what she was fighting against. So let's flashback further, before Ann Marie and Donald Hollinger even met. Before *That Girl . . .*

Chapter 1

Women on TV Before Ann Marie

Mary Tyler Moore says to this day that Marlo opened the door that everybody came through. It was the first step.

—BILL PERSKY, CO-CREATOR AND
CO-EXECUTIVE PRODUCER OF *THAT GIRL*

INTO THAT KITCHEN

In the beginning, there was woman.

Well, in the beginning of TV sitcoms anyway. Right from the start of widespread commercial TV in the late 1940s, female characters took their "rightful" place on television: as mothers and wives and teachers and secretaries. On the whole, females on television in the 1950s and early 1960s can be divided into two categories: the housewives and the career girls.

Perhaps it was Peggy Wood as the fondly remembered *Mama* (1949–56) who first set the antifeminist tone and kept female characters on the small screen in their "place." Her warmth, old-world charm, and strong domination of her family (not to mention her time slot) made it clear that this career as a mother was something to which all women should aspire. Between the Norwegian Mama and the Jewish Molly of Gertrude Berg in *The Goldbergs* (1949–56), matriarchy took the forefront of television situation comedy success. Women as mothers were among the first images that television successfully presented to home viewers.

Then, in 1950, comedian Gracie Allen (with her husband/partner George Burns) entered the fold. Just as she did so successfully in vaudeville, the movies, and radio, Gracie played a scatterbrained, silly, zany housewife (albeit with her own famous name) who came out on top. Her brilliant characterization set the stage for Lucy (*I Love Lucy*, 1951–57) and her carbon copycat, Joan Davis (*I Married Joan*, 1952–55). These TV characters were women who got up in the morning (makeup already in place), cooked breakfast for their husbands (Lucy's toast always popped a foot into the air out of the toaster), cleaned the house (pushing a vacuum cleaner for about a minute), shopped for food and clothes (with whatever money George [George Burns], Ricky [Desi Arnaz], or Brad [Jim Backus] gave them), and got into very amusing scrapes and difficulties along the way, all the while, of course, retaining their femininity. Lucy, Gracie, and Joan didn't work or even seek to (although Lucy was dying to be in show business, it was for the glory of being in front of an audience rather than a need to participate in the workplace or fill her days). But they *were* funny and once in a while Lucy, at least, did seek and find work (think of the classic candy-factory scene), either to prove that she could do as well as a man or to make a few extra dollars. Still it was clear that she was a housewife, and eventually a mother, and happy to be one. Lucy's incredible success paved the way for many other housewives who continue to make us laugh.

Joan Davis as sitcom's Joan Stevens may have been a pale imitation of Lucy Ricardo (without the child, although her real-life daughter [Beverly Wills] appeared as her sister on the show), but she helped to reinforce the housewife as a zany, funny lady. Gale Storm as Margie Albright (*My Little Margie*, 1952–55) presented a younger woman who still lived with her father, Vernon Albright (Charles Farrell). Like other sitcom women of the 1950s, Margie had no ambitions beyond dating her stupid but cute boyfriend, Freddie (Don Hayden), scheming with elderly Mrs. Odetts (Gertrude W. Hoffman), or tricking her dad into sending her on a trip to Bermuda. Later, in 1957, Gale Storm did, however, cross over to the other side in the seldom re-run *Oh Susanna* (aka *The Gale Storm Show*), where she held the position of social director on a cruise ship. But as always with TV sitcom women of that time, hers was a job that was traditionally performed *only* by women.

Which brings us to consider the other type of 1950s sitcom woman: the career girl. Careers for women on TV in this period, as in real life, were quite limited. The year 1952 saw the crossover television debut of a radio favorite, *Our Miss Brooks* (1952–56). Constance Brooks was played by the stylish, acerbic Eve Arden, veteran of countless career girl/second banana roles in the movies. Now cast as the leading lady of her own sitcom, Arden played high school teacher Miss Brooks. Like many female teachers in the movies, Miss Brooks was single (most teachers in the early years of the twentieth century left teaching when they married) and looking for a man. You can bet that if Robert Rockwell as the handsome Mr. Boynton (or Gene Barry, in the 1955–56 season) had married her, she would have quit and settled down to become Joan or Lucy.

Soon Miss Brooks the career gal was joined by Susie McNamara, *Private Secretary* (1953–57), played by the incomparable "Maisie" of the movies, Ann Sothern. Susie was a secretary, that most feminine of careers (she would have been shocked to see male secretaries all over cable today). She took care of her handsome boss, New York talent agent Peter Sands (played by Don Porter), with a mixture of maternal skill and predatory sexuality. And she typed! Of course, being in the inner sanctum she had her own assistant, receptionist Vi Praskins (Ann Tyrrell), who played a quasi Ethel Mertz to her working-girl Lucy. (Susie was, in fact, acquainted with Lucy. According to a flashback in the 1957 *Lucy-Desi Comedy Hour* entitled "Lucy Takes a Cruise to Havana," it is explained that Lucy and Susie started out as secretaries together. On vacation from their jobs—this was supposedly the late 1940s and before Susie worked for Peter Sands—they took a trip to Cuba, where Lucy met Ricky, and the rest is TV history.)

When they had played out all the plots relating to Susie and show business, Susie McNamara became Katy O'Connor, the assistant manager of the Bartley House hotel in New York, on *The Ann Sothern Show* (1958–61). (Most sitcom career gals lived and worked either in New York or Los Angeles because this is where the TV industry was located.) This job was indeed a promotion for Sothern's character, but she still pursued the same man (after casting the older Ernest Truex as her boss, the producers wisely brought back Don Porter, with whom Sothern had great on-camera chemistry) as she did her daily tasks. On the last episode of the series she even persuaded him to propose to her. However, are we to assume that they married and she stayed home while he managed the hotel, or did she abandon him at the altar to marry a penniless French nobleman and show up on *The Lucy Show* (1962–68) as the Countess Framboise? Another secretary resided on CBS-TV from 1952 until 1956, when we were invited to *Meet Millie*, starring Elena Verdugo.

(In the TV world of the 1950s, African Americans were given short shrift. However, we do have at least one woman from each of the categories: the dutiful but shrill wife, Sapphire [Ernestine Wade], on *Amos 'n' Andy* [1951–53] and the wise, wily, but always-in-her-place domestic, *Beulah* [1950–53], performed by Ethel Waters, Hattie McDaniel, and Louise Beavers at different times on ABC-TV.)

Soon other white upper-middle-class housewives began to dominate the airwaves. These were softer, gentler, less abrasive types, the kind who emptied the garbage wearing their good pearls and high heels. We all remember mamas like Harriet Nelson, playing a version of herself on *The Adventures of Ozzie and Harriet* (1952–66) (if we had no idea what Ozzie did for a living, what hope was there for Harriet?); Jane Wyatt as Margaret Anderson, the perfect wife and mother who knew that *Father Knows Best* (1954–60) (today comedian Kaye Ballard does a flawlessly vicious imitation of Wyatt's sophisticated, worldly Eastern accent as she purrs, "Bu-ud, take the gaa-bage out for your faa-ther"); Donna Reed as Donna Stone of *The Donna Reed Show* (1958–66); Barbara Billingsley as the mother of "the Beaver" on *Leave It to Beaver* (1957–63); and even the young and gorgeous Mary Tyler Moore as Laura Petrie, retired dancer and New Rochelle hausfrau on *The Dick Van Dyke Show* (1961–66). Jean Hagen (1953–56) gave way to Marjorie Lord (1957–71) in the Danny Williams (Danny Thomas on *Make Room for Daddy/The Danny Thomas Show*) household, but each wife still catered to Danny. (Ironically, Louise Beavers was now Louise, Danny's maid, an unlikely promotion from *Beulah*, which was at least a "star" maid role as Shirley Booth's *Hazel* would be in the 1960s.) Danny Thomas, of course, would go on to produce *The Dick Van Dyke Show*, which was eventually written by Bill Persky and Sam Denoff, who would create *That Girl* for Danny's daughter . . . but I am ahead of myself.

Although most housewives on television tended to wear jewelry and frilly aprons in their spotless suburban kitchens, we must never forget Audrey Meadows, whose kitchen was also her living room or, as she called it, "frontierland," as the ever-suffering Alice on the mid-1950s version of Jackie Gleason's *The Honeymooners*, or her country cousins on *The Real McCoys* (1957–63) and *Petticoat Junction* (1963–70).

In the 1960s things started to change. Lucy Ricardo went away and came back as Lucy Carmichael on *The Lucy Show* (1962–68), while Ethel Mertz turned into Vivian Bagley on the same new series. Lucy was now a widow (was Ricky dead and who were these *new* kids?) and Viv was a divorcee. The gap in the two characters' ages, which seemed huge on *I Love Lucy* (perhaps due to Ethel's husband, Fred Mertz, being so old—by the way, his portrayer, William Frawley, moved on to playing, from 1960 to 1965, the grandfather, "Bub," on the male-dominated *My Three Sons*), narrowed drastically on *The Lucy Show*. Suddenly these two slightly middle-aged female characters, who had men to take care of them in the 1950s, now had to fend for themselves. They fixed things around the house, joined the volunteer fire department, and still found time to clash over dates. However, mostly, they were mothers trying to make ends meet under the Scrooge-like eye of Gale Gordon's banker, Theodore J. Mooney. Still, the characters were drawn a bit more realistically than they had been in their former incarnations. And, more importantly, *The Lucy Show* was a hit and was still captivating home viewers on Monday nights when *That Girl* premiered in the fall of 1966.

At the same time that Lucy and Viv were installing a shower and performing with Broadway star Ethel Merman (Ann Marie would do that too, but on a more professional stage), Laura Petrie was breaking new ground on *The Dick Van Dyke Show*. While she was a housewife who gave up her career as a dancer to live in the suburbs and raise a son, she was a housewife seen in tight Capri pants! Despite the prerequisite twin beds demanded by network censors of the day, Laura was perhaps the first sitcom woman who we believed had relations with her husband. Laura/Mary was sexy! The network reportedly complained about her wearing those tight, formfitting

Nobody noticed that it was revolutionary. I think that's how good revolutions start. The great advantage of our doing that show about this love affair at the time, in the middle sixties, was there was almost like those wonderful, understated love scenes in It's a Wonderful Life *[1946] between Jimmy Stewart and Donna Reed. The sexual tension was there and all that, but we didn't have to resort to all the crap that you see now about people jumping in and out of bed. It was not necessary for the comedy. The comedy was there. The relationship was there. The understanding was there.*

—SAM DENOFF, CO-CREATOR AND
CO-EXECUTIVE PRODUCER OF *THAT GIRL*

slacks on camera around the house, but she continued to wear them regularly and it was clear that her beauty had much more of a carnal aura than did Donna Reed's Donna Stone for example. In her own small way, Laura Petrie paved the way for a more realistically sexual woman to appear on the home screen. However, it would be a long time before the seeds that Laura's sexuality planted would bear fruit.

In 1964, two seasons before Ann Marie (of *That Girl* to come) left home for the big city, *Bewitched* (1964–72) made its first appearance on ABC. Following the very popular but predominately male *My Three Sons* in the network's Thursday night lineup, super-liberated Samantha Stephens was first glimpsed by the world. She was a pert woman of infinite power who wanted nothing more than to be a normal sitcom housewife and mother. She was a witch with the sex appeal of a Laura Petrie and the potential to be the world's most liberated woman. However, she chose instead to be "Donna Reed." All the forces of nature, including her mother, Endora (Agnes Moorehead), her father, Maurice (Maurice Evans), and all the other witches and warlocks of the universe conspired to make Samantha see the light and not conform to mortal standards, but Samantha chose Darren (or "Durwood," as Endora would call him) and normality. So, for the first time on the television screen, Samantha represented a woman with a choice. That she selected the cookie-cutter suburban life is not the point. What was important was that she had the freedom to pick her life's path. Samantha, with all her powers, was morphed into *I Dream of Jeannie* (1965–70). However, Jeannie (a real "genie," played by Barbara Eden) did not crave the conventional world and made trouble for her "master" (Larry Hagman) and the mortals who surrounded him.

Yet, none of these sitcom women prepared us for what Marlo Thomas would bring to a new generation of women starring on television. She would portray a female character so fresh and deceptively daring that she almost didn't make it to the small screen.

Chapter 2

The Star of Our Own Lives

Believe me, getting That Girl *on the air back in 1966 wasn't easy. Roles then available to women were mostly "the daughter of," "the wife of," or "the secretary of," but never the "of" herself. I made up my mind then that I wanted to play a single girl making it on her own.*

— MARLO THOMAS TO *NEWSWEEK* MAGAZINE IN 1973

THAT MUSCLE

In the theater they say that every show has a star or a "muscle." When Tommy Tune is involved with a musical, whether he stars in it or not, it is "a Tommy Tune show." Whether Marlon Brando starred in *A Streetcar Named Desire* (1947) or not, it was first and foremost "a Tennessee Williams play." In television one must multiply that identification by a thousand.

The muscle of *The Dick Van Dyke Show* (1961–66) was not Dick Van Dyke, but Carl Reiner. Reiner created the premise and the characters (including the lead character of Rob Petrie for himself, although the network thought he shouldn't play it), and it is through Reiner's voice that the show spoke. And *Seinfeld* (1990–98), of course, was always about Jerry Seinfeld.

That Girl was, is, and will always be about Marlo Thomas. She was both the star *and* the muscle of the show. Yes, the show was created by Sam Denoff and Bill Persky. Yes, it was produced by four of the finest TV producers. And yes, the writers included Denoff and Persky, future movie luminary James L. Brooks (known as Jim Brooks at the time), and a host of others who went on to greater fame. But it was always Marlo Thomas and her production company, Daisy Productions, that defined *That Girl*.

"The energy and the force and the whole thing was Marlo," proclaims co-creator and executive producer Bill Persky. "There's no question about it. Without her it never would have happened. Whose voice is it that's permeating it and driving the show? That's who the people will respond to. They will always respond to stars. But there also has to be a sense that there's somebody behind the consistency of a show. I also think that because we had three different sets of producers, Marlo became even more central. But it was her. The whole thing was about her and what she cared about."

The character of Ann Marie was based on Marlo Thomas's thoughts, feelings, and emotions as a young, struggling actress who yearned for independence. When ABC was looking for a program to showcase her talents, they sent her lots of unacceptable scripts. "They were old-fashioned," remembers Thomas. "And I said, this should be so easy. I mean, what about just doing a girl like me? A girl who had graduated as a teacher from college, which I had, who wanted to be an actress, as I did. Whose parents didn't want her to move out, as my parents didn't want me to move out. Whose father was terrified she was going to lose her virginity and who was always concerned [about] whether or not there were men in her apartment, which was what my father was like. And so I said, 'How about that for a premise for a show?'"

It is true that Ann Marie was not of the same social strata from which Thomas had emerged. (Marlo is, after all, the daughter of Danny Thomas, one of the biggest TV stars and producers of the 1950s and 1960s. And although Marlo was born in Detroit, she was brought up in plush Beverly Hills. In contrast, Ann Marie is small-town to the core.) Still, it must be admitted that Ann and Marlo have a great deal in common. And so to fully understand Ann Marie, we must first explore Marlo Thomas.

Mass media shapes our dreams, and television is the biggest of them all. So the show [That Girl] *has been very influential in shaping girls' dreams of what and who they could be.*

—GLORIA STEINEM, FEMINIST, AUTHOR, AND ACTIVIST

MARLO THOMAS
(Ann Marie)

Marlo Thomas wears many hats: actress, feminist, wife, stepmother, frequent flier, producer, public speaker, and multiple Emmy winner. And, of course, daughter. Born Margaret Julia Thomas in Detroit, Michigan, on November 21, 1942, this perky actress, the daughter of showbusiness tycoon Danny Thomas and former band singer Rosemarie, was raised in Hollywood. She has a brother, Tony (a very successful TV producer), and a sister, Terre. They have always been a close-knit family, and the 1991 death of her father (who made two appearances on *That Girl*) was very hard on Marlo.

Although she was surrounded by a high-profile world of theatricality in her youth, she did not have a totally idyllic childhood. "The real disadvantage was not having my parents there when I wanted them," remembered Thomas in an interview. "My father worked in nightclubs so they traveled a lot, and my sister, brother, and I were left home with staff and relatives. It made me appreciate the telephone." Marlo did not begin acting until after graduating from the University of Southern California with a B.A. in teaching. In fact, she aspired to being a teacher at first. "A teacher, like an actress," Thomas wrote in a college paper, "gets her audience prepared, so she can zing in her message or tell a story."

But acting must have been in Marlo's blood. When she was six years old, her father introduced her on stage to a Miami nightclub audience, and little Marlo (her mispronunciation of the nickname Margo) got up and sang "Ain't We Got Fun." She was a hit! After college, Marlo made up her mind to follow in her father's footsteps and at first she found the going rough:

"As far as being an actor and following a famous parent, the biggest disadvantage is that you aren't allowed to fail anywhere. People are watching you too soon. Even when I was doing summer stock, people were writing reviews of me in Variety *[the showbusiness newspaper often referred to as the industry's Bible] because they wanted to see what Danny Thomas's daughter was doing. It gives you too much spotlight too soon. You need the freedom to make a lot of mistakes before you get to be any kind of an artist. I kept looking for places to hide. I went to London, where I had my biggest success at that time—Barefoot in the Park [1965]. It's like everybody expects the boss's kid to be a fool; they expect stars' children to be ungifted. Everyone expects you to be some kind of idiot. There is not the impulse to believe that the offspring of talented people will be talented."*

But soon Marlo's career began to blossom, and in the early 1960s she made appearances on such TV series as *The Many Loves of Dobie Gillis, Dick Powell's Zane Grey Theater* (playing opposite her father), and *Thriller.* Her first major break came when she was cast as Stella Barnes, Joey Bishop's sister and an aspiring actress on the 1961–62 season of the sitcom *The Joey Bishop Show* (1961–65). Coincidentally, although they never wrote any episodes in which Marlo appeared, two of the writers of that show were the future *That Girl* creators, Sam Denoff and Bill Persky. After she left that program, Marlo made guest appearances on such shows as *Bonanza, McHale's Navy, The Donna Reed Show,* and *Ben Casey.* She made her theater debut in 1960 appearing with Fay Bainter in *Black Chiffon* at the Santa Barbara Playhouse, costarred with Fifi D'Orsay in *Gigi* in 1961 at the Laguna Beach Summer Playhouse, and starred at the Civic Playhouse with Ron Harper in *Sunday in New York* in 1963, which was produced by Alan Carr and featured future *That Girl* cast members Bobo Lewis and John Aniston. It was on the stage that Marlo gained a lot of recognition, both good and bad.

This period was creatively frustrating for Thomas. It was during this time that she was devastated by a review that read, "She's good, but who knows if she'll ever be as good as her father Danny Thomas?" Marlo went to her dad and said, "I'll never be me, Marlo. I'll always be compared to you." He said, "I raised you to be a thoroughbred. And thoroughbreds don't look at the other horses. They wear blinders. And they run their own race."

Marlo says, "This was the best advice I ever got in my life. And it's what I've always tried to do . . . run my own race."

Thomas says that she found her inspiration from strong women. "Katharine Hepburn [was a role model], because she was single and independent and feisty, and a wonderful actress on stage as well as in films," Thomas pointed out in an interview. "I always admired her growing up." Another role model for Thomas was her Italian (her mother's mother) grandmother. "All of my *Free to Be* . . . stuff came out of her. She really said to me, by her example, at a very young age that you don't have to be tied down to any stereotypes," said Thomas.

When it came time to help create the character that would immortalize her, Thomas turned to these inspirations.

"When I was a girl growing up, my father used to show us a movie every Friday night and the ones he showed us were usually directed by Preston Sturges and Frank Capra. Jean Arthur, Carole Lombard, Katharine Hepburn were all in those movies. Strong, funny, sassy women. I certainly was that personally. And I wanted to play that. I wanted *That Girl* to be those things."

For five seasons on ABC, *That Girl* was just that and Marlo Thomas became a household name.

THAT BIG BREAK

ABC said, "Gee, I don't know, you know, a woman on her own?" . . . I said, "The Fugitive [1963–67] was on his own. Forget about a family, he didn't even have a city! He went from city to city and it was okay for a guy. Why isn't it okay for a female?"

—MARLO THOMAS

In the mid 1960s, ABC-TV had its eye on Marlo Thomas. Network executives Edgar Scherick and Len Goldberg saw something in her that they were positive could translate into a hit sitcom. As Ron Jacobs, the executive in charge of production on *That Girl* (and Marlo's cousin) has said, "One of the rules in this business is, if you can find an attractive woman who can do comedy, she will become a star." ABC, in the person of Edgar J. Scherick, agreed.

Educated at Harvard, where he got a B.A. and graduated magna cum laude, Scherick first worked for the Dancer-Fitzgerald Sample advertising agency in 1953. He went from advertising into TV in 1955 and helped to create ABC's *Wide World of Sports* in 1957. After a stint in the ABC sales department, Scherick was promoted to vice president in charge of programming. And he was committed to finding a vehicle for Marlo Thomas.

But *That Girl* was not Marlo's first attempt.

She came to Scherick's attention via a near miss, a pilot for Universal called *Two's Company.* Marlo Thomas remembers the experience very well.

"There was a pilot at Universal being done by a man named Peter Tewksbury, who was quite a brilliant writer/director. He had done a wonderful show, coincidentally with Teddy Bessell, called *It's a Man's World* [1962–63]. He was a very gifted fellow and he had this darling show called *Two's Company* [1965]. It was about a young married couple . . . they had been married about eight days or something and she was a model. The photographer was played by Paul Lynde, and the groom was a young man named Ron Hussman. Anyway, I was dying to get the part and I had to screen-test for it. I'll never forget the day I went. It was five blondes and me and I thought, 'I'm never going to get this. They obviously want a blonde!'"

"Anyway, I screen-tested and I got the part. We did the pilot and it was quite good. It almost sold, but it didn't sell."

In viewing the unsold *Two's Company* pilot today, one is struck by the ease and natural warmth that Marlo Thomas brings to the role of Caroline Sommers. The plot (created and written by A. J. Crothers and directed by Peter Tewksbury) concerns a newly married couple, who rather resemble Neil Simon's characters in Marlo's soon-to-be London hit stage comedy, *Barefoot in the Park.* In this pilot test installment, the wife has obviously given up her career as a model to be an old-fashioned homemaker. However, when her husband quits his job, she secretly goes back to work. She pretends to be pregnant to win a modeling job and then the usual sitcom complications ensue.

Our first glimpse of Thomas (it was shot in black-and-white) comes as she romantically lights candles for an intimate dinner with her husband, Bob. Physically, she is the same Marlo Thomas that the world will come to love as TV's Ann Marie. The trademark flip hairdo with bangs is already in place ("That was my hairdo"). The makeup was perhaps a bit more subdued than the glamorous Ann Marie would use, but watching the show today, she is immediately and delightfully recognizable. Her sense of comic timing is already apparent and she plays off old pros like Paul Lynde and Anne Jeffries with the ease of someone twice her age. However, it is in the warmly sincere scenes with Ron Hussman (best known for his Broadway musical performances in such shows as *Fiorello*, *Tenderloin*, *On the Town*, *All American*, and *Irene*), as her husband, that she shines. It is very clear why Ed Scherick and the other ABC executives saw something special in Thomas.

Ron Jacobs remembers screening the pilot at the time and recalls that Marlo was "damned good in it."

But in January of 1965, with the pilot unsold, Marlo Thomas was just one more hopeful actress looking for the big break.

Then, one day, "I got a call from my agent that the head of the network, Edgar Scherick, wanted to see me. So I went to see him, of course. And he said, 'Look, the show didn't sell, but we believe at ABC that you can be a television star.'"

Scherick remembers the meeting and his excitement about her performance in the shelved *Two's Company*. "There was sparkle to Marlo, even on that unsuccessful pilot," he recalled at the 1996 *That Girl* seminar at the Museum of Television and Radio in Beverly Hills. "There really was. There was a sparkle. So we proceeded to make an arrangement, which was that she was going to find a show for her. Scherick believed wholeheartedly that with the right vehicle, Thomas could be a star."

Obviously Scherick had shown the unsold pilot to prospective sponsors, because one of them, Bristol-Myers (which was the parent company for Clairol hair products), became very interested in Marlo Thomas and was instrumental in taking her acting career to its next logical step.

"Marvin Koslow was the head of Bristol-Myers and Clairol, and he saw a chance to sell shampoo products and hair products," recalls Thomas. "He needed a young woman to sell them. There weren't any young women on television, there was *Our Miss Brooks* and Loretta Young. They said, 'We're going to be looking for a project for you and you should look too.'"

Naturally, Thomas was elated. With Clairol's blessings, the network sent her scripts and pitched ideas, none of which were to her liking. Finally, after reading through dozens of bad notions, she thought of the idea of doing a show about the kind of person she really was—a young, aspiring actress who abandons the nest and moves to New York City to become independent. She even had a title for it, *Miss Independence*, a nickname her father had given her when she, in real life, left home to be an actress.

"From day one, I had tried to talk her out of an acting career," wrote Danny Thomas in his autobiography, *Make Room for Danny* (1992). "I told her I didn't want her to have to suffer the heartbreak and rejection I had seen so many times with young women trying to make a go of it in my profession. On the day when she came home from her commencement, Marlo steered me into my office at home. She threw her diploma down on my desk and said, 'This is for you. Now, how do I become an actress?' I told her that I'd do all I could to give her the proper advice. 'Dad, I want to leave home and go out on my own. I don't even know how to open a can of sardines. I've been too sheltered and protected. I've got to become more independent.' That's when I started calling Marlo, 'Miss Independence.'"

When Marlo got her first apartment, she called her father in a panic, "Daddy, it's terrible! The place is overrun by ants!" Danny screamed to his wife, "Rosemarie! Miss Independence has ants." Marlo thought her father's nickname was the perfect title for her sitcom idea.

Despite her enthusiasm, the network was scared of her show idea. After all, there had never been anything like it before on American TV.

"They felt it was way too dangerous to show a young woman without a family unit," recalls Thomas. "In fact, when we first talked about doing it, they wanted me to come to New York [in the story line] and live with my aunt. Or bring my six-year-old brother with me. And I said, 'But that isn't the way girls go to New York to be an actress. They don't go to live with their aunt or bring their little six-year-old brother with them. What parent lets you bring your six-year old brother?' I said, 'The whole importance of this is the fact that she's an independent girl who wants to make it on her own in the big city.' I had to fight really hard not to be attached. Not to be married or engaged. Or living with a family member. Or living in a dorm. But to live in my own apartment. It was a major battle."

In 1965, when Thomas brought this revolutionary idea to ABC, the world was changing for women. By then, not every girl wanted to get married right out of high school or college. Girls and women were finding out that there was more to life than keeping house and having babies. Marlo Thomas was one of these liberated, forward-thinking women.

"I can't remember when the women's movement wasn't a part of my life," said Thomas in an interview with Susan L. Dworkin of *Ms.* magazine in the mid-1980s. When asked how she first became committed to feminism, Thomas replied, "Growing up as a girl made me a 'feminist.' Of course, I didn't know that was the name for how I felt. The low expectations . . . limited life choices . . . stereotyping. When I became an actress, all my feelings were confirmed. I mean, nobody knows better than an actress what it feels like to be put down because you're a woman."

Thomas's friend, well-known feminist author, Gloria Steinem remembers how "the weaker sex" was perceived at the time Thomas was attempting to sell her revolutionary idea.

"We were just emerging from the Kennedy era, so I think the parameters of women's roles were marked by Jackie Kennedy and the pillbox hat on the one side and the various sixties stereotypes on the other. From the seriousness of the civil rights movement, which had not really been absorbed by the media, to the beginning of disco and the kind of frivolous, glamorous image. But the women's movement per se was not a public event yet. The image of women on television, which is always about fifty years behind real life, was really very inaccurate. I think there were no divorced women on television. I believe you had to be a widow in that era. And there were no shows about women alone."

Marlo Thomas meant to remedy that omission. She kept at Edgar Scherick. She remembers telling him, "I don't want to be the wife of somebody or the secretary of somebody. I want to be the 'somebody!' I want to play the person about whom the story is. Who's not an appendage to anything. In our lives we don't feel like anybody's appendage. We always feel like we're the star of our lives. We're our life. I want to do a show like that."

Scherick still had his doubts, but "the next time we met," continues Thomas, "I brought him a copy of *The Feminine Mystique* (1963) by Betty Freidan. I said, 'Please read this, this is what's happening in this country.' And I've always loved Edgar Scherick, to this day, because he *did* read it. And he called me, and the first thing he said was, 'Is this gonna happen to my wife?' I said, 'I don't know, but that's what's happening. It's not about what used to be. It's not about your mother and your wife and my mother. This is about what's happening to women in their teens and their twenties now. And if you want to reach them, you have to tell this.' So he said, 'Okay.'"

Thomas was both thrilled and amazed that her first hurdle had been successfully negotiated. Now she needed the writers to make her vision a reality. She turned to her friends Sam Denoff and Bill Persky.

THOSE CO-CREATORS:
SAM DENOFF AND BILL PERSKY
(Creators, Writers, and Executive Producers)

The duo who would be so instrumental to the success of *That Girl* met in 1955 while working at local New York radio station WNEW. Both were in their early twenties. Persky was in publicity and promotion, and Denoff was in copy and continuity. They joined forces and began writing jokes. Hanging around the Catskill comics at Grossinger's resort hotel (Persky's sister was the daughter-in-law of the owner), they sold a few of their jokes. In 1961, Hollywood beckoned and they began writing comedy for some of television's top programs and personalities: *The Joey Bishop Show* (1960–65), *The Bill Dana Show* (1963–65), a Danny Thomas special, Steve Allen, Andy Williams, and others. They won an Emmy Award for writing *The Andy Williams Show* in 1963.

Their first big industry break came when Carl Reiner, who created and wrote most of the episodes for *The Dick Van Dyke Show*, liked their work. He promptly commissioned them to write as many *Van Dyke Shows* as they could. They were rewarded with two Emmy nominations and full-fledged careers.

They were friendly with Marlo Thomas. "They were part of a group of young, creative friends who played charades and hung out."

When she approached them about what was then called *Miss Independence*, they jumped at the chance to create their own show and to become executive producers. They stayed with the series for its entire five-year run, concurrently writing and producing other TV projects, like *The Sid Caesar Special, The Bill Cosby Special*, and two Dick Van Dyke specials. For their work during in this period Persky and Denoff won two Emmys, for *The Sid Caesar Special* and *The Bill Cosby Special*.

In 1971, they wrote and produced Goldie Hawn's first TV special, entitled *Pure Goldie*. (They had discovered and cast her in their short-lived sitcom *Good Morning, World*, 1966–67.)

After twenty-one years as partners, they mutually agreed to split in the early 1970s, and Persky produced, directed, and wrote an NBC-TV pilot for Ted Bessell, called *Bobby Parker and Company* (1974), while Denoff tried to launch a successful sitcom for Don Rickles. Neither project flew.

Persky went on to create, write, direct, and produce *Kate & Allie* (1984–89), which is a direct descendent of *That Girl*. Both men remain active in television today.

THAT PILOT

Sammy and I had been part of Danny Thomas's stable, so [Marlo] had seen us over the years and seen our work. And when the time came to pick who she wanted to be involved with, she selected us and it was logical that we go along with it.

—BILL PERSKY, CO-CREATOR AND
CO-EXECUTIVE PRODUCER OF *THAT GIRL*

We really were impressed with her, so we sat down and started to figure out what to do. A single girl on her own, wanting to be independent and trying to be an actress. I don't remember that there were any other premises, because that's what she wanted to do. That's what she really was doing— single in New York.

—SAM DENOFF, CO-CREATOR AND
CO-EXECUTIVE PRODUCER OF *THAT GIRL*

With the go-ahead from ABC to do a TV pilot and a commitment to air the results, Thomas didn't have to look too hard for who she wanted to create and write the project.

"I used to play charades with Bill [Persky] and Sam [Denoff], which is how I knew them. I didn't choose them because they worked for my father, I wanted them because they were my friends and they were very talented. I played charades with them at least once a week and they got a big kick out of me. I went to them and I said, 'Look, I have this opportunity, would you be interested in writing it?' We sat down and talked about it and they said, 'Yeah!' They wanted to do their own show. They hadn't had their own show. Because *Dick Van Dyke* was Carl's [Reiner] show. And so this would be created by them."

One of the first things to change was Thomas's title, *Miss Independence.* "Edgar Scherick said it sounded like a 1930s Irving Berlin musical," recalls Thomas. Denoff remembers, "We didn't like that title. It sounded like a Broadway show: *1776.*" Nonetheless, the title seems to have stuck with the show at least until December of 1965. In the *Playbill* for the London production of *Barefoot in the Park*, Thomas refers to her new show as *Miss Independence.* However, in the December 29, 1965, issue of the *New York World-Telegram*, gossip columnist Sheilah Graham refers to the series as *That Girl.* Perhaps the title didn't change until the pilot was officially sold.

But the one thing the team agreed on was Thomas's premise. "Bill and Sam really got that show," says Thomas. "They really understood that this was like a bird flying from the nest. And she wasn't afraid to fly—her parents were afraid for her to fly. That's the conflict." And it was original. As Thomas told the press in 1966, "The single girl is a subject that television has avoided."

In early-to-mid 1965, Denoff and Persky began to refine the idea and develop the characters and situations that would turn a great idea into a solid pilot that would sell: a show eventually called *That Girl.* But where on earth did they come up with that title?

"The fact is there were a lot of things to get across in the pilot," remembers Persky. "Before you even met her, you had to know her parents, you had to know her boyfriend, you had to know what she was doing . . . and that exposition is so weird, so I said let's write three little vignettes that show different sides of her. My parents always referred to my sister [Bunny Persky Grossinger, widow of Paul Grossinger, son of the founder of the famous resort in New York's Catskill Mountains] as 'that girl.' It was always an exasperated phrasing: 'That girl is just doing this and that girl is just doing that.' So I said, we'll do a scene with her parents that shows her from college, and they will end up saying, 'Oh, she's really something, that girl.' And then a scene with her agent who's trying to sell her and he says, 'She's beautiful, she's wonderful, she's an exciting talent, she's new, she's fresh . . . you can't go wrong with *that girl!*' And then there was the scene in the restaurant where the guy said, 'Where's my waitress?' and then he said, '. . . *that girl!*' And in just about forty seconds, we said everything that we had to say. Then push-in-zoom shot and all of that. So it was done as a device. Marlo loved that. And I said, 'We can't do this every week.'"

But they did do it every week. "Sometimes with quite a stretch. So the show became *That Girl* and the device became the signature." Thomas agrees, "We thought we'd do it once or twice, but we wound up doing it a hundred and thirty-six times!"

Thomas remembers handing her pet project over to Denoff and Persky with confidence. "They went off and wrote the script. They wrote the pilot. And then we had a lot of conversations about it." Thomas was not concerned about Denoff and Persky understanding her character. She trusted and knew that "Bill and Sam were really writing a woman of that time. Don't forget, they were married to young women who were my age. Billy was married to an actress, Sam was married to a dancer . . . these were also young women who were struggling and out there and living in their own apartments. It was my whole generation of young women. This is what we were all living."

In mapping out the pilot, one of the first things Denoff and Persky did was to christen their independent lead character "Ann Marie." Although a *TV Guide* article at the time said that the name was a combination of Thomas's real-life parents' names, D*anny* and Rose*marie* Thomas, neither Thomas nor Persky and Denoff remembers it that way at all. But although they didn't mean it that way, in retrospect, Marlo Thomas wishes she had come up with that idea to "pay homage [to her parents], but Billy made that name up. He came up with the name because they thought it was funny to have two first names. And they used it all the time: 'Ann Marie, that *is* my last name.' I must have said it a hundred times."

"I know we liked the idea of a double name. Annie and, in moments, Ann Marie. It's funny, it's such a popular American name now." Denoff agrees, "Billy and I just thought of that. We were kicking names around. I remember we said, 'Marie, I don't know, does it sound like a last name?' We had seen a name something like it. You say, 'That's a good first name, that's a good last name.' You try to think of a name that nobody's going to sue you. We took a disadvantage and made a virtue of it."

Having two first names became a large part of the plot of the pilot they were writing, which was about Ann contemplating a name change.

It was clear from the start that Ann would have an overprotective father and a loving mother, but should she, the creators wondered, have a succession of boyfriends, neighbors, pals, and so forth? Gloria Steinem jokingly recalls that Thomas "wanted to have a new boyfriend every week!"

"We were sure, if you can be sure of anything, that she should have a significant other, a boyfriend," says Denoff. "Because we learned from the geniuses, like Sheldon Leonard and Carl Reiner, that if a main character has responsibility to someone, they're funnier. They're just funnier. Because if you just go off by yourself and do what you want, there are no consequences. Lucy wasn't as funny when Desi wasn't there. Nor was Ralph Kramden or any of those comedy stars. They need somebody that they're afraid of. Same with Dick Van Dyke. We had her father, but he wasn't there all the time. So therefore Donald, a contemporary, was a logical choice. We wanted to have her have a boyfriend."

Persky agrees: "Donald was the most important relationship. The best shows are the romantic comedies, [such as] *Mad about You* [1992–99]. You know what? *All in the Family* [1971–83] was a romantic comedy. When Jean Stapleton left [in 1980], goodbye show! While he [Archie Bunker] was going and raging and screaming, people were just waiting for that thing to come out of her mouth. And that's what this was too. That's why we insisted on having the regular boyfriend. We said, 'What is it going to be, one schmuck after another?' No. It's boring. That's why it was very important that she had Donald. The constants were Donald and her neighbors and her parents (because her jobs were always changing) and the rest of it, all the other bizarre characters you meet out there in the world, that's fine. That's the career."

And so Ann Marie, like most young girls, had a father and a mother and a boyfriend. A boyfriend who was also her agent and, for some reason, was portrayed in the pilot as a Native American.

CASTING THE PILOT

The casting of any production is difficult, but knowing that you are casting roles that may be played for many years on a television series must be excruciatingly difficult.

Co-executive producer Sam Denoff concurs. "I hate casting. The only part that was written for an actor was Ann Marie. Every other part was casting, which is always difficult. And rewarding, because you make discoveries. It's also painful because you hate turning people down. It's more painful when you know people stink. Billy and I had a fictitious bakery. . . . When someone came in that we knew was not an actor we said, 'Let's put this person probably in the bread section.' You try to be kind. I murder casting people who are snotty to actors. I just kill them. They are terribly vulnerable people. Network people do that. They have these readings where they keep schlepping people in front of this jury. I say to them, 'Don't be a jury, you have to be nice. These people will do better for you.'"

There were several characters to cast in the pilot, but the two most crucial would be the men in Ann Marie's life—her father, Lou Marie, and her boyfriend/agent, Don Blue Sky. Of course, after screening the actors and sifting through the ones who were totally wrong for the roles, it was essential to have them read with Marlo Thomas to see if there was what the experts call "chemistry."

"I read with a lot of people," recalls Thomas. "First of all, the guys [Denoff and Persky] would go through them and have me read with the finalists."

One of the finalists for the coveted role of Don was Ted Bessell.

Thomas remembers: "I immediately felt the chemistry with Teddy and also he was funny and he was off-center. I loved him. I loved working with him. He had been on *It's a Man's World* and we had interviewed a lot of guys. They came in and read with me. We had a lot of really wonderful guys come in. There was Bill Bixby, who was great. [Bixby was famous for his roles in *The Courtship of Eddie's Father* and *The Incredible Hulk,* and Thomas had appeared on his sitcom *My Favorite Martian.*] A lot of lovely guys came to read. It wasn't that they weren't good. It's just that Teddy had a soul and a sweetness, as a human being. And it just exuded through his face."

So Ted Bessell was cast as Don Blue Sky.

TED BESSELL
(Don Blue Sky, later Don Hollinger)

Born in Flushing, New York, on March 20, 1935, Ted Bessell was originally gearing up for a career as a classical musician. As a twelve-year-old child prodigy, he performed a piano recital at Carnegie Hall.

However, after graduating from college in 1958, Bessell focused on acting. In 1962 he played college student Tom-Tom DeWitt on the one-season TV series *It's a Man's World.* In the mid-1960s he was regularly featured on *Gomer Pyle, U.S.M.C.* Ted also appeared in such feature films as *McHale's Navy Joins the Air Force* (1965) and *Don't Drink the Water* (1969) with Jackie Gleason.

Ted's best-known TV role was unquestionably as Donald Hollinger—Marlo Thomas's boyfriend—on the hit series *That Girl.* The show began its successful five-year run in 1966.

After *That Girl,* Bessell tried his hand at yet another sitcom, *Me and the Chimp* (1972), in which he played opposite a primate. It was not until the mid-1970s that he played another classic TV role: Joe Warner, the boyfriend Mary Richards was most likely to marry on *The Mary Tyler Moore Show* in its last TV season.

In the 1980s, Bessell appeared in several TV movies, including *Breaking Up Is Hard to Do* (1979) and *The Acorn People* (1981). He also played regular roles on a pair of unusual sitcoms, *Good Time Harry* (1980) and *Hail to the Chief* (1985, as husband to Patty Duke), but both of these programs failed to catch on with home viewers. Incidentally, the latter show was produced by Marlo's brother, Tony Thomas.

Bessell moved into directing, helming episodes of *The Tracey Ullman Show* (1987–90) and *Sibs* (1991–92). In 1989, he shared an Emmy as a producer on Fox Television's *The Tracey Ullman Show*, which was honored as best variety or comedy program.

Sadly, on October 6, 1996, Ted Bessell passed away in Los Angeles. He was sixty-one, and had been preparing to direct the big-screen version of the TV series *Bewitched* (1964–72), the show which was the original Thursday night lead-in on ABC-TV for his most lasting acting triumph. Ted was also in discussions with Marlo Thomas about a *That Girl* reunion telefeature which he would direct and also star in as, once again, Don Hollinger.

....

Casting for *That Girl* was completed with the prime roles of Lou and Helen Marie going to Harold Gould and Penny Santone. Jack Ellinson (who had written and would write many episodes of the 1960–68 TV series *The Andy Griffith Show*) was to produce the show, and Jerry Paris (director of many episodes of *The Dick Van Dyke Show*, as well as the actor who played next-door neighbor Jerry the dentist in that series) was set to direct. (In the July 16, 1965 issue of *Variety*, it had been announced that Carl Reiner would direct *Miss Independence*, which proved to be merely a rumor, not fact.) Ron Jacobs remembers that Paris was second choice. "Nobody knows this, but I called Dick Crenna (Richard Crenna, best known as an actor in such sitcoms as *Our Miss Brooks* and *The Real McCoys*) in Thailand and asked him to direct it. But he was doing a movie and wasn't available."

With the staff and cast in place, shooting was soon to begin on the pilot episode of *That Girl*, entitled "What's in a Name?" But, first, several other business and artistic matters needed to be settled.

The Characters and the Actors Who Created Them, Part One

The Leads

That Girl revolves around Ann Marie. All the characters are related to Ann in some way, and the way they are associated creates the comedy and drama of the series. Although it is a comedy, the characters are more realistically drawn than those on other sitcoms of that time, like *Bewitched* (1964–72) or *I Dream of Jeannie* (1965–70). Lou Marie, for example, on *That Girl* may have some things in common with Endora (Samantha's mother) on *Bewitched,* but in the long run he would never turn Donald into a toad, even if he had the power. People learn lessons on *That Girl* and they grow emotionally.

The four main characters in *That Girl* are Ann, her boyfriend, Donald (he appears in nearly every episode with her), her father, Lou, and her mother, Helen.

Ann Marie

"Diamonds, daisies, snowflakes . . ."

These words don't even begin to describe the character of Ann Marie. The first thing we see is the outer image—a fresh face with big eyes shaded by long, lush lashes and framed by shiny, dark, teased hair with bangs, hair that falls to her shoulders in a graceful flip. In other words, Ann Marie has the image of the perfect 1960s New York City working girl.

Ann is in her early twenties when the series debuts in the fall of 1966. She is fresh out of Brewster College and ready to make good as an actress in the big city. She is Miss Independence. An only child, Ann has been sheltered until now by her loving but overprotective father, Lou, and coddled by her sweetly traditional and wise mother, Helen. It is no wonder she is a bit naïve. She is also very enthusiastic and optimistic. Ann seldom gets depressed, but forges on through every obstacle. She has seen her mother take a backseat to her father's career and find contentment as a homemaker in Brewster, New York.

Ann has decided to be something new: a woman who will support herself and make her own way in the world. In other words, more like Daddy than like Mommy. Ann is a feminist before they coined the term.

Her wardrobe and apartment reflect that she is a woman of both taste and resourcefulness. She must shop at very fancy thrift stores to be able to afford all the clothes and shoes and hats and purses that she obviously relishes. Her apartment is more modest than her wardrobe: Three rooms on the East Side of New York, with a nice-sized living room/dinette area, a spacious (for Manhattan) modern kitchen, and a bedroom, plus, of course, a bathroom. From what we see of the bathroom, there is a sizeable stall shower. Inexplicably, there is a false fireplace that lets one see from the living room into the bedroom. The apartment is nicely decorated, but it's not too chic. It resembles the living space that an actress of her standing might have.

Among the highlights of Ann's career are understudying a famous Broadway actress and playing a murdered bank teller on a TV show. Her most embarrassing professional moment occurs when she opens her eyes while playing a corpse on live TV. Between acting gigs, Ann accepts a wide assortment of temporary jobs, including door-to-door shoe salesperson, dramatic-monologue-spouting roving model at Sardi's restaurant, perfume salesclerk at Macy's, and waitress.

Ann is very sentimental and, despite her independent streak, requires constant love and approval. She gets both, not only from her parents, but also from her steady boyfriend, Donald Hollinger. As the TV series progresses we see Ann grow from a slightly scatterbrained young woman to a truly liberated woman who is sincerely in love with Donald, but is unwilling to abandon her career and life to him. Ann sees herself as Donald's equal. By the time the series goes off the air, she is no longer That Girl—she is That Woman.

Marlo Thomas as Ann Marie

Although Marlo Thomas has gone on to portray many different types of characters in her career, it is almost impossible to separate Ann Marie from Marlo. This is not to say that Marlo is Ann, but that Ann's character is very much like Marlo's was in real life at that time. The pert look, the warmth, the zaniness are all a part of Marlo Thomas. That there is so much more to the dynamic Thomas than that is a testimony to her acting ability. Ann may be a small part of Marlo, but without Marlo there would be no Ann Marie.

Chapter 3

Behind the Scenes

When I was a little girl and I was afraid, my mother used to put daisies in my room 'cause she said it was a happy flower. I used to be afraid of the dark and things like that, so she would bring the daisies in the room because she said they were smiling flowers. And that's why I named the company Daisy.

—MARLO THOMAS, PRESIDENT OF
DAISY PRODUCTIONS, OWNER OF *THAT GIRL*

GROWING A DAISY . . . PRODUCTIONS

The business side of any new television show is a complex matter. A seemingly infinite number of decisions must be made daily. Who will produce? Who will oversee the writing? Who will be responsible for hiring and taking care of payroll? Who, in fact, will be responsible? In the 1960s, as today, the network controlled all the options. They could cancel the show at any time, but they could also keep the actors and creative staff under contract for five years in case they want to exercise the option to keep the show on the air. Of course, someone would have to oversee the show for as long as it aired. But who would that be? The responsibility fell on the delicate but able shoulders of Marlo Thomas.

"When we first started this, I had no thought of producing the show," remembers Thomas. "I was just so excited to have a great job and get a wonderful character. But Bill [Persky] and Sam [Denoff], who were the creators of the show, said that they really couldn't commit to five years. They didn't want to commit to anything for five years. Jerry Davis, who was the producer, said he didn't really want to commit for five years, and the network said, 'Well, somebody has to be there for five years! You can't just put a show on and we don't have anybody responsible for it!' So I said, 'I will.'"

Those two words propelled Marlo Thomas into a position of power and responsibility. She had to form a production company, which she named Daisy Productions, to oversee and handle the nuts and bolts of producing a new half-hour sitcom every week. No small task! Thomas approached her attorney, Leo Ziffren, and asked his help in setting up the business. Ziffren had some very good ideas for Thomas and the company.

"He said to me, 'If you're going to take the responsibility in this way, I think you should set it up so that you own the negatives.'"

Owning the negatives meant that Daisy Productions would not only control the destiny of *That Girl*, but would also share heavily in the future revenues that came from reruns, syndication, merchandising, possible spin-offs, and so forth. For Thomas, up to now an actress with no voice in how she was presented to the public, it meant having "a seat at the table." It meant being able to shape the TV program along with the other creative artists. This appealed to Marlo Thomas greatly.

"Because I had really thought of the original concept," says Thomas, "and because I had taken it to the network and sold it and then gotten Bill and Sam to write it, I really was already performing as a producer. Though I didn't even know you called it that at the time. I was just hustling. But I guess it was the next step. I had done the work and I liked it because I had control."

But in those pre-women's lib days, having a woman in charge of a huge television show was just as revolutionary as the character of Ann Marie. There was Lucille Ball, and that was it.

"It was very hard for people to take the fact that a woman had a lot to say in those days, especially a very young woman," said Thomas at the Museum of Television and Radio's *That Girl* seminar in 1996. "It was a very unusual time. Lucille Ball was a freak of nature, this gifted woman who owned a studio and ran a show and produced a show and had all this power. It was really very unusual. So along comes bouncy me in my twenties. There was a joke that used to go around the studios. In fact, my brother told me this just a few years ago. Whenever I would be late or something to get to the set, they'd say, 'Oh, she's in the men's room, talking to Lucy.' That's what I had to put up with!"

During the same seminar in Los Angeles, co-creator Bill Persky acknowledged Marlo as a pioneer businesswoman. "There are all these shows on the air but nobody who really knows how to run them. I was interviewed and they said, 'What's happened to television?' I said, 'Television is in the eleventh generation of cousins marrying cousins. The gene pool has gotten so . . . the people doing it learn from people doing it.' Well, she was the first one to do it. She started a company. It was a whole other time. There was a sense of responsibility and an excitement. People had come from other areas of the entertainment world. They came from theater, they came from a lot of different places. Everybody in the business only knows what they saw on television and they are doing switches on switches."

So with Daisy Productions in place, the other decision was about how to shoot the show.

ONE CAMERA AND A LAUGH TRACK

People sit alone to watch TV. A laugh track is put on so that people won't feel so alone.

—MARLO THOMAS

Since 1951, when Desi Arnaz revolutionized television by helping to invent the three-camera system of recording a television show, most programs have followed this format. Before that time, television was broadcast live and the only records were kinescopes, films of the live performance shot from television-monitor screens. These filmed records sometimes distorted the features of the actors, emphasizing their noses or chins, but were the only way to preserve live TV performances for transmission on the West Coast.

When Lucille Ball and Desi Arnaz contemplated entering television in the early 1950s, most sitcoms were broadcast live from New York City. The Arnazes didn't want to move their newly growing family away from California. (When they made the pilot, Ball was pregnant with Lucie; Desi Jr. would follow two years later.) But they also wanted a record of their work. It was Desi who had the idea of filming the sitcom in front of a live audience with three cameras, each camera shooting the scenes from a different angle, and then editing the three films together to create a more visually interesting episode. This concept revolutionized the industry and single-handedly created the rerun market. When *I Love Lucy* became a huge success, other shows switched over to this method.

In mid-1965, when the pilot for *That Girl* was set to go into production, there were two choices available for shooting a sitcom. Either you shot your show the Lucy-Desi way or else you filmed it with one camera and without an audience (the laugh track to be added later). The trend at ABC was the latter format, as it produced more realistic-looking shows and allowed for better lighting. And so it was determined early on that *That Girl* would be shot with one camera, on film, like a movie, and without the supposed benefit of an audience.

"It wasn't an audience show," comments Denoff. "Marlo didn't want to do that. She preferred to have it on film. A lot of women, especially in those days, preferred that. Lighting when you do a multi-camera show is not as flattering and so she preferred to do that. A lot of comedies in those days were shot that way . . . *[I Dream of] Jeannie* and all of those."

But Marlo Thomas's reasons for filming the show this way actually had nothing to do with vanity. She remembers having "two reasons: one was that I had done a lot of theater and I didn't have experience with the camera. And I wanted to get it. Because if you do a three- or four-camera show or a five-camera show, it's like doing a stage work. And I had done a lot of that. I'd worked on the London stage in *Barefoot in the Park* [1965]. I'd done *Two for the Seesaw* [1961]. I did *Sunday in New York* for nine, ten months [in 1963] in Los Angeles. And I really wanted to learn camera work. That was one reason and the other reason was I didn't want to do a show that had to be 'ha, ha, ha, ha!' I didn't want to do that kind of show. I wanted to do . . . a softer show than that, a show that had more feel-ings between me and Teddy. With the family. I just wanted it to have more heart. . . . It felt like that was the right way to go. I didn't want to do *The Lucy Show* [1962–68]. I mean, *The Lucy Show* was the great show of all time, but it wasn't what I wanted to do. I wanted . . . a show that had more story, that was more story-oriented and less dependent on 'ha, ha, ha' every fifth line. And so that was our deci-sion. We talked it over and decided that that really was the show. It wasn't a unilateral decision. I had my own reasons, because I wanted to work with one camera. But Billy and Sam and I really made that decision together, that this was the show we wanted to do."

The only drawback of filming a sitcom this way is having to use a laugh track, a group of laughing people on tape that is dubbed into the soundtrack wherever it is deemed appropriate.

"You've got to have something because you have to tell the audi-ence [where to laugh]," says Denoff. "It's not like sitting in the the-ater. People sit here in this room and look up at that thing and they're by themselves. And you feel like an imbecile if you laugh." It makes people feel better to know where the laughs should be. Thomas is realistic about the function of the laugh track.

"I grew up with laugh tracks. It didn't really bother me. The guy who did the laugh track did it for all the shows. Sweetening, they called it. He sweetened my dad's show and Lucy's show. He did all those shows, all those comedy shows, even when they were live. Not only that, with live audiences sometimes you had to take the laughs out and put smaller laughs in. He was a master at it—at get-ting rid of laughs, putting in laughs, and knowing where they were. The big problem is that they not get overanxious and overdo it, so that they're not laughing at nothing. A guy walks in and says 'hello' and 'ha, ha, ha.'"

The advantages of filming a show this way outweighed the dis-advantages. Marlo Thomas looked fabulous! The character of Ann Marie was an idealized character who needed to look beautiful and glamorous on every show. (Thomas: "We really went for it. It was a fantasy time. It was like Doris Day movies.") So, in the summer of 1965, with all these elements decided upon, the pilot for *That Girl*, described in the *New York Herald Tribune* as a modern-day version of *My Sister Eileen*, was ready to go before the camera. (*My Sister*

Eileen started life as a memoir [1939] by Ruth McKenny about two sisters from Ohio and their experiences in New York City. It was turned into a play [1941] by Joseph Fields and Jerome Choderov, which was subsequently filmed [1942, 1955]. This, in turn, was adapted into a musical called *Wonderful Town* [1953] by Fields and Choderov, Betty Comden and Adolph Green, and Leonard Bernstein who wrote the music.)

"The pilot was such a beautiful show," declares co-executive producer Persky. "It was a perfect pilot!" Thomas agrees that the pilot showed what the series would be like: "[Ann Marie] was a wonderful character. When you look at that pilot you can see it, you can really see it. I have friends who are doing pilots, and I sometimes give them the *That Girl* pilot as a stencil and say, 'You can see in the pilot, you can see the five years. You can see where the stories are going to go. There's the parents, there's a boyfriend, there's a career. . . .'"

The plot of the pilot ("What's in a Name?"), written by Persky and Denoff, centered around Ann Marie (Marlo Thomas) getting one of her first professional acting jobs on television. Although she would only be onscreen for a few moments, this big break meant that Ann would get her first onscreen credit and the name Ann Marie would be established. Several of Ann's friends, especially her agent and boyfriend, Don Blue Sky (Ted Bessell), suggest she think about changing her name, as two first names seem to confuse the general public. Ann takes their advice and begins looking for a new name. This gets her parents, the Maries, into an uproar, especially her proud and overprotective father (played by Harold Gould). This rift between Ann and her parents so upsets the young actress that she changes her mind at the last minute and keeps her family name.

"The subject matter was great, about changing her name," says Persky. "I decided I wanted to be a director because of that show. (Persky went on to direct several *That Girl* episodes and to create and direct the hit series *Kate & Allie*.) Because we wrote this scene . . . I always believed that, well, we learned this from Carl [Reiner], but I believed it, that you had to be doing something in addition to what the scene is. There was that confrontational scene between her and her father. I said, 'Let's have her wash all of her sweaters so that they have nowhere to walk. Every woman in the world would recognize that situation.'" (The plot of the pilot [which was not aired until recently], sweater scene and all, was reused in Episode #11, also titled "What's in a Name?")

The pilot was directed by Jerry Paris, who cut his directing teeth on *The Dick Van Dyke Show*. Despite later cast changes, the pilot established the tone that the series would stick to: a combination of broad humor and slapstick, leavened with reality and warmth. The sweater scene in which Ann and her father fight over her changing her name is a perfect example of what became the style of the entire show. Ann has laid out all her sweaters to dry, and she and her father have to hop over the wet garments in order to communicate face to face.

The creators were all happy with their efforts, but they had no idea whether ABC would like what they offered. Marlo Thomas was particularly nervous.

Thomas: "When you make a pilot, all you feel is, 'Is it good enough? Is it good enough?' I remember saying to Billy [Persky], 'Is it any good?' He said, 'Are you kidding? It's great!' I said, 'Really? Was the scene yesterday with the sweaters on the floor, was that any good?' 'Oh, it was adorable! It was great!' I couldn't tell. First of all, I was used to being in front of an audience and I'm not getting any laughs. I have no idea. It's like working in a time warp. Nobody's laughing and we're doing jokes. It was just very hard to tell."

With the pilot in the can, there was nothing now to do but wait for the go-ahead from the network. For Marlo the waiting period involved being onstage in London's West End, where she was committed to star opposite Daniel Massey in the London cast of Neil Simon's Broadway comedy hit *Barefoot in the Park* (Piccadilly Theatre, London; opening date: November 25, 1965). It was while she was entertaining audiences in London's West End that Thomas learned the good news and the bad news.

The Characters and the Actors Who Created Them, Part Two

Donald Hollinger

He is tall and cute. Not handsome in the traditional sense, Donald is boyish and manly at the same time. His hair is blondish and curly, but cut short enough at the beginning of the series to be conventional. He is no 1960s radical. Donald is in his early thirties and is fully established as a writer for *Newsview* magazine, a weekly not unlike *Time* magazine. He went to college in his hometown of St. Louis, Missouri. (Initially, it is indicated that Don comes from Toledo, Ohio, then Shelton, Ohio, until finally the writers decide upon St. Louis as Don's birthplace.) He wears sports jackets or suits to work and is usually still wearing them when he picks up Ann for their dates. He wears contact lenses and owns a car. He is sometimes a klutz. Nonetheless, Ann finds him endearing.

Naturally, Donald finds the pretty and stylish Ann to his liking and she takes to him fairly quickly too. They first meet when Ann is doing one of her many survival jobs as a candy salesperson (who is also doing a TV commercial) in the high-rise office building in which Donald works. Although he does not see himself as courageous, heroic, or chivalrous, Donald gallantly tries to save Ann's life when they first meet. That her life is in no real danger, because she is only filming a TV commercial and pretending to be abducted, has nothing to do with the fact that Don undertakes to rescue her.

Donald tries to take care of her throughout the rest of the TV series. Whenever she is in a scrape, Ann calls upon him. Thus, the pattern of their relationship is set: Miss Independence needs Donald. After all, she is proving her self-sufficiency to her father, not to her boyfriend. Ann also tends to dominate Donald. She is very much her father's daughter. Although Ann occasionally dates other men, Donald does not seem to be interested in anyone else but Ann and it is assumed by him that, one day, they will marry.

His parents are Midwestern provincials who probably envision Ann and Donald moving to a small town where he would run the newspaper and she would act in little theater while raising their children. Ann does not see it that way at all. The fact that he is tolerant and supportive of her bid for success makes Donald pro-feminist. By the end of the five seasons (1966–71) of *That Girl,* when Donald and Ann are engaged to be married (an event that is never to occur), Donald is actually attempting to understand women's liberation. He is doing what he can to be the kind of man Ann Marie wants, while maintaining his own masculinity.

Ted Bessell as Don Hollinger

Unlike Ann Marie and Marlo Thomas, the role of Donald Hollinger was not created expressly for Ted Bessell. Over the years, Bessell brought his own personality to the role. His personal warmth and regard for Thomas translates beautifully in the way his Donald speaks to and looks at Ann. And his natural zest for realistic romantic comedy (as well as physical comedy) helps to shape Donald for viewers of the series.

Chapter 4

Changes

The testing said that Ted was very unattractive. In the original premise he was her agent and an Indian.

—SAM DENOFF, CO-CREATOR AND
CO-EXECUTIVE PRODUCER OF *THAT GIRL*

GOODBYE, DON BLUE SKY

There was good news and there was bad news. ABC loved the pilot, but . . . they hated three of the four leads! And the first one they wanted to be recast was Ted Bessell's role as Native American Donald Blue Sky, Ann Marie's agent/boyfriend.

"Before they ever tested it," remembers Persky, "Sammy and I were talking, and we realized that we had made a terrible mistake with Teddy's character. Her boyfriend should have been a strong, handsome, solid guy and her agent should have been a schmuck, so that you could get the laughter out of it. By giving both parts to the same guy, he could be neither. So he didn't function well. They were going to buy the pilot, but research and all that insisted that we get rid of Teddy because they didn't like him. But we had realized when we looked at it that we had created a schizophrenic character."

Denoff agrees: "It hurt the actor. He wants her around and yet he gets her jobs and sends her away. You weren't sure where he was at. The testing said that he was very unattractive. In the original premise he was her agent and an Indian."

We all went to Edgar [Scherick] and said, "We hurt Teddy. It's our fault. Give us a chance." And he fought the whole network and got Teddy on the air.

—BILL PERSKY, CO-CREATOR AND
CO-EXECUTIVE PRODUCER OF *THAT GIRL*

When asked why an Indian, Denoff laughed and tried to justify their choice. "At that time we were attracted to Indians. [Co-creator Bill Persky] was going on his second wife, who was part Indian. We thought it was a character thing. You think of all these things, thinking this'll be funny and after a while it goes away. The best intentions when you create a show. . . ."

There seemed to be a trend that TV season to present Native Americans in a contemporary setting. Burt Reynolds would appear in *Hawk* (1966) playing a full-blooded Iroquois and, if it had worked out, Don would have joined the tribe. But it didn't.

"They said we had to replace Teddy," continued Persky. "We went to Edgar [Scherick]. 'Supposing we keep this guy as her boyfriend and get a different guy as an agent?' Scherick, who was a smart guy, said, 'Yeah, okay, do that.' And the guy [Ted Bessell] had a job."

And Marlo Thomas, of course, fought like blazes to keep Ted Bessell. "The network didn't want him to be an agent," Thomas recalls. "They felt the boyfriend should be a romantic figure and not be somebody who was earning money off of what Ann Marie would earn." Bessell was told that they thought his being Marlo's agent would make him too unsympathetic a character. Thomas agreed with the network on that but felt that Bessell would be just perfect for the altered role of the boyfriend.

"In the pilot there was a lot of conflict about him. But once he was no longer the guy who was the agent, he became an independent identity. And since he wasn't making money from her, he stood on his own and the audience really liked him. Teddy was a sexy guy. Girls liked him. Guys could identify with him. He wasn't a dope. A lot of guys were dopes on shows with girls. That was kind of the way they did it." But not on *That Girl*. With the change of character from Don

Blue Sky, agent, to Don Hollinger, *Newsview* reporter, Ted Bessell retained his role as "that guy" to *That Girl*. (Standup comic George Carlin was hired to play Ann's talent representative, George Lester.)

"That made us feel good," says Denoff.

The creators and star were not as successful in saving the two actors who were the first Lou and Helen Marie: Harold Gould and Penny Santone.

"I thought Harold Gould was great," declares Marlo Thomas. "That was a network decision. That was never our decision. I was very happy with Harold Gould."

But perhaps casting Harold Gould, a talented but very "New York" actor, as Lou Marie was a mistake. Gould's persona was softer than the character of Lou Marie, who, although not based on Danny Thomas, shared some of that star's personality traits. Gould as Lou Marie came across as a father who would always accede to his daughter's wishes. In the long run, Gould might have diminished the required tension between father and daughter. But was this the real reason behind the recasting of Ann's parents?

"He was too Jewish!" says Denoff. "Harold Gould was too Jewish. The euphemism was 'too New York-y.' He's a wonderful actor. Lew turned out to be wonderful too. Lew is as Jewish a guy as you can get, but he wasn't *that* Jewish. These people who tell you these things at the network are Jewish."

Persky felt that Gould would have been wonderful in the role and agrees that the network didn't want it to appear that the Maries were Jewish. "No question about it. The parents ended up being Rosemary DeCamp and Lew Parker and they were terrific. But Hal Gould was fabulous." (Coincidentally, Harold Gould was the original father in the pilot version of the long-running *Happy Days*, which first aired as a segment on *Love, American Style*. Gould's career did not suffer from these recastings and he is well-known to television audiences as Rhoda's father on *Rhoda* [1974–78] and as Rose Nyland's suitor, Miles, on the hit series *The Golden Girls* [1985–92].)

During all this time of *Sturm und Drang*, Marlo was triumphing in London in *Barefoot in the Park*. The London critics fell all over themselves to describe her: "gangling ferocity" and "popping vitality." They said that she was composed of "nine parts quicksilver" and threw around such superlatives as "irresistible," "infectiously funny," and "sizzling." Although Thomas had pulled a ligament in her leg on stage in the provincial tryout, she stalwartly refused to miss her London opening night. She told the press that she would only be staying with the show for eight months, because of her commitment to ABC and her new television series. She became the toast of London.

And in the middle of creating the character of Donald Hollinger and thinking about recasting the Maries, Denoff and Persky went to London to see their star. Although they knew how wonderful she was in the pilot, they were further thrilled with her comic range on the stage.

Denoff recollects, "She was brilliant! And the one thing I remember about that that was great was, here she was the daughter of Danny Thomas, that's how people knew her, Danny's daughter. She got rave reviews in London and one of them said, and I'll never forget it, 'We understand that she is the daughter of an American comedian.' So she did it really all on her own."

"My father hated that review," remembers Thomas with a smile.

Persky and Denoff began screening and reading actors for the roles of Lou and Helen Marie and looking for someone to produce the new TV series.

Thomas explains why they had to regroup. "We made the pilot and then I went to London. . . . And while I was in London the pilot sold . . . and then we couldn't go right away, because I had this other commitment. [She stayed with *Barefoot in the Park* for eight months, returning to New York in early May 1966]. Everybody was kind of gone. I mean, Jack Ellinson [producer of the pilot] took another job. Everybody moved on."

Although Denoff and Persky were instrumental in the writing and producing of the pilot, they, too, were suddenly too busy to wear those hats on the series.

"We never meant to write all the shows or produce them," says Persky.

Denoff remembers it differently. "We thought we would write more of them but, coincidentally, we sold another show the same year, which we were committed to Procter & Gamble to be more involved with. It was *Good Morning, World,* an ABC-TV sitcom starring Ronnie Schell that ran from 1967 to 1968. We thought that was going to be a huge hit and it lasted only a season." Despite the show failing, Denoff recalls that there was a sunny side. "The victory of that show was that we found a girl that came in to audition for the next-door neighbor of the star and his wife and family. She was a dancer and she turned out to have a pretty good career: Goldie Hawn."

Denoff continues with his reminiscence of *That Girl*. "We were doing both shows at the same time. The first year, to help us, we had a great fellow named Jerry Davis as the producer. In those days there were no staffs. There was a producer and in some cases executive producer. Billy and I were executive producers. You had a producer who took care, with us, of having the story meetings with the writers. Most of the writers were freelance writers. There was no staff. Which wasn't necessary, because we also had the luxury of having enough lead time to get the material ready. Jerry [Davis] was a great, witty, bright man. He was also a director."

"We were like a family," continues Denoff. "Jerry Davis was terrific."

Davis, who had produced the very successful *Bewitched* (1964–72), is credited with writing ABC-TV's July 15, 1966, press release called "Producer's Platform." In it he praises Marlo Thomas and expresses the hope that the show will turn out to be "a daisy of a series." He muses about the show and the character as he sees her. "*That Girl* is looking for answers. She is bright, funny, and lovable; sometimes a troublemaker, sometimes a victim. The dialogue will be light and kookie—in keeping with her character." When referring to Ann's relationship with her parents, Davis took the safe route, "She's growing up but not away from them."

With Jerry Davis hired to produce the first season's shows, the executive producers turned their full attention to recasting the important roles of Ann Marie's parents. Especially her father. Many actors read for the part and several of them auditioned with Thomas. But for Marlo, there was one audition that stands out in her memory.

"I remember one day Billy [Persky] called me and said, 'Groucho Marx wants to come to read.' I said, 'Groucho Marx?!!? I'm not reading with Groucho Marx! Groucho Marx! My God! Groucho Marx is like God! How do you read with Groucho Marx? It's humiliation that he has to read!' So Billy said to me, 'It's going to be more humiliating if he doesn't read with you.' It was just awful. I did it. I had to. If he was going to come in and read, I realized that I couldn't make him read with the casting director. I would have to go and read with him.

Well, it wasn't right. First of all, I was so intimidated. I mean, Groucho Marx! It's Groucho Marx for God's sake! I grew up on Groucho Marx! I couldn't believe it. When I walked into the room I practically knelt. My father always played the Marx Brothers' movies. So I read with him and it was apparent that it wasn't right for him. That was the biggest star who came in. We had a lot of other good actors, but he was a major star of all time. It was just ridiculous."

Then one day Denoff and Persky called Thomas in to read with Lew Parker and it was immediately apparent that Parker was the right actor for the role and that the ever-elusive chemistry between the two of them was right.

"I loved him," states Thomas. "He just loved me and I loved him." It was that simple. Parker's musical comedy/vaudeville panache melded perfectly with the character's outsized, bombastic tendencies and his natural warmth lit up the small screen whenever he looked at his daughter.

Parker commented about his audition for the role of Lou Marie in an August 1966 ABC network press release. "Marlo couldn't possibly have been sweeter," said Parker. "She took my arm and said, 'We'll tape this until you feel comfortable in the part. I'll stay until midnight if necessary.' I think she is a great talent. I find I'm developing a strong, fatherly feeling toward her."

Persky admits that Lou Marie's character is based on Danny Thomas. (Marlo Thomas disagrees with Persky: "It wasn't based on my father, but on our relationship. Neither character was based on my parents. My parents are outrageous. My mother's her own sitcom.") So he thought that the switch from Harold Gould to Parker was the right move. "Well, he had a resemblance to Danny in that he was bombastic and strong. Hal was flustered somewhat. Lew was very strong and very solid and a patriarch. Someone to be reckoned with."

LEW PARKER
(Lou Marie)

Lew Parker was born April 30, 1909, in upstate Connecticut. His father was part of a vaudeville team called "Parker and Decker," so show business was in his blood. Making his debut in the chorus of a

1920s musical called *The Ramblers*, Parker was nearly fired from this job for being late on opening night. His comedy talents were immediately apparent and Parker was encouraged by one of the stars of the show, Paul McCullough, the lesser-known half of the famous comedy team of Clark and McCullough (Bobby Clark was the other half). McCullough told Parker to try his wings in vaudeville. Parker doubled on the road and in such Broadway shows as *Girl Crazy* (1930), which introduced Ethel Merman to the world. While in *Girl Crazy*, another comic star, Willie Howard, put him into his act and they played the fabled Palace Theatre in New York City. Parker's comedic talents, coupled with this singing and dancing ability kept him working in such Broadway shows as *Roberta* (1933, with Bob Hope), *Red, Hot and Blue* (1936, with both Hope and Merman again), *Hellzapoppin'* (taking over on the road in the early 1940s for Ole Olson), *The Front Page* (revival production, 1946), *Are You with It?* (1946, as well as appearing in the 1948 film version of this play), and *Ankles Away* (1955). It was in *Ankles Away* that he met his wife, Betty Kean (one of the famous Kean sisters; sister Jane was best known for her stint as Trixie in the color TV version of *The Honeymooners* in the mid-1960s). It was perhaps because of his close friendship with fellow funnyman Danny Thomas that Parker was given the chance to audition and win the role of Lou Marie in *That Girl*. On January 22, 1972, shortly after *That Girl* ended its run, Lew Parker died.

....

For the smaller, but still important role of Ann's mother, the team tapped veteran actress Rosemary DeCamp, who practically made a career out of playing mothers on-camera.

"I've played everybody's mother," recalled DeCamp in a 1967 ABC press release, "but since 1942 when [in *Yankee Doodle Dandy*] I played Jimmy Cagney's, my children have been getting younger and now I get the prize in Marlo Thomas, who is captivating and extremely talented."

DeCamp brought a natural warmth and intelligence to the role of Helen Marie that otherwise might have become a cliché and taken a backseat to Parker's Mr. Marie. But whenever DeCamp was on the screen, she infused it with vitality and warmth. Both DeCamp and

Parker were perfect for their roles and it is hard to imagine that anyone else could ever have done them.

ROSEMARY DECAMP
(Helen Marie)

A native of Prescott, Arizona, Rosemary DeCamp was born November 14, 1913 (some sources list 1910). Known for playing mothers, she made her film debut playing a sixty-five-year-old woman in *Cheers for Miss Bishop* (1941). She was twenty-eight. Her lengthy career encompasses radio, television, and movies. She is perhaps best remembered on film for playing the mothers of two of America's great composers: George M. Cohan in *Yankee Doodle Dandy* (1942) and George Gershwin in *Rhapsody in Blue* (1945). Her television work includes her role as Bob Cummings' sister on *Love That Bob* (the title of the daytime run, from 1959 to 1961, of *The Bob Cummings Show* [1955–59] and also the title used when that show went into syndication); Jackie Gleason's wife in the original *The Life of Riley* (1949–50); the occasional role of Shirley Jones's mother on *The Partridge Family* (1970–74), which was the lead-in show on ABC-TV for *That Girl* in its last season; and, of course, Marlo Thomas's mother, Helen Marie, on *That Girl*.

Rosemary was also the spokesperson for 20 Mule Team Borax for several years on TV's *Death Valley Days* (1952–75). She has been married to Los Angeles Superior Court Judge John Shidler for nearly sixty years and resides in Redondo Beach, California, about eighteen miles southwest of downtown Los Angeles.

....

As important as the Maries were to be to the new TV series, it was Bonnie Scott as Judy Bessamer who would be the more constant character that first season, appearing in nineteen of the first thirty episodes. Lew Parker appeared in only eight that first year (1966–67) and Rosemary DeCamp appeared in only nineteen episodes altogether (between 1966 and 1970).

In the series Judy is a housewife married to obstetrician Leon Bessamer (played by a very young Dabney Coleman). They and their infant baby, Stanley, live next door to Ann. The minute Ann moves into her apartment, Judy is there, ready to make friends and, at least for that first season, whenever there is a crisis or good news, it is Judy to whom Ann immediately turns. Judy seldom figures in the plots, but she is present to respond to Ann's day or present her with new problems, for example, throwing a monkey wrench into Ann's audition by making her babysit Stanley. The Bessamers allow Ann to sleep on their couch when her cousin comes to stay for his honeymoon. They are true friends. Judy also serves the purpose of having a contrasting lifestyle. While Judy takes care of the house and the baby, Ann takes care of herself. Judy is the past, just down the hall, while Ann represents the future.

BONNIE SCOTT
(Judy Bessamer)

Born in Philadelphia in 1934, Bonnie Scott moved to Hollywood at a very early age. (She had made her professional debut singing and dancing in Atlantic City at the age of two and a half.) At sixteen she appeared on television's *The Soap Box Theatre* (1950) and began recording for RCA Victor Records. Her motion pictures include *Vicki* (1950), *Beware, My Lovely* (1952), *Love Is Better Than Ever* (1952), and *Dondi* (1961). Before *That Girl*, she appeared on television on *The Jerry Lewis Show*, *Playhouse 90*, *The Adventures of Ozzie and Harriet*, *American Bandstand*, and *You Bet Your Life*.

Bonnie appeared in several stage musicals in Hollywood, including *Vintage '60*, which came to Broadway and won her the coveted role of Rosemary opposite Robert Morse in *How to Succeed in Business without Really Trying* (1961). Her success in that Broadway musical led directly to Ms. Scott winning the role of Judy Bessamer, Ann's next door neighbor on *That Girl*.

Appearing only seven times as Jerry Bauman during the first season, Bernie Kopell would become more important as the series progressed, and would be the only regular besides the two stars and Lew Parker to span all five years of *That Girl*. Jerry Bauman would change from the guy Donald worked with to a married man who lived next door to Ann and still worked with Don. In effect, Ruthie, his wife, would take the place of the departed Judy Bessamer during the last four seasons and Jerry would become Don's foil and Ann's friend.

BERNIE KOPELL
(Jerry Bauman)

Bernie Kopell was born on June 21, 1933, in New York City. He began surfacing on television in the middle-1960s and wound up doing double duty as Conrad Siegfried (agent of K.A.O.S.) on several seasons of *Get Smart* (1965–70) and as Jerry Bauman on *That Girl*. During this same period, the versatile Kopell appeared in 1970–71 on *The Doris Day Show* as the Italian neighbor of Day and the husband to Kaye Ballard's character on that TV comedy. However, it was as Dr. Adam Bricker on the long-running *The Love Boat* (1977–86) that Kopell is best remembered by his fans today.

....

Other recurring characters that first season were Dabney Coleman (b. 1932) as Leon Bessamer (in what amounted to eight short walk-on scenes) and Billy DeWolfe (1907–1974) as Jules Benedict (he made such an impression as Ann's acting coach that it is hard to believe he appeared on the entire series only three times, twice in the first season).

THAT WARDROBE

Oh, the hell with it! Let's make her au courant!

—MARLO THOMAS
SPEAKING OF HER CHARACTER, ANN MARIE

There are myriad decisions to be made when producing a television show, and *That Girl* was no exception. Creating a character involves more than just the contributions of the writers, the director, and the actress. It also encompasses how the character looks on-camera. And Marlo Thomas wanted Ann Marie to look great and very much up-to-date. She wanted her to be of her time and not like the usual ingenues on television who never seemed to dress with any style.

That first season the credits read "Clothes by Werle." It was the responsibility of Werle to make sure that Marlo as Ann looked of-the-moment. The 1960s started a great fashion revolution, which began in London. Marlo, having lived in London the year before, performing onstage in *Barefoot in the Park*, brought that influence back to America and to television for the first time. Mini skirts, hats, over-sized earrings, fishnet stockings, white boots. Ann looked as if she'd stepped right off the pages of *Vogue* magazine.

From the start there were arguments among the creative team over this facet of the show. The executive producers and creators, Sam Denoff and Bill Persky, were used to *The Dick Van Dyke Show*, where Laura Petrie wore clothes appropriate to her life as a New Rochelle housewife (despite the "ever-offensive" capri pants). And here was Ann Marie, supposedly just making ends meet, wearing clothes that any fashion model would have envied. "She would change hemlines in the middle of a show," recalls Persky. "That's how on top of that stuff she was. None of the guys understood it."

Who paid for all this? Donald? Her father? Mrs. Brentano down the hall?

"It was a great fashion time," says Thomas today. "Twiggy. London. Mod. And the girls who watched loved it. It was fantasy. Do [the characters on] *Friends* really live that way? I mean, nobody lives the way you see it on television. The apartment was small, but probably more than she could have afforded. And certainly the clothes were way more than she could have afforded. But I think that we just thought, 'Oh, the hell with it! Let's make her *au courant*.' I mean, we're talking about the sixties and the seventies, with clothes and boots and fishnet stockings and all this stuff. It was a great time and we just went for it. It added to the time. It added to being really right on the spot. Billy used to always worry that it would mean that when we got to syndication it would be out of fashion. And the funny thing is, we never were out of fashion. Because fashion has built on the fashions of the sixties, but it's never dismissed the sixties and the seventies. It's really interesting. Now they're back totally."

To the viewers it didn't matter a bit whether or not Ann could afford her wardrobe. Ann/Marlo looked fabulous. And all the girls who watched her wanted to be *That Girl*.

In retrospect, Persky and Denoff understood that Thomas was right about wanting a striking wardrobe for Ann.

Persky: "She was totally feminine and yet she knew what she wanted. I mean, the thing we started about the clothes, how could a girl afford this? We'd spend more time going over wardrobe sometimes than over story ideas, but the fact is her clothes were vital. And everybody said, 'How can she afford it, a girl with an apartment?' Well, no one cares. This is show biz. We're showing an idealized version of stuff. The fact is, girls tuned in . . . young women tuned in and saw the clothes. They loved it."

Like Lucille Ball, Thomas was the power behind her hit television show and in those pre-women's-lib days, men felt threatened.

Bill Persky was a man who understood people, men and women alike. ("I have three daughters of my own. I have a sister. So I have always been very much aware of women's roles in life.") From the start, he understood Marlo Thomas's needs and wants as an actress and producer.

"There was a defining moment in the whole thing," Persky remembers. "About the makeup person and the trip to New York. This is symbolic of how things get mixed up. We did a shoot in New York. We did the titles and it was on a very tight budget. Marlo very much wanted to take Tom Case [makeup] and Lynn Masters [hair], who were doing the hair and makeup for her every day on the show. All the shots in New York were just establishing shots—Marlo running around and getting into cabs. There were no closeups. So no one could understand, because it was a lot of extra money to accommodate her. They wanted to use local people. Sam said, 'We gotta make a stand real early,' because it was the first season, 'we can't let her be excessive and we can't this and we can't that.' I agreed, but I said, 'There's something going on here.' You always know that actresses and their makeup people have a very special bond. So there was a lot of fighting and yelling and 'you can't!' and 'I'm gonna!' Finally I sat down with Marlo and said, 'Why is it so important? You realize they're gonna be long shots. And I know you want to look great all the time, but it's really not going to matter. You know that.

You're smart enough. So what's really going on here?' And she said, 'The fact is that ABC sends a lot of people around for photographs and interviews and all that while we're shooting there and I want to look good.'

So I said okay, and I called ABC and said, 'Look, we're going there, we have makeup and hair people and it's gonna cost a lot more for us to bring the people we use here, but because of the publicity things you're gonna use her for there, she feels she wants to look her best and, blah blah blah, will you pick up that tab? And they said yeah.' So what happened was everybody got what they wanted.

But there were people, Sam [Denoff] and Jerry Davis and the people around who said, 'You gave into her.' And I said, 'No, I didn't. I accomplished what everybody wanted. Everybody won.' There was a reason behind what she wanted. So I guess that was like a template of how I dealt with Marlo. I always knew that there was something more at stake for her than what appears. There was always a good reason."

THAT MAKEUP

That was my real hairdo. The makeup was a little more. We made her more glamorous. I mean, I didn't wear eyelashes in real life, and she had *eyelashes!*

—Marlo Thomas
speaking of her character, Ann Marie

There were also "enormous arguments about makeup in the beginning," Persky recalls. "Tom [Case] and I were experimenting and trying to come up with just the right balance of color." Marlo remembers the situation: "Not too red with the rouge, not too much pink or yellow in the makeup base. It was hard to get it just right."

Persky continues his reminiscence. "We had an opening night party. [TV producer] David Wolper was a very good friend of Marlo's, so he threw us a party. They had about five television sets and Sammy always said to her, 'Marlo, you're so worried about makeup [but] on everybody's set you're gonna look different,' and she said,

'No, no, no, no!' And there at the Wolper house, on every set . . . one she was orange, one she was green, one she was blue, one she was red. I mean, it was hysterical. But as with all things, it doesn't matter how it translates coming out, it has to be perfect going in. It's going to get confused and lost and aborted and destroyed and compromised, but the stronger it is when it starts, the stronger it's going to be when it finishes."

Perhaps in those pre-cable days of unstable TV reception Persky and Denoff were right, but with her usual foresight and perfectionism, Thomas was proven correct. With the advent of cable TV and better uniformity of color on sets, Thomas's makeup was exactly the way it should be.

....

With the hair, makeup, and clothes now established, the cast and crew of *That Girl* were ready to begin production. Freelance writers such as Joseph Bonaduce, Sydney R. Zelinka, Peggy Elliot and Ed Scharlach, Milton Pascal, Tom and Helen August, Dale McRaven and Carl Kleinschmidt, Jim Parker and Arnold Margolin (who wrote the first-aired episode), and the soon-to-be-famous Jim Brooks were commissioned. (According to Persky: "[This was] Jim Brooks's first script ever. That was the one where they stayed in the bed-and-breakfast, and they were in bed together and her father came. . . . And it was the best script we ever had. We never changed anything. We never fixed anything. He had been an editor at Wolper. This was the first thing he wrote and it just was great. Right away!") The scripts were written and rewritten. Then the ceaseless one-camera shooting began on August 7, 1966, with what would become episode #10: "Break a Leg."

So, with the look defined and the family complete, both in front of and behind the cameras, the race began. ABC announced *That Girl* (for the first time under its new series title) in a March 21, 1966, press release that boasted that the TV series "promises to be one of the most talked about new comedies of '66–'67." The network ordered a season's worth of episodes from Daisy Productions. In those days, a season of television lasted much longer than it does today (usually twenty-two episodes). The season truly began in early September and didn't end until spring. Thirty half-hour episodes were ordered for that first season of 1966–67. Thirty chances for someone to call Ann Marie, *That Girl*. Thirty chances for an audience to fall in love with Marlo Thomas and her character. But would they?

"It was very scary," recalls Thomas. "All the research said that we would fail. In fact, they used to do a piece of research called 'Intention to View,' where they would list the names of shows, the people starring in them, and a sort of thumbnail sketch of what the show was about. So it said, 'This is a show called *That Girl*' [certainly not a big title; it's not *Blithe Spirit*], starring Marlo Thomas [that no one ever heard of], and it's about a young, single girl who moves to New York to become an actress.' The 'Intention to View' was the lowest of the entire upcoming season."

ABC remained undeterred as everyone geared up for the 1966–67 television season. All that remained was to monitor how the home TV audience would take to this revolutionary small-screen heroine who lived alone and wanted a career more than marriage. The date was set for September 8, 1966, for the world premiere of Marlo Thomas as *That Girl*.

The Characters and the Actors Who Created Them, Part Three

Lou Marie

Lou Marie is like his name, both masculine and feminine. He is a contradiction in terms. He is first and foremost a husband and father. He is also a small-town restaurateur and takes great pride in his culinary skills. (He knows what goes into a good stuffed cabbage.) It is no wonder that Ann is a talented actress, since her father also has an artistic streak. His restaurant in Brewster, New York, is called La Parisianne and serves French cuisine with an American flavor. Lou loves to sing and performs "Minnie the Moocher" at the drop of a hat, but thinks very little of the theater as a profession for his daughter.

He is a man stuck between the old and the new. He loves having his wife, Helen, at home and thinks that a daughter should live with her parents until she is married and taken care of by her husband. However, when Ann moves out on her own to pursue an acting career in New York City, Lou supports her as best he can. He trusts her, but not the men of Manhattan. Thus, Lou takes an instant dislike to Donald while at the same time appreciating and accepting him. More than anything, Lou loves Ann and wants her to be happy. The fact that his version of happiness is not hers is not the point. Lou Marie is a father. He may have wanted a son, but he is thrilled to have raised a daughter—and that job isn't over yet!

He is a man of great pride and vanity. He is flattered when a great star like Ethel Merman seems to be flirting with him, but terrified by the thought that his wife might not like it. Lou is a family man, but still a lustful man.

Lew Parker as Lou Marie

Lew Parker brings his own humorous, bombastic quality to Lou Marie. It is as difficult to separate Lew from Lou as it is to separate Ann from Marlo. His takes and slow burns (the result of years of vaudeville and Broadway experience) are masterful and his warmth on-camera is inestimable. We truly believe that he loves Ann and Helen, and grudgingly endures Don.

Chapter 5

The First Season (1966–67)

The single girl is a subject that television has avoided.

—MARLO THOMAS, 1966

THAT PREMIERE

In the mid-1960s, there were only three nationwide consumer TV networks in the United States: ABC, CBS, and NBC. And the competition was fierce indeed. The 1966–67 television season was packed with shows, all vying for home viewers who would buy the products that were hawked during the commercial breaks.

The new shows included a one-hour version of *Tarzan*; a prehistoric science fiction sitcom called *It's about Time* (CBS), starring popular comedian Imogene Coca; and *The Green Hornet* (ABC). NBC offered a witless sitcom entitled *Occasional Wife*, and sought and won the youth market with *The Monkees*, a clever takeoff on the currently popular Beatles' movies. NBC also premiered a critically panned show that would surprise everyone with its staunch fans and longevity: *Star Trek*. The very popular pop-art *Batman* began its second season on ABC (*Batman* was so popular that it aired two half-hour episodes a week, one on Wednesday and one on Thursday) and

Garry Moore appeared on CBS in his long-run variety show. Burt Reynolds, not yet the movie star he would become in the 1970s, appeared in the ABC action show *Hawk*, and David Carradine starred in *Shane*, the ABC-TV version of the classic 1953 film. Among the most eagerly anticipated shows for the new season were star vehicles for Tammy Grimes and Jean Arthur (the latter the very same luminary whom Marlo Thomas sought to emulate in her character on *That Girl*). Both *The Tammy Grimes Show* and *The Jean Arthur Show* soon proved to be ratings disasters for ABC and CBS respectively.

And among the ten new situation comedies that ABC offered its viewers for the 1966–67 season was *That Girl*, the show with the lowest ratings on the "Intention to View" poll among home viewers.

Upon examining the fall 1966 Television Schedule, one sees a mixture of the old and the new. CBS's *The Lucy Show* appears alongside NBC's *The Monkees*. There's *Perry Como* (NBC) and *Green Acres* (CBS), *Lost in Space* (CBS), and *Star Trek* (NBC). Thursday nights on ABC began with the second weekly installment of *Batman* at 7:30 P.M. Unlike today, prime time began at that hour, usually with a program that was suitable for children or the entire family, such as that season's *Gilligan's Island* (CBS, on Monday), *The Monkees* (NBC, also on Monday), the aforementioned *Batman*, *Lassie* (which began at 7:00 P.M. on Sunday), *Flipper* (a Saturday offering from NBC), or *Voyage to the Bottom of the Sea* (ABC's 7:00 to 8:00 P.M. offering on Saturday). On Thursdays, *Batman* was followed by *F Troop*, a semi-popular spoof of Civil War days which, in turn, was followed, at least for a brief time, by *The Tammy Grimes Show*. The CBS network countered with the hour-long *Jericho*, the male-dominated *My Three Sons*, and the *CBS Thursday Night Movie*. In its turn, NBC had the western *Daniel Boone*, *Star Trek*, the situation comedy *The Hero*, followed by the *Dean Martin Show*.

Filling the 9:30 P.M. slot that was occupied the previous season by *Peyton Place II* was *That Girl* (against the second half of *Star Trek* and the beginning of the *CBS Thursday Night Movie*). Having the truly delightful and popular *Bewitched* as a lead-in was no mistake and showed what Thomas has called "a great vote of confidence from the network." The powerful Samantha Stephens of *Bewitched* was the perfect prologue to the revolutionary Ann Marie of *That Girl*, and ABC programmers certainly must have known it. Viewers were ready to embrace these two females—one with her feet planted in the fantasy world of witches, warlocks, and suburbia, while the other had hers rooted in career, family, and New York City.

The networks were fiercely competitive and anything that would win ratings was deemed appropriate strategy. For the fall of 1966, ABC's strategy hinged on two promotional stunts. First, the network moved up its fall premiere week to begin just after Labor Day, giving their shows a week's head start against the other networks. ABC called this their "advance premiere" series and sent out press releases about Thursday's "Ladies Night" bloc of shows, starting with *The Tammy Grimes Show*, moving on to *Bewitched*, and culminating with *That Girl*. (They even advertised the trio of shows as "Dollhouse 90, ninety minutes of light comedy with the ladies leading.") This is why the first episode of *That Girl* is dubbed by Thomas as a "special preview episode." At the end of the show Thomas comes onscreen as herself and says, "Hi, I'm Marlo Thomas. Hope you liked our first show. Well, actually, it wasn't our first show, it was our preview show. Our real first show will be on next week when the season actually begins. Tonight you saw how *That Girl* met her boyfriend and in next week's show you'll meet Ann Marie's parents in the episode that shows what happens when she leaves home and goes to live in New York. And wherever you are, I hope you'll watch *That Girl* in color . . . or black-and-white. I just want you to watch."

The other part of ABC's strategy worked like gangbusters. ABC slotted blockbuster movies such as *The Bridge on the River Kwai* (1957) to air during the crucial first weeks of the new TV season, thereby "front loading" its new schedule with exceptionally attractive specials. Between the special preview week and the impressive array of feature films, ABC ran away with the psychologically important first ratings period. And their most successful sitcom was *That Girl*.

"It was a big risk for ABC to do it," says Thomas, "but at the time they had less to lose because they were a small station. They were a beginning station. And they didn't have any big stars. They had Elizabeth Montgomery, but they made her a star. They didn't have Lucille Ball and my dad and [Dick] Van Dyke. They were all on CBS. ABC had *The Fugitive*, with a little-known David Janssen up until then, and *Bewitched*, with a little-known Elizabeth Montgomery. It was really the fledgling network. So that's why they could take the chance."

That first-aired installment was entitled "Don't Just Do Something, Stand There" and was billed as a "preview episode," one of the twelve advance premieres that ABC was offering. Although not chronologically the first show, the choice of episodes was a good one. This half-hour not only introduced us to Ann Marie, but also to several of the ongoing themes that characterized the series.

We find Ann at one of her many survival jobs in Manhattan and quickly learn that she is really an aspiring actress. The two sides of her professional life are neatly established before the first commercial. Next we meet the character who will figure in every episode, the revamped Donald Hollinger, played by Ted Bessell. No longer her agent, he is now a young reporter for *Newsview* magazine who happens to work in the building where, currently, she is selling candy behind the counter. Unlike other TV series, which take the back story for granted, we actually see Ann and Donald meet for the very first time.

And they meet cute. Ann gets a part in a TV commercial that requires her to be abducted and dragged off by two thugs. Having previously met her as she sold gum behind the candy counter, Donald thinks the abduction is real and saves her by knocking down the abductors and taking bound-and-gagged Ann into a waiting elevator. Of course, Ann is far from amused by Donald's heroic action.

In the course of the installment, their paths coincidentally re-cross when they both want to buy the same antique rolltop desk. Of course, they discover their mutual attraction and, by the end of the thirty minutes, they are on an official date at their favorite Italian restaurant, Nino's. The only characters not yet introduced to viewers are Ann's parents, who will soon round out the regular foursome.

That Girl *was like the birth control pill and* The Feminine Mystique *[1963, rev. 1997]. They helped to obliterate the happy housewife.*

—SUSAN L. DWORKIN, FORMER
CONTRIBUTING EDITOR, *Ms.* MAGAZINE, 1998

As the first reviews of the sitcom premiere came in, it was evident that ABC's risk paid off. The reviews were wonderful.

"ABC-TV has that winner in *That Girl*," proclaimed *Variety* on September 14, 1966. "That was evident in the first episode, in which Marlo Thomas proved herself a delight." *Variety* went on to praise Persky and Denoff for giving Thomas "a vehicle that crackled with good fun, that went clicking along without a no-fun stop. It wasn't too sophisticated to lose its corny charms, nor was it so outlandish as to be unbelievable. . . . The series looks like it will land well up in the Nielsens."

Cleveland Amory in *TV Guide* proclaimed, "There is one very good thing about *That Girl*—well, that girl. Ann Marie is not just pretty funny—she is very pretty and very funny. She looks like Paulette Goddard, which is a good way to look to begin with, and on top of this she has the most engaging smile you're likely to find."

Ben Gross of the New York *Daily News* wrote that "Marlo Thomas is a charmer," and called the series "a delight." He ended the review by saying, "Danny Thomas had better watch out. He may soon be known as the father of a famous daughter."

The *Chicago Tribune* reported that Marlo Thomas was "very funny" and that the show had "good dialogue, a lively story line . . . the real treat is the lively Miss Thomas, who could become one of the stars of this season."

Allen Rich of the *Citizen-News* in Hollywood called Marlo Thomas "a first rate comedienne. She also has the Thomas flair for perfect timing and switching from high comedy to serious moments in a second's time." He called it "a likely hit."

The *Denver Post* said that "Miss Thomas has class." They also called her "sparkling, vivacious, and energetic." And the *Baltimore Sun* judged that Marlo was "the most delightful series newcomer and overnight star to appear in many a season."

Everyone involved with the show breathed a sigh of relief. Especially Marlo Thomas. "We went on opposite, strangely enough, a [NBC] show starring Richard Mulligan called *The Hero* [which, it turned out, lasted just half a season], which was touted as being 'the show of the season.' And we beat him huge! The interesting thing is we had the great good fortune of having *Bewitched* as our lead-in, which was a great vote of confidence from the network. But we had a movie on CBS opposite us at nine o'clock and they were throwing all these great movies, Steve McQueen, all these kind of big movies against us."

But *That Girl*, the one-woman revolution, triumphed.

"What it really proved was that, in fact, *That Girl* wasn't a revolutionary figure the way all the bigwigs thought, but that it was a *fait accompli*, that every family in America had a That Girl in it. And if they didn't have it, everybody wanted to be a That Girl. And by That Girl I mean an independent young woman who could call her own shots. That was the desire. It was no longer 'I've got to be married by the time I'm twenty-one or I'm an old maid.' We were riding that wave. Not because we chose the wave, but because, in fact, I was one of the young women of my own time who was part of the wave."

Co-creator and co-executive producer Bill Persky looks back on the success of the show from a different angle, but agrees with Thomas about "the wave."

"The climate was correct for that to happen. Marlo may have known it. I don't think I did. I just thought it was a chance to do an interesting show. I have three daughters of my own. I have a sister. So I have always been very much aware of women's roles in life. But I don't think we ever set out to say 'here's something that's going to do something.' I think if we had, we might have missed. It would have put a pressure on it that wasn't there. We just let the characters grow up and we just happened to catch the wave of things starting to change."

Feminist writer Susan L. Dworkin agrees that "Marlo just nailed it. It was exactly the right time."

Playing opposite Thomas's Ann Marie in that first "preview" episode was the under-appreciated Ted Bessell in his first appearance as Donald Hollinger. Though he never received the great reviews and accolades, Marlo Thomas has never denied his enormous contribution to the show. "There's no two ways about it," states Thomas emphatically. "Ted Bessell was half of that show. It's called *That Girl*, but it could very well be called 'Those Kids.' And in the beginning we weren't sure how much we were going to use him. But it was so apparent once we started that he was so much fun to play off and that the two of us were so good together."

In fact, except for episode #2, which is really the first chronologically, Ted Bessell appeared on almost every segment of *That Girl* and even went on, in 1968, to direct one episode, thus beginning a new career as a director.

Bessell enjoyed his role of Don Hollinger and especially liked working with Thomas. He was quoted as saying, "One of the nicest possible things is Marlo. There's a tremendous rapport." Even in 1966, Bessell understood that the show was called *That GIRL.* "There's no question it's her vehicle," he told the press, "I knew that when I took it." However, Bessell was confident that he could make a mark as Donald. He had always hoped to do a series character who grows and matures, and early in the series' run he told reporters that with this program it was possible.

"There have already been indications of maturing character in some of the scripts," Bessell reported to the media in the first season. "And I would hope that big changes come as the relationship between Don and Ann Marie gets stronger."

David Wolper, the famous TV producer and a very good friend of Marlo's, had a party at his Beverly Hills home for the viewing of the opening show of *That Girl.* Besides all the creators of the show and bigwigs from ABC, Marlo's proud parents, Danny and Rosemarie, were there with their nervous, but thrilled, daughter. Marlo, who seemed well on her way to becoming a significant role model— among other things—told *Catholic Miss* magazine that "many tears of joy were shed" when the show aired for the first time.

Bill Persky remembers that special party well and that, for some reason, Ted Bessell "was very uncomfortable about being there. He felt very awkward. When he walked out and said 'goodnight,' he walked into the closet. And stayed there. And then he came out and said, 'Now I'm really leaving.'"

But for Marlo Thomas and company, the triumph of the evening meant that the next day they were back to work.

"We really, really liked each other," remembers Thomas wistfully. "We had so much fun on that show. The makeup man that I used on that show is still my makeup man to this day. And he's worked on different series . . . Tom Case. And he does all kinds of movies with wonderful stars. And he always says to me, 'That was the happiest time of my life.' We had such fun."

But the fun was also hard work. Filming a new half-hour TV episode every week with the one-camera technique was often grueling work.

"It was very hard," concurs Thomas. "I got into makeup at five o'clock, rehearsal was at seven . . . and we worked long hours. We really worked sixteen- , seventeen-hour days. But I was twenty-four years old, so I could do it. But it was hard work."

Rosemary DeCamp remembers it was tough work too, but she cheerfully recalls the "6:00 A.M.s in makeup with Marlo and hair-dressers and the morning gossip and wardrobe discussions. I was well paid, the company good, the scripts excellent."

Thomas continues, "I discovered very quickly that there is no time in this work for you to be tired or moody, especially if you're important to the show. You can't come on the set and 'sluff it off.' There are a lot of high-priced, professional people involved with the show and dozens of people are depending on it. They care. I care."

THAT BUSINESSWOMAN

Besides caring for her performance, Marlo Thomas had to operate Daisy Productions. The business end of show business was forever rearing its head.

Co-executive producer Sam Denoff explains how a television show was run. "The network gives you a certain amount of money to do the show and if it costs you more than that, you owe that to the bank. You owe it."

Thomas and her lawyer, Leo Ziffren, were on top of these matters. Although the show cost a lot to produce, they made it work. Ziffren also found a way for Thomas and Daisy Productions to "own the negative."

"What we did in those years," explains Thomas, "it's not true anymore, but in those years you could get a guarantee of twenty-two reruns, which is fantastic, because reruns are like found money. Once you pay the residuals, you still have a lot of money left. And so what I did was I put my salary up, so that if we went over in a deficit, I paid with my salary and then at the end of the year I got it back when the rerun money came in. So it was pretty much like postdating a check. It was guaranteed. And the twenty-two reruns were guaranteed. Today you can't get that. That was a different time and also it was a fledgling network. So that entitled me to owning the negative. That was what gave me, in the end, a tremendous amount of knowledge. Because the more you *have* to be responsible, the more you *are* responsible, the more you have to know. So I learned a lot about syndication and editing and sponsorship and, really, everything to do with production. And it was a real education. A tremendous education! And it made me a good producer."

That debut season, audiences saw Ann Marie leaving her parents' Brewster, New York, home for the first time and moving into her own apartment in Manhattan. (Brewster is a real city, about forty miles directly north of Manhattan, near the Connecticut border.) Ann's apartment building (after she moved from the East Side Hotel) was a typical New York City brownstone with a front stoop that neighbors would sit on during hot nights. First-season viewers saw Ann's determination to become an actress and the temporary jobs that she took to make her dream come true. They witnessed her initial meeting with Don Hollinger (Ted Bessell), a writer from *Newsview* magazine, and saw her begin to date him. They watched her study her craft with acting coach Jules Benedict (Billy DeWolfe), play a singing mop on a kids' TV show, star in an off-off-off-Broadway production of *A Preponderance of Artichokes*, wait tables, understudy a Broadway luminary, have a flashback about her former career as a grade-school teacher in Brewster, get killed for the first time on a television drama, sell shoes door-to-door, become a regular on a soap opera, have an article written about her for *Newsview* magazine, try standup comedy, and accept an award with a bowling ball stuck on her toe.

All this hard work on-camera was paying off. *That Girl* was a hit with the public. And off-camera, things were going along smoothly.

The series was filmed at the Desilu-Cahuenga Studios near Sunset Boulevard in Hollywood. The studio that was created to produce *I Love Lucy* now rented space for other television productions. Bill Persky remembers that it "was the most incredible place in the world. It had five stages and [at one time] five shows in the top ten. *The [Dick] Van Dyke Show* and *Make Room for Daddy* had been shot there. *Gomer Pyle [U.S.M.C.]* was there. *[The] Andy Griffith*

[Show] and *I Spy* were there. We had the most wonderful studio in the world. The people who were there were [producers/creators] Garry Marshall and Jerry Belson, when they were a team. They were doing *[The] Joey Bishop [Show]*, which was not easy. They used to come over to our show and say, 'Can we visit you? We're in so much pain.'" But, although Danny Thomas had once said "you show me a happy set and I'll show you a boring show," *That Girl* was the exception to his rule.

"We had such fun," recalls Thomas with a smile. "At four o'clock in the afternoon I always needed some sort of sugar fix, and I used to say to the prop man, 'Go get sixty hot fudge sundaes!' And he'd bring back this big barrel of ice cream. I couldn't have a hot fudge sundae in front of the crew without giving them one. So we had a lot of fun. Every Thursday night after we shot, we had a poker game. And we'd all drink margaritas and beer and stuff and play poker till two in the morning. We just had a party every week and it was just fun."

VIEWERS RESPOND

When you are living a certain kind of life but you never see it reflected in the mass media, you feel that perhaps you are alone or crazy. And so even though millions of women are leading that life, to see it finally reflected made a big difference.

—GLORIA STEINEM, FEMINIST, AUTHOR, AND ACTIVIST

Television is a dead-on mirror of the times.

—SUSAN L. DWORKIN, FEMINIST, AUTHOR, AND ACTIVIST

Viewers began to respond to this Thursday night TV show phenomenon of a single girl on her own. And Marlo Thomas began to hear from a grateful audience.

"It was amazing because we got so much mail. *So* much mail. Three thousand to five thousand letters a week! From young women, saying, 'Oh, I know just how you feel. Don't get married to Donald! You just have to stay single. I'm married and I have two children and I'm twenty-three years old and I wish I was like you, in New York with a boyfriend.' And then from much older women, saying, 'Oh, when I was a girl I used to think that too.' It was just an amazing vein. It was a mother lode of a vein of gold. Because it was the truth. It wasn't a gimmick. It didn't come out of an idea of how do we succeed, but it came straight from my generation. What we felt. Everybody needs somebody to sort of tell them they're not freaky. I got so many letters from women saying, 'My mother always thought I was crazy, that something was wrong with me that I didn't want to get married. And I can say to her now, Marlo Thomas doesn't want to get married and she's not crazy.' So we started to realize that what we were doing was important . . . groundbreaking."

Although the sitcom appealed mainly to young women (the polls said from the ages of eighteen to thirty-five), the strongly defined character of Ann's father, Lou Marie, as played by Lew Parker, gave mature viewers someone to identify with as well. Parker was struck by the similarities between the role and his real-life situation and, thus, immediately identified with Lou Marie who had to cope with his daughter leaving the nest.

"The same thing was happening at the time in my own home with my nineteen-year-old stepdaughter, Deidre. The scripts dealing with the Maries' reactions to their daughter's leaving home are so realistic, you'd think they had placed a tape recorder in my own home."

Although she did not appear as often as Parker did, older female viewers had Rosemary DeCamp as Ann's mother, Helen, with whom to identify. As the mother of four daughters of her own, DeCamp certainly understood her on-camera role.

"I think the handling of Ann's departure is pretty bona fide," said DeCamp in 1967. "You're supposed to raise them, then throw them out of the nest. It's not easy to do nowadays. You are never prepared for the departure of your children. The series has taken this heartbreaking situation and made it into a truly delightful comedy." DeCamp was also pleased that the program did not overlook the parental visits with their offspring in the story line of *That Girl*.

"Since kids are crazy about the series, I feel that it is a good influence that Ann Marie is drawn back to home and the old folks from time to time."

Another measure of the show's success was Thomas's first *TV Guide* cover story in the November 12, 1966, issue. Thomas had had

TV Guide features written about her as early as May of 1962, but to earn the cover was a coup. Entitled "The Velvet Steam Roller" (Bill Persky's pet name for Thomas), the article highlighted Thomas's commitment to quality and some of the small off-camera battles that ensued during that first season. Thomas was quoted as saying, "I'm very strong, but I don't manipulate. I come out and say what I think. I'd rather be blatantly honest than softly manipulative." Series director Bob Sweeney (a former actor) is quoted as saying, "Marlo has one of the most professional approaches I have ever seen. She studies, she prepares, she refuses to settle for second best in herself."

On February 16, 1967, Marlo Thomas was named "the most popular female television personality" by the Hollywood Foreign Press Association and accepted her Golden Globe Award in a televised ceremony. (Her competition that year was Phyllis Diller *[The Pruitts of Southampton]*, Barbara Eden *[I Dream of Jeannie]*, Elizabeth Montgomery *[Bewitched]*, and Barbara Stanwyck *[The Big Valley]*. Thomas was also named "Most Promising New Star" by *Photoplay*, *Motion Picture Daily*, and *Fame* magazines. *Fame* also listed the show as one of the "Top Ten of Television".

As 1966 turned into 1967, TV series came and went. Highly touted sitcoms like *Occasional Wife, Love on a Rooftop, The Tammy Grimes Show,* and *The Jean Arthur Show* became part of flop history but, like Ol' Man River, *That Girl* kept rolling along.

In early May of 1967, while *That Girl* was shooting on location in Philadelphia (episode #37: "The Philadelphia Story"), the 1966–67 Emmy Awards announced their nominations. There was good news and bad news: Marlo Thomas, already a winner of the Golden Globe Award, was nominated, along with Lucille Ball (*The Lucy Show*), Elizabeth Montgomery, and Agnes Moorehead (both for *Bewitched*), for Outstanding Continued Performance by an Actress in a Leading Role in a Comedy Series. But *That Girl* was not nominated for Outstanding Comedy Series, edged out by *The Monkees, The Andy Griffith Show, Bewitched, Get Smart,* and *Hogan's Heroes.* (*The Monkees* won.) When it came time to announce the winner, it was that other female executive and perennial favorite, Lucille Ball, who won the trophy.

Meanwhile, Paramount Pictures announced that they had signed Marlo Thomas to a multi-picture deal and hoped that she would star in the film version of the Neil Simon play *The Star-Spangled Girl*. (When the film, now titled *Star Spangled Girl*, was finally released in 1971, because of scheduling problems for Marlo it was Sandy Duncan who played the role that Connie Stevens had originated on Broadway. Interestingly, Jerry Paris, who directed the *That Girl* pilot episode, directed the big-screen comedy.)

But Emmy-awarded or not, *That Girl* seemed a solid hit with critics and viewers alike. However, by the end of that first season (1966–67), Bill Persky, Sam Denoff, and Marlo Thomas knew that changes had to be made in the staff.

The Characters and the Actors Who Created Them, Part Four

Helen Marie

Of all the regulars on *That Girl,* Helen Marie is the one about whom we know the least. She is Ann's mother and she possesses great natural warmth. She is attractive but does little to make herself seem younger at a time when other women are doing just that. Her hair is naturally gray and worn in a modest style. She dresses well, but not too elegantly. She and Lou live very nicely in a large suburban house befitting his status as one of the most successful businessmen in Brewster. Helen is used to playing second fiddle to her strong, overbearing husband, and takes his bombastic tirades totally in stride. She loves him for his virtues and his faults. Their relationship is typified by the way Helen is able to accompany him on the piano when he sings "Minnie the Moocher." She knows how to play along, but also how to lead.

Helen has been a good mother, but it is clear that Ann is a daddy's girl. All of Ann's independent ways are the opposite of Helen's. However, Helen is pragmatic and believes that her daughter should have her freedom. Helen is used to being in the middle of fights between Ann and Lou. Although she might take her offspring's side, Helen frequently tries to make Ann understand Lou's ego and vanity and urges her daughter to capitulate. Helen loves her husband more than she loves her daughter. If need be, Helen can avoid ugly scenes by getting a convenient headache.

She wins her battles gently, but she does win them. When she is threatened, she becomes a tigress. When it seems that her handsome husband is being wooed by a famous Broadway star, a jealous Helen takes action in the only way she knows: she acquiesces, because she loves Lou and wants him to be happy. She decides to go home to her mother, who lives in Arizona. However, before she retreats, she confronts her rival and—in her own sly way—puts her competition down ("I could never begin to wear so much makeup"). Helen wins the foray as usual, and it is clear that she and Lou have a very solid marriage.

Helen likes and appreciates Donald from the start, while realizing that the relationship roles she and Lou have enjoyed over the years are reversed in Ann and Donald. Ann is Lou and Donald is Helen. Above all, Helen is calm, clear, and collected, and we love her immediately.

Rosemary DeCamp as Helen Marie

Much of the responsibility for Helen's qualities must go to Rosemary DeCamp. Having the least defined character on *That Girl*, DeCamp imbues Helen with her own strong, warm qualities and builds a character that otherwise might never have emerged.

Prior to *That Girl*, Marlo Thomas had already enjoyed some success. This publicity shot of Thomas shows off one of her rave reviews for *Barefoot in the Park* at London's Picadilly Theatre in 1965.

Actor/producer Danny Thomas wishes his soon-to-be-famous daughter luck on the first day of shooting for her new sitcom on Stage 8 of the Desilu-Cahuenga Studios (now Ren-Mar Studios) in Hollywood.

FROM TOP:
Thomas in 1965 shooting the New York City location credits for the *That Girl* pilot; From the original pilot credits, Ted Bessell points to his credit graphic on a street outside of Central Park.

CLOCKWISE FROM TOP:
The original logo for *That Girl*, with the flip and bangs; Marlo Thomas as a thrilled Ann Marie in the opening credits of the series; Thomas as Ann mussing her hair at the end of the opening credits.

A publicity shot of Marlo Thomas and Ted Bessell.

FROM TOP:

A second-season publicity shot of the Marie family: Lou, Ann, and Helen (Lew Parker, Marlo Thomas, and Rosemary DeCamp); Almost the entire Thomas family appeared in Episode #79, "My Sister's Keeper." In a scene in a church hallway, when Marlo as Ann accidentally bumps into a clergyman (played by her real-life father, Danny Thomas, in a cameo role), she says, "Oh, excuse me, Father." He replies, "That's all right, my child."

**THE SHOW OFTEN BOOKED
CELEBRITY GUESTS**

CLOCKWISE FROM TOP:
Danny Thomas, Marlo, and Milton Berle in Episode #127, "Those Friars"; In
Episode #59, "The Drunkard," Ann appears with Sid Caesar in a commercial.
In Episode #31, "Pass the Potatoes, Ethel Merman," the Merm teaches Ann
to sing.

Chapter 6

The Second Season
(1967–68)

I think we are fortunate in being in the only business in America where we start out doing the absolute best that we can, to get as close to perfection as possible.

—EDGAR SCHERICK, FORMER HEAD OF
PROGRAMMING AT ABC-TV, AT THE 1996 *THAT GIRL*
SEMINAR AT THE MUSEUM OF TELEVISION AND RADIO

SECOND-SEASON CHANGES

As Edgar Scherick states above, show business is a profession in which people do strive to achieve perfection. Some fall short of their creative marks, but it is rare that anyone sets out to do mediocre or bad work. On the *That Girl* set and behind the scenes, the quest for a better product was never-ending and the desire for doing well came from the show's originator, Marlo Thomas.

Some TV properties retain the same staff and cast for the entire period of production. However, sometimes after a season has wound down, it becomes apparent that things require fixing. Even with a hit show like *That Girl*, this fact of TV life held true. The first major change was the replacement of producer Jerry Davis.

Bill Persky recalls, "Jerry Davis was terrific, but his social life was very important. He kept screaming, 'Who knew this job would take so much time? It's just terrible. I don't want to be this. I want to be Harry Ackerman!'"

Ackerman was a very successful television bigwig who was executive producer of such shows as *Dennis the Menace* (1959–63), had helped to launch *I Love Lucy* on CBS, and created *Bewitched* (1964–72). (Producers Jerry Davis and Danny Arnold had both worked under him on *Bewitched*.) Harry had a reputation for delegating authority and not being a hands-on producer. Definitely not the way the *That Girl* set was run.

Persky continues, "We kind of talked [Jerry Davis] into doing the show. Jerry didn't want to do it. He was never that much of a fighter or a worker, so the first group of shows that Jerry did were a struggle and Sam [Denoff] and I had to be very deeply involved."

Thomas remembers the late Jerry Davis (he died in April 1991) fondly but realistically. "He was adorable. But we needed somebody stronger in writing. We needed a real writing producer."

So Davis left *That Girl* after its first season, and on April 12, 1967, *Daily Variety* announced his replacement: Danny Arnold.

Arnold had produced TV's first successful rural sitcom, *The Real McCoys* [1957–1963] on ABC-TV, starring Walter Brennan, and had also produced the first couple of seasons of *Bewitched*. "Marlo didn't know him," says Denoff. "She said, 'Who is he, who is he? Does he know how to do it?' We finally convinced her to meet him, and they liked each other."

"Danny Arnold was one of the toughest hombres that ever lived," recalls Thomas. "He [later] created *Barney Miller* [1975–82] and wrote all those shows. In fact, when it was discussed for him to be the fellow who would take over from Jerry Davis and produce the show, people said to me, 'Oh God, you two will kill each other! He's so tough! He's so strong!' [Arnold's *Bewitched* reputation had preceded him. He and creator Harry Ackerman had fought over the future stories. It seemed Ackerman wanted Samantha, the witch, to gradually lose her powers and Arnold, correctly, thought that there would be no show anymore if that happened.] And Danny came to see me and he said, 'You know, everybody tells me we're gonna kill each other, 'cause you're so strong and I'm so strong.' And we sat down for about five minutes and fell totally in love with each other and we never ever had any arguments. I told him, 'Never lie to me and I'll be happy.' And he never did."

"His way of producing was a lot more extravagant than others," claims Sam Denoff. "Those two years cost us as much as the other three years. He was re-editing, re-shooting, re-editing, re-doing, re-editing. . . ."

But for Marlo Thomas it was the results that counted, and she loved how Danny Arnold handled the show and how he took care of her.

"He was so smart, he was so good, he was so kind. And he was a real protector. He took all of his strength and all of his talent and used it, not only on the show, but to protect me [from all the pressures put on a star/producer]. It was a wonderful time to be with him. He directed them too. I totally adore him."

Denoff remembers Arnold, who died in August 1995, with a chuckle. "Danny Arnold . . . we hired him and after two weeks he told us not to bother him, we didn't know what we were doing. But that was Danny. He was always that way. He was a dear, sweet man. He knew better than anybody on any given subject in the world. Aside from that, he was a very talented writer and director, so he knew what he was doing."

Arnold's first order of business as producer, and one that endeared him to Thomas, was the addition of another key staff member with a title credit that didn't exist in *That Girl*'s first season: script consultant.

"Since there were so many men on the show, at one point I said, 'You know, I really feel that we need a woman on the staff," says Marlo Thomas. "It's just crazy. All these men and me. I was constantly saying, 'Well, a girl wouldn't say that to her father. Or a girl wouldn't say that to her boyfriend.' So Danny Arnold brought in Ruth Brooks Flippen." (Flippen was the wife of character actor Jay C. Flippen, who appeared in episode #45: "'Twas the Night before Christmas, You're under Arrest." He died in 1971.)

Ruth Flippen was not only "a very gifted writer and wrote a lot of wonderful shows, but she was there and she became a buffer and a real conscience for the show. Because it had been me all alone saying, 'No, she wouldn't say that and girls don't feel that and that's not the way it goes.' So now Ruth was there to say, 'No, that's not what women say, that's not how they feel.' So it was very helpful. Very, very helpful!"

Throughout the years, Flippen wrote or co-wrote fourteen episodes, beginning with episode #35: "The Apartment" and ending with episode #82: "The Defiant One," and contributed to many other installments during the seasons (1967–69) for which Danny Arnold produced the series.

The other new credit read "Clothes by Cardinelli." Cardinelli was actually a designer named Marilyn Lewis, and Ann Marie's look became even more high fashion under her guidance. And although Marlo/Ann did not change her hairdo, there *was* "a change in the hair."

"The first year that was my own hair (which was a dark brown flip with bangs). But as Lynn Masters [Thomas's hairdresser] can tell you, no human hair can take the beating that my hair took. By the end of the first year I didn't *have* hair. It was just hanging there. So I started to wear falls. Then I didn't want to have bangs anymore, so I let my bangs grow out. But Clairol [the sponsor of *That Girl*] didn't want them grown out. So then I had to wear a bangs wig—it was like a big moustache on my forehead!—so that in real life I could let my hair grow out and wear bangs on the show."

There were other alterations to the working format on *That Girl*. Even though Ann didn't move from apartment 4D at 344 West 78th Street, the physical layout changed from the first season to the second. In the premiere season, her kitchen was located to the left of her doorway (and hidden from view except when needed). In the second year (1967–68), Ann's apartment was restructured to provide a kitchen off the living room and a dinette which was in full view. Only the bedroom remained a separate room, still viewed through the see-through fireplace. Nonetheless, there were occasional scenes in Ann's bedroom where we saw her asleep in her single bed (perfectly coifed and made up!). On only one episode was Ann's bathroom shown, and, while no toilet was visible, viewers did get a glimpse of Ann in her shower.

With the disappearance (when the network did not renew the actors' contracts) of Ann's next-door neighbors and friends, the Bessamers (Bonnie Scott as Judy Bessamer is last seen on episode # 29: "Author, Author" and her husband, Leon the obstetrician, takes his final bow on episode #28: "This Little Piggy Had a Ball," in which Ann gets her toe stuck in a bowling ball), there was a need for new neighbors/best friends.

Although Bernie Kopell (of whom Marlo has said, "He was wonderful . . . he was a great foil for Teddy [and] they liked working together") had been with the show during its first season (and would remain until the end), his character was finally solidified in the second season as Jerry Bauman and he was given a wife, Ruthie, played by Carolan Daniels.

"I started out as just the neighbor next door," recalled Kopell at the Museum of Television and Radio's *That Girl* seminar in the mid-1990s. "I had three different wives. It was very strange. There was Arlene Golonka. We had a tremendous wedding on [*That Girl*, although actually only Don and Ann attend their wedding, in episode #21: 'Rain, Snow, and Rice'] and then she wasn't available for the second show, so we moved in Carolan Daniels, but never referred to it. We stuck a blonde wig on Carolan. She had some problems with a feisty, pesky husband and Alice Borden [she didn't show up until season four] was found. And then I got to be Teddy's coworker at the magazine so he could keep me up to date on the romance. It was a very creative time for me. I was doing *Get Smart* at the same time. I never had a contract with Daisy Productions or with Talent Associates [who did *Get Smart*]. It was a very busy five years. I would find out if I was working on Marlo's show and I'd become very friendly with the assistant directors. I said, 'Okay, I'm working on Marlo's show Tuesday and Thursday, you've got me on Monday, Wednesday, and Friday.' In five years I never had a conflict once. No conflict, no contract. It would never happen today."

More and more, Jerry and Ruthie Bauman would slip into the next-door neighbor/best friend roles that had been filled the first season by Judy and Leon Bessamer (Bonnie Scott and Dabney Coleman). Coleman, of course, went on to greater fame as the comic heavy in many 1970s and 1980s films, such as *Nine to Five* (1980), and to star in several of his own series, including *Buffalo Bill* (1983–84). Scott, who had come from musical theater (she had starred opposite Robert Morse in the original 1961 Broadway cast of *How to Succeed in Business without Really Trying*, but was replaced by Michelle Lee both on Broadway and in the film, even though Robert Morse got to repeat his role in this 1967 film version of the hit Broadway musical) seemed to vanish from public view after her season on *That Girl*.

In an effort to provide Ann with a sidekick comparable to the role Judy played on the first season of *That Girl*, comedienne Ruth

Buzzi was cast as Marge "Pete" Peterson. She appeared in several episodes in the 1967–68 season (episodes #34: "To Each Her Own," #37: "The Philadelphia Story," #42: "The Mailman Cometh," #54: "Great Guy," and #58: "The Beard"), then disappeared, only to resurface in a 1968 mid-season replacement show on NBC-TV called *Rowan & Martin's Laugh-In* (1968–73). That landmark comedy variety show made Buzzi a household name.

In addition, there were other casting changes on *That Girl*. Ann Marie had two agents disappear in one season (1966–67): Ronnie Schell as Harvey Peck and George Carlin as George Lester. In the second season, on episode #42: "The Mailman Cometh," she acquires a new ten-percenter, one Seymour Schwimmer, played by Don Penny. She keeps him as her representative until Morty Gunty as Sandy Stone appears in episode #101: "Ten Percent of Nothing Is Nothing" in the third season (1968–69). Thank goodness the on-camera Ann has the good sense to retain tart Jules Benedict (played brilliantly by Billy DeWolfe) as her acting coach. And, of course, she was smart enough to keep Donald as her faithful boyfriend.

....

Besides bringing Ruth Brooks Flippen on board and, in mid-1967, writing and directing some of the episodes of *That Girl* himself, Danny Arnold also brought fresh blood in the writing and directing departments of the hit sitcom.

The first show that Arnold produced was written by Jim Brooks (who had debuted as a sitcom writer with his *That Girl* scripts for episode #16: "Christmas and the Hard Luck Kid" and episode #21: "Rain, Snow, and Rice" the season before) and guest-starred Broadway's Ethel Merman. She had been a major star in New York for over thirty-five years and starred in such hit musicals as *Girl Crazy* (1930), *Anything Goes* (1934), *Annie Get Your Gun* (1946), *Call Me Madam* (1950), and *Gypsy* (1959). She had recently turned her oversized talents to television.

"This is the first time I've played myself in a television series and I'm thoroughly enjoying it," Merman had said on the *That Girl* set. (Perhaps Merman was forgetting the two-part episode she did on *The Lucy Show* in 1964, in which she also played Ethel Merman, albeit under the pseudonym of Agnes Schmidlap.) In the same press statement, the Merm, as she was known, also commented about Thomas's thoughtfulness.

"Marlo is sweet as well as bright and talented. The first day, she sent me a beautiful arrangement of daisies with a note about how happy she was to have me on her show."

Episode #31: "Pass the Potatoes, Ethel Merman" turned out to be one of the highlights of *That Girl*. Merman and Thomas had such a good chemistry (Thomas: "She was so much fun!" Merman: "It was one of my favorite guest shots ever") that the singing star was asked back to do another guest shot on episode # 50: "The Other Woman."

Although *Variety* wasn't too keen on the second season's premiere (". . . the plot lines are not designed to give anyone a brain strain"), they at least appreciated Bessell that second season, noting that he turned in "a solid acting job." The *Hollywood Reporter* observed that the second season "promises to be even better than its first." They reported that "Marlo Thomas has blossomed into one of the sharpest comediennes in the business and certainly the most attractive on any web's femme roster." Bessell also was lauded as "now giving deeper dimension to his role and projecting more colorfully as a guy in love, but with a sense of humor and a will of his own." And, most importantly, the audience flocked back to see Ann Marie's exploits. In fact, on September 20, 1967, *Variety* reported that *That Girl* was second for that week in the top forty television shows, with 27.5 percent of the audience.

The fall 1967 TV season saw *That Girl* moved into the prime 9:00 P.M. slot (still following the popular *Bewitched*) opposite the second half of a new NBC one-hour police drama series starring Raymond Burr entitled *Ironside* (1967–75) and the CBS *Thursday Night Movie*. The new shows that season included several hour-long programs featuring big names: *The Carol Burnett Show* (1967–79, which brought variety shows to their apex and made Burnett a household name), *The Jerry Lewis Show* (1967–69, a comedy-variety format), and a new NBC program starring Marlo Thomas's father, *The Danny Thomas Hour* (1967–68). New sitcoms included Bill Persky and Sam Denoff's new baby, *Good Morning World* (1967–68), Paula Prentice and Dick Benjamin (he directed Marlo Thomas in the London Production of *Barefoot in the Park*) in *He & She* (1967–68), Sally Field as *The Flying Nun* (1967–70), Eve Arden and Kaye Ballard in

The Mothers-in-Law (1967–69), and *Accidental Family* with Jerry Van Dyke (1967–68). Of these, only *The Flying Nun* would survive the ratings wars as a hit program.

In season two of *That Girl*, viewers got to see Ann move on in her profession. Right off the bat she gets cast in a revival of *Gypsy* with Ethel Merman. We then see her do a commercial for Twinkie soda pop (Don gets in on that one too!), try a telemarketing job, win a role in a Broadway play that closes in Philadelphia, collaborate with Donald on a play about her life (he, meanwhile, has written his first novel), win the lead role in an Italian movie (only to turn it down because of a requisite nude scene), model clothes at Sardi's restaurant (as a roving model, spouting little dramatic monologues in the process), become a high-fashion model for a famous photographer (models were big in the 1960s, for example, Twiggy), showcase fur coats (this is before fur activism), do commercials as the Creamy Soap Girl, and, finally, make her Broadway debut. A lot of on-camera action for one season!

And in October of 1967, all of Marlo Thomas's attention to fashion and good taste paid off when she tied with Candice Bergen for the New Star to Fashion award given out by the Costume Designers Guild.

OVERSEEING THE WRITERS
AND DIRECTORS

Danny Arnold was working out very well in his new capacity on *That Girl* and, although Marlo Thomas kept her hand in as usual, she felt she could trust Arnold, Sam Denoff, and Bill Persky to get the job done.

"Billy and Sam and Danny Arnold really ran the writers. Danny especially was bringing in writers from everywhere. Billy and Sam would rewrite . . . Danny would rewrite . . . it was heaven. They were all so talented and caring."

Persky and Denoff would always be around to make sure that their series characters stayed true to what they had created. They had strict rules.

"Our guidelines [for the writers] were what we mainly learned from Carl Reiner and Sheldon Leonard [the creator and producer of

The Dick Van Dyke Show, among others]," explains Denoff. "Above all, if you start out from a basis of truth, you can do all kinds of wonderful, silly things. Put people in precarious predicaments, but don't start out stupid! Carl Reiner warned me and Billy. It was the third year that we were working on the show *[The Dick Van Dyke Show]*. We had written something that he said, 'Look, let me tell you something, you two guys are the most neurotic, crazy writers I have ever worked with. And I've worked with a lot. You are as disturbed people as I've ever known. Taking that into consideration, never let Rob Petrie [Dick Van Dyke's character] do anything you wouldn't do.' And that took the stupid out of it."

Being the creators and writers themselves, Persky and Denoff not only advised the staff writers but, as Persky puts it, "wrote 'on' every one. You know what I mean? We contributed on everything we did. We were involved in all the stories. . . ."

Denoff remembers telling writers on *That Girl*, "Keep your stories real. Keep your stories about things that are important. In the show we had certain rules. . . ." These rules included deriving humor from "people in life. There are no funny cops. There are no funny plumbers. These people are *not* funny. What they do is make *you* funny by making your life complicated and difficult and expensive and all of those things. And salespeople, they don't do jokes. People like that don't do jokes. People in show business do jokes! Yes, getting a job, that's what made *A Chorus Line* [1975] a hit. It wasn't about dancing, it was about getting a job. Everybody relates to that. And everybody related to her [Ann Marie]. So that was our prohibition to those writers. No stupid! Once in a while we made mistakes. In five years, you do. There are some shows that are better than others. If we saw a script we didn't like, we said 'fix this.' The other thing we insisted on is that we not make contemporary references to people or things happening now. Because that becomes old in twenty-four hours. You always think of syndication because that's how you make money."

Thomas concurs about the quality of the *That Girl* scripts. "I think the shows were very good because we had all those writers [Arnold, Denoff, and Persky]. We would talk about it and they would say, 'We're thinking of doing a two-parter in Las Vegas. How would you feel about having a guy come and be a rival for Donald?' We would talk about it in those kinds of terms and then we would always sit down and read the scripts two or three weeks in advance. We either would think the script wasn't good enough and throw it out, or give it to another writer to rewrite. And I would have input then. I had a lot of input. But they were very talented people."

Thomas always believed (and still does) in hiring the best people for the job and giving them the room to accomplish their work. She learned this axiom from being around one of the best television producers in the business: her father, Danny Thomas.

"It isn't any fun to be the only guy on the block who's got any brains. I remember one time, my father had Jack Benny as his guest star on a television special. I was very young. I must have been twelve years old. We were walking out of the studio at NBC and the show had just been over. And somebody yelled out at my father, 'Hey, Danny! Jack Benny almost stole the show from you!' And my father said, 'He'd better! That's what he got paid to do!' And that's the truth of it. You don't hire people around you to be weak. You don't hire them around you *not* to be good. You try to hire and steal the best people you can find, so that you can have a great ensemble cast and great writing."

The same was true of directors, some of whom came and went quickly. Although Bob Sweeney, Hal Cooper, John Erman, and Danny Arnold directed many episodes each, the first three seasons (1966–69) alone saw twenty different directors guiding the show.

"That was the way it was in those days," recalls Thomas. "Somebody did three. Somebody did four. Somebody did five. Some of them [had different ideas], but Danny [Arnold] would be there to guide it. We would rehearse on one day. We would have a read-through and a rehearsal, and next day would be a rehearsal. So Danny and Bill and Sam would be there watching to be sure the director— and in those days they were all men—knew what he was doing. And also because we'd been on awhile by that time, so directors knew who the characters were."

Thomas remembers some of the different *That Girl* directors with affection. "We had good directors. We had John Rich, who was wonderful and very funny. He directed a lot of *Van Dyke Shows*. And Bob Sweeney was inventive and sweet. And Hal Cooper, terrific and adorable. We had many really good comedy directors and most of them gave us a lot. Teddy [Bessell] directed a few. Billy [Persky] did, Danny [Arnold] did. Billy and Danny were so much fun. It was great when Danny or Billy or Teddy directed, because they knew the show and us so well that it made it really easy."

Besides dealing with Ann's burgeoning career, the second season, as did the first, dealt with the relationships between Ann, Donald, and their respective parents (mostly hers). The second year on the air saw the reappearance of Mabel Albertson as haughty Lillian Hollinger, Don's mother. (She had visited him in episode #12: "Soap Gets in Your Eyes" and mistaken Ann's real character for the evil one she played on a soap opera. On that installment Mrs. Hollinger's first name had been Mildred.)

"I thought Mabel Albertson was just hilarious," recalls Thomas about the late actress. "She was so dry . . . like Bea Arthur. I loved her."

In the second season, Albertson reappears in two hilarious installments. First, the Thanksgiving episode (# 41: "Thanksgiving Comes But Once a Year, Hopefully") and then the one in which she finds the pants!

In episode # 53: "Odpdypahimcaifss" (translation: "Oh Don, Poor Don, Your Pants Are Hanging in My Closet and I'm Feeling So Sad"), Mrs. Hollinger arrives at Ann's apartment to find a pair of her son's pants hanging in that girl's apartment. Horrors! Thomas laughs at how much mores on television and in real life have changed today.

"It was a major thing. That was a funny show. We couldn't even consider doing that show today. *Friends* [1994–], which is one of my favorite shows, actually did a show about the wet spot on the bed. We could never do that. Donald and I could never even *sit* on the bed, or be anywhere near the bed in that room."

Bill Persky always felt that Don and Ann not doing anything sexually explicit on the show was an advantage. "In the exclusion of being able to have two people jump into bed on the show, your creativity becomes heightened because you have to do something else. Nothing was ever sexier than Cary Grant coming out of the bedroom in a pair of perfectly ironed pajamas. It allowed you to wonder what happened and not have it thrown at you."

Marlo Thomas recalls that the prudish atmosphere of 1960s television provided fun behind the scenes. "We always had to make sure that the audience knew that Donald never spent the night at Ann

Marie's. So practically every show would begin with me going to the door and letting him in. Well, for Teddy this was irresistible. I'd open that door and find Teddy dressed as a gorilla or Superman or whatever costume he could find to make us laugh."

In January 1968, *That Girl* was doing very well in the Nielsen polls, with 45.4 percent of the TV viewing audience tuning in to her antics on Thursday evenings at nine. And Yale University's Skull and Key Club named Marlo Thomas "Girl of the Year" that February. By April 1968, *That Girl* was the only sitcom in the top five TV shows on the air, and in May it was number five in the ratings for two successive weeks.

During this season Marlo Thomas also appeared as a guest on *ABC's Hollywood Palace* (hosted by Sid Caesar, Thomas presented a fashion show), was interviewed on the May 10, 1968, installment of *The Dick Cavett Show*, and signed for her first major film role (earlier she had turned down the lead in *Rosemary's Baby* [1968]; it went to Mia Farrow) in what was then called *Did You Hear about Jenny Shapiro* (later changed to *Jenny*), with Alan Alda.

The 1967–68 TV season ended in late April for *That Girl* and the reruns began immediately. Soon after that, the Emmy nominations were announced and once again the series was passed over for a nomination for Outstanding Comedy Series (*Get Smart* won the Emmy Award), but Marlo Thomas was nominated for a second time for Outstanding Continued Performance by an Actress in a Leading Role in a Comedy Series. This year her competition was Barbara Feldon *(Get Smart)*, Elizabeth Montgomery *(Bewitched)*, Paula Prentiss *(He & She)*, and the formidable Lucille Ball for her last year as Lucy Carmichael in *The Lucy Show* (next season she would play the same on-camera character, but with a different name in *Here's Lucy*, 1968–74). As the sentimental favorite, Lucille Ball won for the second year in a row.

Danny Arnold earned two Emmy nominations. The first was for Outstanding Directorial Achievement in Comedy for episode #35: "The Apartment." He lost to Bruce Bilson for *Get Smart*. (Bilson, incidentally, had also directed *That Girl* episode #39: "The Collaborators" in the fall of 1967.) Arnold's second nomination was shared with Ruth Brooks Flippen for Outstanding Writing Achievement in Comedy for episode #42: "The Mailman Cometh." They lost to Allan Burns and

Chris Hayward of *He & She.* By the time Burns and Hayward got their Emmy on June 4, 1968, *He & She* had been cancelled.

Meanwhile, *That Girl* rolled on into its third season, with Danny Arnold still at the helm under the sure eyes of Bill Persky, Sam Denoff, and Marlo Thomas.

Resumé
Ann Marie

Actress/Model

Height:	5 feet, 5½ inches	Dress Size: 6
Weight:	104 pounds	Shoe Size: 6A
Hair Color:	Brown	
Eye Color:	Brown	

Address: 344 West 78th Street or
           627 East 54th Street
           Apt. 4D
           New York, New York

Phone Number: Plaza 3-0598

Education: Brewster College, Brewster, New York
Member: Brewster Community Playhouse

Prizes:

Gold Medal Winner for Best Actress at Camp Winipoo

Representation:

Gilliam and Norris Talent Agency
Contact: Sandy Stone, George Lester, Harvey Peck, or
   Seymour Schwimmer (In an extreme emergency,
   call Don Blue Sky at BRyant 9-9970)

Current Member of the Benedict Workshop of the
   Dramatic Arts (Taught by Jules Benedict)

Professional Experience:

Stage

* *Gypsy* (Lincoln Center, New York City, revival starring
  Ethel Merman), as Girl at the Picnic
* *And Everything Nice* (Pre-Broadway tryout, played Colonial
  Theatre in Philadelphia and closed there)

* *The Revolutionary Heart* (Broadway show starring Barry Sullivan, New York City)
* *The Knights of Queen Mary* (Broadway show at the Empire Theatre, New York City)
* Untitled play (Understudy to Sandy Stafford on Broadway, New York City)
* *Honor's Stain* (Off-Broadway play, New York City, starring Sharon Hackett)
* *A Preponderance of Artichokes* (Experimental drama off-off-off-Broadway, New York City)
* *North of Larchmont* (Broadway show, New York City)
* *Funny Man* (Las Vegas Sands Hotel, Las Vegas, Nevada, starring Marty Haines)
* *The Queen of Diamonds* (St. Louis, Missouri), as Megan, the Queen's Sister

Miscellaneous Credits

Director of Annual Show at the Brewster (New York) Country Club

Appearance at the Friars Club (New York City) with Milton Berle and Danny Thomas

Television

* Guest Mop on *The Merry Mop-a-teers*
* Recurring role as Sheila in untitled daytime soap opera
* Recurring role of Doris the Ding-a-ling in untitled daytime soap opera
* Debut as Bank Teller on untitled TV show (credit reads The girl . . . Ann Marie)
* Dead Girl on *The Ladykiller*
* Contestant on *The Mating Game*
* Hit in the face with a pie on an untitled comedy show
* Cindy on The *Barry Forbes Show*
* Contestant on *Get Rich Quick*

Television Commercials

* Jungle Madness Perfume

* Twinkie soda pop
* Beer commercial with Marty Nickels
* Creamy Soap Girl
* Series of commercials for Action Soda
* No-Freeze Antifreeze commercial
* Appeared as "Duchess Ducky of Diet Soda Land"

As Spokesmodel

* Spokesperson for Chicken Big; Played Miss Chicken Big (coining the phrase "We Fry Harder")
* "Miss Everything" at the "New York Has Everything" exhibit at the Coliseum
* Spokesperson for Women in Space Air Force Program

Modeling Jobs

* New York Automobile Show at the Coliseum
* High-fashion layout for Noel Prince
* Fur coat campaign
* Roving model at Sardi's restaurant (New York City)
* Model for Girl Friday Productions
* Model at Belmont Race Track (Belmont, Long Island, New York)

Special Talents

Plays the violin and tap dances

Chapter 7

The Third Season (1968–69)

I think Marlo is just simply amazing to be in every shot and look good and to hire the people, see all the rushes, and sign the checks! As for me, I must just be pleasant and be there.

—ROSEMARY DeCAMP, IN THE JULY 5, 1969, ISSUE OF *TV GUIDE*

STARTING THE NEW TV YEAR

The autumn of 1968 saw the three American TV networks again preparing to fight for industry supremacy. CBS revamped its biggest star, Lucille Ball, and put her in a sitcom with a new title *(Here's Lucy)*, gave her a new character (Lucille Carter), and sent her out there to do what she had been doing since the early 1950s: make 'em laugh! Perennial hick Andy Griffith finally decided to hang up his sheriff's badge after eight successful TV seasons, but the town of Mayberry continued with some new cast (Ken Berry) and a new title *(Mayberry R.F.D.*, 1968–71).

Also at CBS, *The Doris Day Show* began its five-year run. Many books on television history credit Doris's show with being the first of the "single woman" television series to have benefited from *That Girl's* revolution, but that first season Doris played a widow with two kids, living on her uncle's farm. It was only the next season

(1969–70) that Doris's character got employment as an executive secretary for San Francisco-based *Today's World* magazine (but she still lived on the farm). It took two more seasons for Doris to chuck the kids and become a carefree swinging single on her TV program. Any resemblance to *That Girl* was purely coincidental. It would take more time before Ann Marie's influence really took hold, in particular, until *The Mary Tyler Moore Show* debuted in September 1970.

The one really revolutionary TV offering that premiered that fall was on NBC. Called *Julia*, it featured a single, African American, working mother, and starred actress/singer Diahann Carroll. The revolutionary move here was having an attractive, young, black star in the white world. Not since *Beulah* (1950–53) had a black woman headlined a sitcom. And never had she *not* played a maid! Taking risks was something that the fledgling ABC-TV could do. However, it seemed that giant NBC would now take some of its own.

And *Julia* was as much a risk as *That Girl* had been three seasons earlier. It lasted until 1971. The other new sitcom entry to endure was *The Ghost and Mrs. Muir* (1968–70), still cashing in on the supernatural craze in sitcoms *(Bewitched, I Dream of Jeannie, and, in 1970, Nanny and the Professor)*. *That Girl* held its prime 9:00 P.M. Thursday night time slot and was still opposite the second half of Raymond Burr's police drama, *Ironside*, and the beginning of CBS's weekly showcase movie.

In an ABC press release titled "The Topical Look for *That Girl*" and dated August 23, 1968, Marlo Thomas announced that in this, its third season, the program would have "a new look of realism."

"Our series is a situation comedy, but situations change," observed Thomas at the time. "What is happening now is that people, particularly the younger generation represented by Ann Marie, are concerned with what's going on about them." She went on to write that "comedy should be a playback of the times" and announced several of the "newly realistic" story lines: Ann preparing to vote in her first presidential election (episode #66: "Secret Ballot"), Ann serving on a jury for the first time (episode #63: "Eleven Angry Men and That Girl"), Ann confronting a possible plane hijacking (episode #62: "The Hi-Jack and the Mighty"), Ann being accosted (episode #68: "A Muggy Day in Central Park"), and a two-part episode dealing with violence in films (episodes #64 and 65: "7¼").

THIRD-SEASON CHANGES

The network press release for *That Girl*'s third season also presented an idea that never came to fruition: an episode in which "a Negro applies for an apartment in the building in which Ann Marie lives." (This idea was obviously recycled into episode #82: "The Defiant One," in which Ann learns timely lessons about race relations.)

Thomas ended her 1968 media statement by saying, "We've always based our show on the belief that the best comedy stems from truth, but the first season concentrated on Ann's romance and was pretty domestic. Last season, the show opened up a great deal and there was more adventure and realism about a girl living alone in New York. This season, the series will also be topical."

Tom Macklin of the *Newark Evening News* noticed a distinct change, in his June 26, 1968, article "*That Girl* Grows Up": "In the first season of *That Girl* there was an episode about a woman who got her big toe caught in a bowling ball. Last season, there was a segment on obscene telephone calls to women, another on a mugging in Central Park." (Actually, the mugging segment, episode #68: "A Muggy Day in Central Park," was in the third season which was being filmed then.)

In the same article Thomas explains that "TV is growing up. We started our show with romantic fluff, now we're dealing with reality. Our audience, mostly women from eighteen to thirty-five, wants something they can relate to."

But, of course, whatever issues emerged, Ann Marie continued to confront them in high-fashion clothes: Halston, St. Angelo, Courreges.

In addition to a new associate producer, Eddie Foy III (he was hired in April of 1968), there were new staff writers, including Stan Cutler and Martin Donavan, Arthur Julian, Carl Kleinschmidt, Jinx Kragen, Paul Wayne, Howard Leeds, John Whedon, Milt Rosen, Skip Webster, and John McGreevey. Some wrote only one script and others, like Cutler and Donavan, wrote several. Of course, Danny Arnold and Ruth Brooks Flippen still kept their hand in and wrote or co-wrote many of the entries.

The treat of the season was a return to the writing fold of *That Girl*'s creators, Bill Persky and Sam Denoff. They scripted what became, for very personal reasons, a favorite entry for Thomas: episode #79: "My Sister's Keeper." In this show, Marlo's real-life sister, Terre, plays a singing nun who is managed by her brother, played by their own brother, Tony. (Tony Thomas went on to become a very successful television producer under the banner of Witt-Thomas Productions. One of their hit TV series was *The Golden Girls*, 1985–92.)

"The whole plot was Ann Marie wanting to represent this singer and put her in show business," recalled Denoff at the *That Girl* seminar, "not knowing she was a nun. In the last scene at the parish, we had Danny Thomas walking by as a priest. And as Ann Marie bumps into him she says, 'Excuse me, Father,' to which Danny Thomas replies, 'That's all right, my child.'"

Thomas had hoped to get her whole family in on the fun.

"Only my mother didn't do it, because she *wouldn't* do it. She was just too shy, she wouldn't. I desperately wanted my mother to play the mother superior in the convent and she wouldn't do it."

But Marlo got her mother into the show by naming her sister's character (Rose) Cassinetti, which was her mom's maiden name.

Because of the emphasis on topical subjects, we saw less of Ann as an actress this third season, but when we did, she was still on her professional roller coaster.

The start of the 1968–69 season saw Ann winning a role in a Broadway play starring movie star Barry Sullivan (playing himself). Her career then took a downslide as she did a commercial for an airline, a series of ads for Action Soda, and another for POP soft drink in which her voice was dubbed by a singing nun. (By the way, how many soda commercials did Ann do?). Things were looking up when she earned a part on a TV comedy show, but she did have to get hit in the face with a pie (shades of *Rowan & Martin's Laugh-In*). The season closed with Ann accepting a job doing public relations promoting women in the space program.

No new running characters came to *That Girl* this go-round, but the Baumans became Ann's permanent neighbors and Jerry Bauman worked with Donald at *Newsview*. We also got to meet Ann's landlords, the Brentanos, several times. (Mr. Brentano was first played by Franco Corsaro and then by Frank Puglia; Mrs. Brentano was always the delightful Renata Vanni.) Comic actor Jesse White appeared this season as two different producers: the packager of the Action Soda commercial (episode #65: "7¼") and the producer of the comedy show on which Ann gets hit by a pie (episode #80: "There Was a Time Ann Met a Pie Man"). (The season before, White had appeared as both the producer of another of Ann's commercials and as her unscrupulous press agent, Eddie Edwards.) And for just one second-season episode (#81: "The Subject Was Rabies"), Ann got a new agent: Jules Munshin as Harry Fields.

As usual, there were veteran guest stars on the series like Jules Munshin and Barry Sullivan and Broadway actress Benay Venuta, but no really huge names. At this point, the very popular program did not require them.

"To me, the show was really the parents and me and Teddy," Thomas says. But she certainly welcomed additional star power.

"The one [guest star] I wanted that we never got together with was George Burns," says Thomas. "I really wanted to work with George Burns."

After three seasons on the air, the network still kept their hand in the *That Girl* pie. Thomas recalls: "They would come and talk to the guys and me and say why something [on the sitcom] they felt didn't work. It wasn't like an ultimatum [being] set down. It was more, 'How could this be better? What's really going to enhance the show?' You didn't really fight the network too much in those days. Also, we were a hit. So they were very protective of it."

Being a hit TV show made big demands on everyone. And doing a one-camera shoot made the demands even bigger. As Rosemary DeCamp related to *TV Guide* that season, whenever she shot an episode as Helen Marie, she had to get up at 4:30 A.M. to leave Redondo Beach by 5:30 A.M. to get to Paramount-Cahuenga's Stage 8 (the Desilu lot had been sold by then to Paramount) by 6:15 A.M. to put on her makeup. DeCamp chuckled as she said, "You have to get there earlier as you grow older."

Co-executive producer Bill Persky recalls, "It was tough. There was a lot of work. There were a lot of demands." However, Persky also admits that all the work and pressures made him a better producer, director, and problem solver.

"There was one moment I will always remember, when nobody was there [at the production office] but me. And I got a call—there was one camera, so there was always shooting—I got a call to come down to the set because there was a problem. And I walked in and I sat down. There was some dialogue that didn't work. Something didn't work. And I sat down in the first chair I came to and it happened to be a chair that . . . [was] in a spotlight. The whole stage was dark and there were hundreds of people standing around, the crew and all that stuff. She [Marlo Thomas] said, 'We hate this and we can't do it and it's not working.' I said, 'All right, just calm down,' and I looked around and I said, 'Holy shit! I'm sitting here with everyone in the world watching and I'm supposed to fix the scene now.' . . . So I said, 'Why don't you do this and this and this and this and that, and when you say that you say this.' And Marlo and everyone said, 'Wow, that's great!' And I just got up and walked out and never looked back."

While everyone else noticed the hard work, Thomas, who thrived on it, prepared for her big-screen debut in *Jenny*, a drama about a filmmaker (Alan Alda) who weds a pregnant young woman (Thomas) to avoid being drafted. As soon as production on *That Girl* ended for the season in late fall of 1969, Thomas went before the cameras on location in New York City. The movie was produced by ABC Pictures and was the first independent film produced by Thomas's champion, Edgar J. Scherick.

Although ABC-TV still had two years remaining on its five-year commitment to *That Girl*, as the third season started to wind down, Thomas began to worry as to how long they could last . . . artistically.

"I was very concerned that we just didn't have a fourth and fifth year of ideas. I mean, how many shows can you do about a girl who wants a job and a relationship with a boyfriend?" Having done eighty-six episodes, Thomas felt that "we've already made, like, seventeen movies about the same subject!"

When the Emmy nominations were announced in the spring of 1969, for the first time in three seasons, Thomas's name was *not* among the nominees for Outstanding Continued Performance in a Comedy Series. This reflected a new Emmy ruling to prevent stars of long-running TV shows from being nominated *too* many times. (It was abolished the next year after an outcry from the press.) Despite the Emmy ruling, *Variety*, on April 30, 1969, announced that the ABC network had acquired the daytime (rerun) rights to *That Girl* and that it would premiere on June 30, 1969, at 12:30 P.M. Now *That Girl* would be aired daily as well as once a week in the evening.

As if to prove how popular the show and Marlo Thomas had become, even such a small item as Ann Marie's classic 1960s sunglasses being auctioned for charity was picked up by the *That Girl*-hungry press.

Thomas was excited about the future and the prospect of shooting some of the upcoming episodes in Europe. (Ultimately, the budget didn't allow for it.)

And then, producer Danny Arnold announced that he was leaving the show.

Chapter 8

The Fourth Season (1969–70)

It was a solid hit. They wouldn't keep it on if it was not doing well. The bottom line is money. We had Bristol-Myers and they were very solidly behind it. Because their audience, the people that they needed, they loved that show. It had that young female audience.

—SAM DENOFF, CO-CREATOR AND
CO-EXECUTIVE PRODUCER OF *THAT GIRL*

MORE CHANGES

It is said that in all of show business there are twenty people and they just keep moving around . . . very quickly. Sheldon Leonard (1907–1997), one of the great character actors of film and television, was also one of the medium's most prolific and successful producers. With and without Danny Thomas, Leonard produced some of television's biggest hits, including *The Dick Van Dyke Show* (1961–66), from which sprang Bill Persky and Sam Denoff who went on to create *That Girl*. So it was somewhat ironic that, when Danny Arnold left *That Girl*, he left to produce a new sitcom for NBC, with Sheldon Leonard as the executive producer.

The show was called *My World and Welcome to It*. It was based loosely on the life and writings of humorist James Thurber (1894–1961), and starred William Windom. Unfortunately, NBC placed the sophisticated and innovative entry in the 7:30 P.M. time slot, normally reserved for very light children's or family shows. Having the perennially successful (fifteen years on TV and counting) *Gunsmoke* as its competition did the critically acclaimed show no good. At the end of the season, *My World and Welcome to It* closed shop forever. And then went on to win the Emmy Award for Outstanding Comedy Series!

So as *That Girl* entered its fourth season, the show got its third set of producers. It was announced in *Variety* on March 12 that the series would have yet another team at the helm: Bernie Orenstein and Saul Turteltaub. Orenstein and Turteltaub were no strangers to *That Girl*, having written episode #26: "You Have to Know Someone to Be Unknown," episode #40: "When in Rome," and episode #52: "He and She and He."

Luckily, they were well known personally to Persky and Denoff, who had the task of hiring the new team. Bill Persky remembers that although they were writers, Orenstein and Turteltaub were novice producers. "They had never done a situation comedy before, really, but they were old friends of ours. So we talked Marlo into them and they turned out to be terrific. . . ."

Marlo Thomas was now increasingly leery about how much longer her series could last on the air. She told syndicated columnist Marilyn Beck, "We're running out of ways to go, creatively. We've hired two new producers for the upcoming season and I think that will help." However, Marlo added prophetically that she didn't think "anything could convince me to go into a sixth year."

When Orenstein and Turteltaub came on board they became the story editors, but they contracted Ruth Brooks Flippen, whom Thomas adored, to write seven *That Girl* episodes (although she ended up with only one installment on the air, #94: "Write Is Wrong"). Flippen had left her position as script consultant on *That Girl* to be the story editor of ABC's *The Brady Bunch* (1969–74). Bernie and Saul also signed Ed Scharlach and Warren Murray, Joseph Bonaduce, and Sydney R. Zelinka to script other entries. Lew Gallo was brought on as their new associate producer and Earle Hagen (who wrote the theme) was tapped to take care of all the musical chores on *That Girl*. The show was solidly sponsored by Bristol-Myers, Noxell Corp, and Lever Brothers.

Besides *My World and Welcome to It*, the autumn of 1969 saw the premieres of such sitcoms as *To Rome with Love* with John Forsythe (CBS, 1969–72), *The Debbie Reynolds Show* (NBC, 1969–70), *Room 222* with Lloyd Haines (ABC, 1969–74), *The Brady Bunch* with Robert Reed, Florence Henderson, et al (ABC, 1969–74), *Mr. Deeds Goes to Town* with Monte Markham (ABC, 1969–70), and *The Governor and J. J.* with Dan Dailey and Julie Sommars (CBS, 1969–72).

That Girl moved its time slot to 8:00 P.M. The series was now the lead-in for *Bewitched* (which was entering its sixth season) and was preceded by *The Ghost and Mrs. Muir* (which was in its second and final year). The competition included the second half of NBC's six-year-old *Daniel Boone*, with Fess Parker as the historical American frontier legend, and CBS's highly touted new variety show, *The Jim Nabors Hour* (1969–71). (Coincidentally, Nabors's first sitcom, *Gomer Pyle, U.S.M.C.* [1964–69], was a spin-off of *The Andy Griffith Show* [1960–68] and had been produced by Sheldon Leonard and Danny Thomas, as well as featuring "that guy" Ted Bessell from 1965–66.)

As was its custom for all TV shows, *Variety* reviewed *That Girl*'s first entry of the new season. They reported, "The series has opened the season with a two-parter, evidently in the hopes that the story will have hooked viewers to keep them from the [Jim] Nabors preem [premiere] this week." To translate *Variety*-ese, ABC once again started their season a week earlier in hopes of catching the audience and keeping them hooked.

After the two-part episode (#87 and 88: "Mission Improbable") Orenstein and Turteltaub did double duty, both writing and producing episode #89: "My Part Belongs to Daddy."

Besides Flippen, Turteltaub and Orenstein brought in new writers, such as Fai Harris and Lynn Farr, Alex Barris, Jerry Ross and William Lynn, Coslough Johnson, and Broadway veteran Arnold Horwitt. (Horwitt had written the lyrics to the 1955 musical *Plain and Fancy*, which included the hit song "Young and Foolish.") But the new story editors still wound up scripting eleven out of the twenty-six episodes and contributing to the rest.

FINDING NEW WRITERS

In a *Hollywood Reporter* piece titled "Lotsa Lousy Writers Here," dated September 18, 1969, Turteltaub and Orenstein told journalist William Tusher that they were bringing in newcomers for *That Girl* because they weren't getting enough satisfactory product from experienced scripters.

"There are a lot of writers in Hollywood," Orenstein explained, "but I don't think there are a lot of good writers." Turteltaub agreed and added, "There may not be so much of a problem in getting fresh ideas for new shows, but there is a crisis in fresh ideas for a show that's been on the air four years. When the leading characters are two single people living in New York, you get to a point where you've done that, you've said that, or if you haven't after four years, some other show has."

So Orenstein and Turteltaub turned to untried TV writers. As script supervisors, they explained, "We end up doing most of the writing anyway. That can't be avoided because your best writer can bring in the best script, and it may be long or somebody may be unhappy with it who's performing it, or they can't direct it, and it ends up therefore having to be rewritten. Since we are the ones who have to sit down and spend those extra ten hours rewriting, we like to find that story we can best handle."

Perhaps to counterbalance the novice TV writing talent, the producers mostly hired directors who were familiar with the veteran series, like John Rich, Richard Kinon, Russ Mayberry, and Hal Cooper. Saul Turteltaub made his directing debut and helmed four installments that season. The season also marked the *That Girl* directing debut of one of its creators, Bill Persky, with the February 12, 1970, entry (episode #106: "Stocks and the Single Girl").

The first entry filmed for the season started shooting on location in Las Vegas on June 6, 1969. It was a two-part piece with Jack Cassidy as the guest star.

Professionally speaking, the fourth season began with Ann once again modeling, directing a show at the Brewster Country Club, playing the dancing Miss Chicken Big in a series of personal appearances for a fried chicken franchise, doing a commercial while suffering from a bad cold, getting a part in yet another Broadway show, performing in Las Vegas, and playing "straight man" in a Catskill's comedy act.

The 1969–70 season brought Ann yet another new talent agent, Sandy Stone played by Morty Gunty (who had played himself in episode #98: "She Didn't Have the Vegas Notion"). There was also a new Ruthie Bauman in the guise of actress Alice Borden.

Borden remembers being discovered "doing a Sani-Flush commercial." In fact, she had been a singer on Broadway and had done numerous backers' auditions with her friend composer/lyricist Jerry Herman for his hit show *Hello, Dolly!* (1964).

This was also the season when TV home viewers were treated to the singing talents of Lew Parker. As Ann's father, Lou, he warbled "Minnie the Moocher." (Parker came by his musical comedy panache naturally, as he had starred in vaudeville and on Broadway in such musicals as *Girl Crazy* [1930], *Are You with It?* [1945], and *Ankles Away* [1955].) Now we know where Ann got her talent. Sadly, this season also saw the last appearance of Billy DeWolfe as Ann's acting coach, Jules Benedict. DeWolfe would go on to appear as a regular (from 1970 to 1972) on *The Doris Day Show.*

Viewers also saw a rare flashback of Ann's working days before she moved to New York City (we had seen her as a teacher in the first season). In episode #103: "That Meter Maid," we find out that she had also been a meter maid (this is one of the two episodes this season directed by Ted Bessell). Strangely, when Ann is recalling the story of corruption in a small town, she tells us that it took place not in her hometown of Brewster, New York (which really exists), but in the fictional town of Fenwick, New York. It is clear that the powers behind the show did not want to offend, even remotely, the actual town of Brewster. However, after so many episodes telling us about Ann's childhood and adolescence, this change did play havoc with the logical sense of the series. Where did Ann Marie grow up anyway? Fenwick or Brewster?

Christmas Day of 1969 brought a new milestone to *That Girl*, when ABC aired the hundredth episode of the series. It was entitled "I Am a Curious Lemon" (a pun on the title of the notorious 1967 Swedish film *I Am Curious [Yellow]*) and was written by Alex Barris and directed by Russ Mayberry. A huge cake frosted with the *That Girl* logo was brought onto the set during the filming and Thomas cut slices for all.

February 19, 1970, also was a milestone of sorts. It was the last time that Rosemary DeCamp appeared as Helen Marie (episode

#107: "The Night They Raided Daddy's"). Although Helen Marie was referred to in the last season (1970–71), she was never seen. According to Marlo, the writers just found it more interesting to write for the character of Lou Marie. Although DeCamp had appeared in only nineteen *That Girl* episodes in total, she had definitely left her mark. Recalling DeCamp as Ann's mother, Thomas says, "She brings a sweetness, a real sweetness."

When *That Girl*'s fourth season ended, it was clear that Bernie Orenstein and Saul Turteltaub were in for the long haul. Like Danny Arnold, they were the needed creative forces known as "writing producers." Orenstein and Turteltaub fully understood that each new episode required a solid premise, an idea.

"To us, basically the whole story is the idea," Saul Turteltaub told William Tusher of the *Hollywood Reporter* (in the article entitled "Lotsa Lousy Writers Here, say Turteltaub, Orenstein") on September 18, 1969. "There's a terrible need for new ideas, simply ideas that haven't been done. The biggest problem in getting these shows out, and I'm sure it's true in every situation comedy, is the initial idea for a story. The dialogue is not that hard. It's the basic concept, that little gem in there, the nub, whatever you want to call it. If the idea hits us that's the whole ball game. Then we say, 'Fine, let's sit down and outline it.'"

After skipping a year, and with new changes in its rules, the Emmy nomination committee once again put Marlo Thomas's name back into the running for Outstanding Continued Performance of a Leading Actress in a Comedy. (Nevertheless, Hope Lange won that year for *The Ghost and Mrs. Muir.*) *Photoplay* named Thomas their favorite actress of 1969–70 and gave her their Gold Medal Award. And to top off the show's success, it was picked up for airing in Germany.

But with the end of the five-year contract in sight and a new three-year contract waiting to be signed, Marlo Thomas made the decision that the fifth season of *That Girl* would be its last. Not everyone was happy about quitting.

Thomas recalls that ABC's network executives pushed them "to commit to three more years. And the guys wanted to. Billy and Sam and Teddy all wanted to."

According to Sam Denoff, "They [ABC-TV] were willing to renew and do a whole new deal because the five years were up. And we would have all made a lot more money, but Marlo didn't want to continue." Thomas explains her rationale. "I said to Billy and Sam, 'I'm not a girl anymore, I'm a woman now. It's five years later. Girls grow into women, boys grow into men. I can't play *That Girl* anymore. It's really over for *That Girl* in me. And now I'm either going to move on to being 'That Woman' with Donald, or stop." So the decision was made to pull the plug.

But Clairol, the sponsor, and ABC thought if you have to go, why not go out in real style? How about . . . a wedding?

Ann Marie's Relatives

Lou and Helen Marie—Ann's parents. Helen never appears in the last season, but she is still referred to.

In episode #22: "Paper Hats and Everything" we hear about the unseen relations named:
>   Aunt Gladys
>   Uncle Oscar
>   Aunt Rosie
>   Uncle Henry

Competitive and old-fashioned Aunt Harriet appears in episode #25: "Leaving the Nest Is for the Birds."

Cheap cousin Harold Turner appears in episode #27: "The Honeymoon Apartment" with his new bride, cousin Edith Turner.

Lou's brother, Uncle Herbert Marie, appears in episode #125: "An Uncle Herbert for All Seasons."

Uncle Harry Marie is dead at the start of episode #127: "Those Friars." He leaves Ann his vaudeville trunk.

Chapter 9

Last-Inning Stretch

We had wonderful sponsors. . . . It was the days of single sponsorship too and that made a big difference. She [Marlo Thomas] looked great and that's all they wanted.

—BILL PERSKY, CO-CREATOR AND
CO-EXECUTIVE PRODUCER OF *THAT GIRL*

THAT NON-COMMERCIAL GIRL

For all of its five-year run, *That Girl* was sponsored by, among others, Bristol-Myers, parent company to Clairol. As Thomas pointed out, "They wanted a young girl to sell hair products." However, although Thomas's TV show sold the products, the young girl herself did not.

According to Marlo, "They asked me to [do commercials] but I didn't want to do it. Clairol wanted to put out an entire line of cosmetics called 'That'—That Shampoo, That Foundation, That Lipstick, That Hair Conditioner—and I just really didn't want to do it. I used always to say, 'Well, Katharine Hepburn wouldn't do it.' I thought it was cheap."

Would Thomas feel the same way now, when everyone from presidential candidates to the ghost of Fred Astaire does TV commercials?

"I think it's changed now. Paul Newman does commercials, Jack Lemmon, Michael Douglas . . . everybody. But in those days, to me, it just felt like hocking the product. I also thought it was odd to do it in your own show, because they wanted me to do it *in* my show. And I just thought, 'Oh God, I'm going to step out of character and become this other person and sell something? I don't want to do that.'"

There were also personal reasons why Thomas avoided the commercial route.

"I've been very political and I was concerned about speaking for something and getting paid for it, and speaking for something and believing in it. And I was just afraid that as a political person . . . I mean, I was campaigning for Bobby Kennedy in those years, and speaking out for women's rights . . . it seemed to me that it would confuse my voice if I made money from speaking as well. Then how do you know which one is the voice that's real? That confused me. That was an innocent feeling on my part. So I never did it."

There was lots of money to be made then too, not only from doing commercials, but also from the actual licensing of the *That Girl* trademark. However, Thomas once again took the high road and very little merchandising appeared.

"They wanted to do a dress line," she recalls, "they wanted to do a sunglasses line, they wanted to do makeup and foundations."

But none of these "That Girl" products ever materialized, as Marlo says, "Because I didn't want it."

Today, Bill Persky and Sam Denoff kind of wish they had followed the lucrative merchandising route. Persky: "I think the cosmetic line would have been astronomical!" Denoff: "Aahh! What would we have gotten? Just a lot of money! Feh!"

But some items did start popping up in the 1960s and early 1970s. Things like the *That Girl* board game, several different *That Girl* coloring books, paper dolls, a novelization using Ann Marie as a character, and a $500 Madame Alexander *That Girl* doll. In 1970, one Western department store chain was found selling an unauthorized "Marlo Wig" for $30, but it was quickly taken off the market.

"I let them do things for children," says Thomas. "Dolls, paper dolls, cutouts, that stuff—the stuff for the kids. We made no money. Coloring books and paper dolls. But the big money to be made in the dress lines and the makeup and the shampoos and all that, I didn't want to do it. It's different now."

THOSE LETTERS

*I would get letters from young women who said, "I'm sixteen
years old and I'm pregnant and I can't tell my father. What
should I do?" or "My husband is beating me. I'm twenty-five
years old and I have three children and I don't have any
money and my husband beats me. Where should I go?" And I
thought, "Why am I getting these letters from these people?
I don't even know these people."*

—MARLO THOMAS

As the *That Girl* seasons went on, fan letters continued to flood
Thomas's production offices. "Marlo got tons," remembers Sam
Denoff, "mostly to her. We were never aware of the mail. It goes to
ABC and they send it over. . . . The producers below us may have
read something and gotten an idea for a show. Fan mail is usually for
autographs and pictures and stuff like that."

Actually, from the beginning, Marlo Thomas's mail was different.
Along with the requests for autographs and photos were notes from
young women, letters she has kept to this day. Her friend, feminist
author Gloria Steinem, is touched by the correspondence Thomas
received.

"I think if you read the mail that Marlo got," says Steinem, "it's
clear that *[That Girl]* was influential, because young women wrote
her with enormous gratitude. They saw possibilities for themselves,
besides immediate marriage or staying home with their parents,
which had not been on television before."

Soon Marlo Thomas's secretaries began to notice a difference in
some of the letters' contents. As Sam Denoff points out, up until then,
viewers had written asking for the usual things and telling Thomas
that they were like her character or that they *wished* they were. And
as Steinem emphasizes, women expressed their gratitude. They
thanked Ann Marie for being a reflection of their contemporary lives.

"Television is at least fifty years behind," says Steinem. "There
had been women living alone in apartments, having boyfriends and
jobs, for much, much, much longer. But it was revolutionary for
showing it."

But little by little other kinds of letters arrived. Letters that changed Marlo Thomas. "The mail that we got on *That Girl* made me an activist," stated Thomas at the Museum of Television and Radio's *That Girl* seminar in 1996.

Thomas had hired several secretaries just to manage her huge amounts of fan mail, which averaged three to five thousand pieces a week. "I had said to them from the very beginning," says Thomas, "'We answer every letter. Everybody gets an answer.'"

At first the secretaries found that they could handle the mail, but every once in a while they would get an unusual letter to which they had no way of responding. So they brought it to Ms. Thomas. Beseeching letters about teenage pregnancies and fathers' rejections, or horrible letters about husbands beating them. "What should I do? Where should I go?"

Thomas was amazed.

"They just identified with this person [Ann Marie]," says Marlo. "They believed that this young woman, who was an independent woman in charge of her own life, would have the answers to these questions that they did not have the answers to. And I didn't have the answers."

Thomas instructed her assistants to find out, for example, where unwed mothers in Illinois should go, to find out where battered wives ("We didn't even have the word 'battered wives' in those days. We didn't have any of these terms.") from Ohio could seek refuge. What she found out shocked her.

"There wasn't any place for a woman who got beaten up by her husband. There were no battered-wives centers. There was no place for a girl to go who was pregnant, not for an abortion, not to place her baby. Everything was just a shame. Everything was a disgrace . . . and everything was the woman's fault. They were totally at the mercy of their parents and their husbands. Because in 1966 and 1967 there wasn't anywhere to go."

"And it really politicized me! It was my first touch with the women's movement in this country."

By paying attention to her mail, Thomas had hit upon some of the key problems that women around the country were experiencing. "In trying to find places for the people who wrote me letters, I found my way to these little tiny spots, little oases in the country where somebody could go if their husband beat them up. They were just beginning. It was just the beginning of the wave and I was getting in on it because I was trying to find help for somebody, 'cause I'm an obsessive person who answers my mail."

And Marlo Thomas, who was a feminist before there was such a word, now became a true activist. She campaigned for Bobby Kennedy. She spoke out for women's rights. She cared!

Gloria Steinem remembers asking Thomas to make a speech in front of homeless women. Thomas was nervous at first. Having been brought up in Beverly Hills she felt that she couldn't possibly know what to say to a group of homeless women. Steinem told her to "just tell the truth." And, in her discussion of self-empowerment, Thomas did just that. From then on she had no problems at all communicating with her listeners.

Looking back from today's viewpoint, Thomas is proud of the progress women have made over the decades and her role in it.

"There weren't any organizations at that time," reflects Thomas. "A woman who got beaten up in the 1960s and 1970s was just unlucky. She wasn't a battered wife. She wasn't a displaced homemaker. Those words . . . reproductive freedom . . . none of those things existed. It's amazing when people say, 'Do you think we've made any strides?' I say, 'Are you serious? Are you kidding? I mean, come on!'"

Mixed in with all those letters that transformed Marlo Thomas were letters that changed Ann Marie.

"We have had many letters from viewers asking when Ann Marie will marry Don Hollinger and we have talked about it," reported Thomas in the *Newark Evening News* in June of 1968. She went on to emphatically state, "The producers and I have agreed that marriage would change the concept of the series so much that it wouldn't be *That Girl*."

Actually, they thought about getting Ann and Don engaged for the fourth season, but did a viewer poll and, surprisingly, the viewers did *not* want Ann to marry. They liked her just as she was and wanted her to remain single.

But with stories difficult to come by, and Thomas definitely not wanting her series to go any longer than five years, *That Girl* and company were ready, if not to marry Ann off, to at least get Ann engaged. On March 10, 1970, the *Hollywood Reporter* made the announcement that, in the fall of 1970, Miss Ann Marie would become engaged to Mr. Donald Hollinger. And, after finding Don's pants hanging in Ann's closet, won't Mrs. Hollinger be relieved!

Ann Marie's Friends and Neighbors

Throughout the five seasons of *That Girl* we get to meet several of Ann's friends and neighbors, some for a brief moment and others for several seasons. Here are some of their names and their places in Ann's life:

Judy and Leon Bessamer
The Bessamers live in Ann's building and Judy is her best friend for the entire first season. They apparently moved away, because from the start of the second season Ann's best friend becomes . . .

Ruth Bauman
Ruth Bauman and her husband, Jerry (Don's best pal and colleague at *Newsview* magazine), live in Ann's building. Although Ruth is played by three different actresses, Ruthie and Jerry remain Ann's best friends until the very end of the *That Girl* series.

Marge "Pete" Peterson
In episodes #34: "To Each Her Own," #37: "The Philadelphia Story," #42: "The Mailman Cometh," #54: "Great Guy," and #58: "The Beard," Ann's best friend (besides Ruthie Bauman) is fellow actress, and plain-Jane, "Pete" Peterson. She and Ann work together in the Philadelphia tryout of the ill-fated play *And Everything Nice*.

Marcy

In episode #113: "Counter-Proposal," #117: "Rattle of a Single Girl," and #120: "That Cake," Ann's new friend is Marcy. Since she only appears in the last season, she is the least developed of Ann's social circle and, with her plain-Jane looks, seems only a "Pete" replacement and an earpiece for Ann's dialogue.

Sandy Stafford

In episode #10: "Break a Leg," Sandy is touted as one of Ann's best friends. When Ann becomes her understudy (Sandy is starring in a Broadway play), the friendship is sorely tested. Sandy never appears again on the series.

The Brentanos

Ann's landlords live in the same brownstone building and Mr. Brentano also fixes things around the building. They are old-world Italians and are more neighbors than friends.

Mrs. Morrisey

We only see Mrs. Morrisey, a neighbor whose son has a habit of locking himself in bathrooms, in episode #8: "Little Auction Annie."

Mrs. Bridges (episode #31: "Pass the Potatoes, Ethel Merman"), **Mrs. Stern** (episode #96: "Fix My Screen and Bug Out"), **Janie** and **Harry** (who never appear, even though they are mentioned in episode #112: "All's Well That Ends"), and **Mrs. McCarty** (episode #121: "That Girl's Daddy") are some of Ann's neighbors in her apartment building over the years.

Charlotte, Sharon, and **Linda** (Pilot episode: "What's in a Name?"), **Margie** (episode #9: "Time for Arrest"), **Sheila Harmon** (episode #13: "All About Ann"), **Sharon Hackett, Carl,** and **Estelle** (episode #28: "This Little Piggy Had a Ball"), and a party full of friends in episode #73: "Should All Our Old Acquaintance Be Forgot" complete Ann's circle of pals.

Chapter 10

That Last Season (1970–71)

Clairol wanted that wedding. Oh, they really wanted that wedding! But I felt it was just the wrong thing to do.

—MARLO THOMAS

NOT GETTING MARRIED

The first show (episode #113: September 25) of season number five was entitled "Counter-Proposal." It was written by Saul Turteltaub and Bernie Orenstein and directed by Turteltaub, both of whom, of course, were still the producers. And in it we finally saw Don pop the big question to his longtime girl friend (remember, they had met on the very first episode) and give her an engagement ring.

Variety watched the first show of the new *That Girl* season and gave it a grudgingly good review: ". . . the parts were somewhat better than the whole, thanks to Miss Thomas's effective portrayal of the warm but witless female lead." They went on to predict that "its last season might just be its best."

"A television series is a funny thing," mused Thomas at the *That Girl* seminar a few years ago. "For five years [Ann and Donald's] relationship never got any hotter and she never got a [permanent] job.

I mean, I played a singing mop and a dancing chicken . . . the most awful jobs in the world. And when the network wanted us to renew . . . I said, 'Who can stand it any longer? We're either going to have to have her make it as an actress or have her get married. And in either case it wouldn't be *That Girl* anymore. This is really about that time in a young girl's life when she's trying to figure out who she is.' That was really, to me, what that story was about. And also I was approaching thirty. I thought, I'm really not That Girl anymore. I mean, I'm a woman now. I feel like an impostor, with this little bangs-wig and everything, running around not having ever seen Donald's ankles. How long can you keep that up? So, anyway, we thought the engagement gave us some kind of progression."

Ann and Don's engagement not only put the show on the Nielsen Company's top-ten list (#7) once again, but also opened up the fifth season to some fresh story lines.

In episode #114, "Donald, Sandi and Harry and Snoopy" (October 2, 1970), we get to meet Donald's sister, played by Cloris Leachman who would go on to win an Academy Award for *The Last Picture Show* (1974). She was already playing the wonderfully brittle Phyllis Lindstrom on *The Mary Tyler Moore Show* (1970–75), which would lead to her own spin-off, *Phyllis* (1975–77). Another time, we witness the engaged couple going to a pre-marital counselor to ensure a long, happy marriage (episode #117, "Rattle of a Single Girl," October 23, 1970), and also we follow the young couple on their trip to St. Louis to see Don's parents. (This two-part installment, episodes #118 and 119, jointly titled "There Sure Are a Bunch of Cards in St. Louis" and airing on October 30 and November 6 respectively, would be the last segments for the marvelous Mabel Albertson as Mrs. Hollinger).

In the very next episode (#120, "That Cake"), aired November 13, 1970, Ann, in her best Lucy mode, loses her engagement ring in a cake that is to be served to Governor Nelson Rockefeller. It was hoped that the governor would appear as himself and talk to Ann in a split-screen effect, but Rockefeller ultimately declined to make his acting debut on the show. In another installment (#128, "A Limited Engagement," January 15, 1971) Donald gets cold feet and breaks off the engagement. But he recovers in time for his stag party in episode #133 ("Stag Party," February 26, 1971).

AND THE SPIRAL GOES ON

History goes in forward ellipses. Cycles that go and then come back . . . but not all the way. Like a spiral, not staying in the same place, but like a Slinky slowly climbing the stairs. People watch the show today because the spiral is still moving.

—Susan L. Dworkin, feminist, author, and activist

That Girl was becoming like a ring of that spiral. If the 1970–71 season was to be the finale for *That Girl*, it was fitting that Ann Marie pass her "Miss Independence" crown to Mary Richards of CBS-TV's *The Mary Tyler Moore Show*. It is astonishing to remember that Ann and Mary shared a prime-time season. How fitting that Ann's last TV year be Mary's first. From the beginning, Mary Tyler Moore said, "Ann Marie opened the door and Mary Richards walked through."

Actually, Sam Denoff and Bill Persky planted the seed that grew into *The Mary Tyler Moore Show*. Having written many of the later episodes of *The Dick Van Dyke Show*, in 1969 the boys (according to Persky, "All writers who are partners are always known as the boys. . . . and when young women started to write, the network executives called *them* 'the boys'") came up with an idea for a one-hour TV special starring Van Dyke and Mary Tyler Moore, entitled *Dick Van Dyke and Other Women*. Moore, whose career on Broadway and in films was not catching fire and who was fresh from a Broadway disaster (the show was a musical version of Truman Capote's *Breakfast at Tiffany's*, entitled *Holly Golightly*, and had Mary costarring with Richard Chamberlain), accepted the special. CBS was so enamoured of her performance in that special that they contracted her for a TV series. So, although Bill Persky and Sam Denoff had nothing to do with *The Mary Tyler Moore Show*, they can be considered the godfathers.

It was actually Jim Brooks, who had cut his teeth on early *That Girl* scripts, who co-created *The Mary Tyler Moore Show* with Allan Burns. At first Mary Richards was to be a divorcee, but CBS feared that viewers might think that she had divorced Rob Petrie, her husband on *The Dick Van Dyke Show*. As a consequence, she was made . . . a single thirtysomething girl on her own. Fleeing an engagement gone sour, she comes to a new city (Minneapolis) and begins living in her own apartment and, at least on the first episode, looking for a job. Sound familiar?

But Mary was thirty and no longer a girl, so, in a way, she portrayed what might have happened to *That Girl* if Ann and Donald had broken their engagement and Ann had moved to a Midwest metropolis. The ultimate irony occurred in Mary's final season (1976–77), when Ted Bessell joined the cast as Mary's boyfriend, Joe Warner, the one man she might actually marry. And just like *That Girl*, *The Mary Tyler Moore Show* left the romance up in the air, without a clean-cut ending, when it voluntarily went off the air in the spring of 1977.

THAT SEASON

For the final season (1970–71) *That Girl*'s time slot was moved once again and, for the first time, the show was seen on Fridays at 9:00 P.M., instead of Thursdays. A new ABC show starring Shirley Jones and David Cassidy, *The Partridge Family* (1970–74), was the lead-in property and *That Girl*, in turn, led the way for the second season of *Love, American Style* (which had been a mid-season replacement in 1970). Back on Thursday night, *Bewitched* (now in its seventh season) was the lead-in for another new ABC sitcom, an adaptation of Neil Simon's play *Barefoot in the Park* (1964), the very same play in which Marlo Thomas had starred in London during that fateful period when the *That Girl* pilot was sold. Thus, the circle continued. Unfortunately, the all-African-American sitcom version of *Barefoot in the Park*, starring Scoey Mitchell and Tracy Reed, was not as lucky as the stage and film adaptations had been and lasted only half a season.

Other new shows that season included *The Don Knotts Show* (NBC, 1970–71), *The Odd Couple* (ABC, 1970–75)—another Neil Simon adaptation, this time wildly successful, starring Tony Randall and Jack Klugman—*Nancy* with Renne Jarrett, John Fink, and Celeste Holm (NBC, 1970–71), *The Headmaster* with Andy Griffith and Jerry Van Dyke (CBS, 1970–71), *Arnie* with Herschel Bernardi (CBS, 1970–72), and Danny Thomas in *Make Room for Granddaddy* (ABC, 1970–71). Mary Richards may have continued the revolution that Ann Marie had begun, but in January 1971 CBS slipped in a mid-season replacement show that was as revolutionary and influential, in its own way, as *That Girl* had been. It was *All in the Family* (1971–83), starring Carroll O'Connor and Jean Stapleton, with Sally Struthers and Rob Reiner.

In a way, Norman Lear's pathbreaking *All in the Family* represented a return to the old days of television, before *That Girl*. It had one basic set, a small cast, and little reliance on guest stars. In addition, it was the first sitcom to be videotaped, which gave it a gritty, realistic, yet stagy look. And, unlike the majority of 1960s sitcoms (including *That Girl*), it was performed before a live audience. What distinguished it from all its brethren was the fact that it was the first American network sitcom to deal openly with bigotry, prejudice, and politics. Hot issues that Thomas was dealing with in her role as an activist, such as abortion and birth control, were skillfully handled on *All in the Family*. It was as if the letters Thomas received were passed on to Norman Lear and *All in the Family*, where serious subjects were dealt with humorously and intelligently.

All in the Family represented what Thomas once had said about *That Girl:* "A whole new era. It's brand new." So with Mary Tyler Moore to carry the torch when Thomas left the small screen, and *All in the Family* to guide the way for future sitcoms, *That Girl* went about entertaining its faithful audience for the last twenty-three times.

LAST-SEASON CHANGES:
THAT HAIRDO, THAT THEME SONG,
AND THOSE WRITERS

Fall 1970 brought Ann Marie not just an engagement ring, but also a new hairdo! For the first time on *That Girl*, gone were the bangs (or the bangs-wig) and gone was the logo-like flip. Ann/Marlo had a new look—less 1960s and more 1970s. Banished to reruns were the miniskirts and the flip hairdo, and replacing them was long, straight hair, parted in the middle—and the midi and maxi look. No one can ever say that Ann Marie was not in fashion! And to go with the new look, the wonderfully memorable theme by Earle Hagen that was played over the opening titles every week was re-recorded—and this time there were lyrics, by *That Girl* creator Sam Denoff.

"I kept thinking about it," recalls Denoff. "'We should say something, because it [adding lyrics to the song] would make her different.'"

Denoff, who had originally wanted to be a songwriter, came up with a lyric that described both Ann Marie and Marlo Thomas. It was a lyric full of contradictory imagery: Diamonds, daisies, snowflakes . . . chestnuts, popcorn, sable. . . . It caught the spirit of *That Girl* and ended by telling the male half of the audience, "If you find one girl to love, only one girl to love, then she'll be That Girl too!"

Even though the lyrics were only used during the last season's opening credits, they made the theme song more memorable and kept the title in audience's ears for decades. It has the power to make you think of the time and place and innocence of a whole television era. As recently as 1997, Earle Hagen and Sam Denoff were called about reusing the theme.

"Earle got a call, because he's the publisher [actually, EDJ Company is the publisher of the *That Girl* theme], from NBC, who wanted to take the *That Girl* theme to promote [the short-lived] *The Jenny McCarthy Show*. I said, 'What?' He said, 'Yes, they want to change the lyric to promote Jenny. I'll fax you the lyric, but I've got to tell you before I do, I think it stinks and I don't think we should do it.' The theme is so identifiable they wanted it to promote a show that's on NBC this season."

Not surprisingly, Denoff and Hagen turned them down.

"I said, 'How about your own theme? It's wrong! It's stupid! I don't care what they want to pay us, it ruins our theme.'"

Besides Saul Turteltaub and Bernie Orenstein, who wrote eleven of the twenty-three final episodes (including the first and last segments), some old hands were back to write the entries for *That Girl*'s last hurrah: Peggy Elliot, Ed Scharlach, Arnold Horwitt, Bruce Howard, Rick Mittleman, and Warren S. Murray (the son of comic Jan Murray). Some new voices included Gordon Farr, Bob Garland, Marvin Walkenstein, Bud Grossman, and Sam Nicholas. Since there was to be no pat, happy-ending, wedding scene for Ann and Donald, and the series was not to be neatly tied up with a ribbon, it was fitting, perhaps, that Persky and Denoff did not write the last episode. But one wishes, for posterity's sake, that they had.

At least two story ideas were taken from real-life situations. Episode #123: "Super Reporter" (December 4, 1970) was directly

inspired by a practical joke that Marlo Thomas played on pro-
ducer/writer/director Saul Turteltaub. She presented him with a
Superman costume and then hid his clothes, forcing him to attend
a meeting dressed as the hero. Turteltaub and Orenstein turned this
prank into a funny episode, substituting Don for Turteltaub and making Ann more innocent than Marlo. The other story idea stemmed from
a talk that Mexican actor Ricardo Montalban gave at the Writers Guild
calling attention to the poor treatment of his countrymen. Episode
#124: "That Senorita" (December 11, 1970, written by Turteltaub and
Orenstein) was the result of their sensitivity to the subject.

Besides the episodes that dealt with the Marie/Hollinger engagement, Ann's story-line career went on as usual. She appeared on a TV
show called "Get Rich Quick" where she is asked to "Know Your
Neighbor" (episode #116: "No Man Is a Manhattan Island," October
16, 1970), appeared in a play in St. Louis, combining the trip with a
pre-nuptial visit to the Hollingers (episodes #118 and 119: "There
Sure Are a Bunch of Cards in St. Louis," October 30 and November
6, 1970), wrote articles for a women's magazine, though Donald actually wrote them for her (episode #122: "Stop the Presses, I Want to
Get Off," November 27, 1970), performed in a revue that denigrated
minorities (episode #124: "That Senorita," December 11, 1970), met
Milton Berle and Danny Thomas (although Danny had appeared as a
priest in episode #79: "My Sister's Keeper," back on February 6, 1969,
this was the only credited appearance of Marlo's father on *That Girl*)
and performed with them at the Friars Club (episode #127: "Those
Friars," January 8, 1971), and modeled twice—once at the Belmont
Race Track (episode #134: "Two for the Money," March 5, 1971) and
once wearing nothing but a staple, as a centerfold in "Playpen" magazine (episode #115, "I Ain't Got Nobody," October 9, 1970)—surely
a long way from a singing mop!

And in the finale episode (#136: "The Elevated Woman," March
19, 1971), after twenty-two weeks of being engaged, Ann and Donald
finally get . . . *stuck in an elevator!*

Thomas recalls the decision to disregard convention and *not*
have Ann and Donald get married on the show.

"I thought it would be wrong. Because an engagement you can
break, but a marriage is . . . [forever]. Hey, I'm a Catholic. I really felt
that That Girl getting married sent a wrong message to the girls of

America. They had really counted on her for a certain stand. If her story ended with a marriage they might think that it meant that that was the only way to have a happy ending. And though marriage is wonderful—I'm happily married for eighteen years—I just felt that it was the wrong message. So the last show is about taking Donald to a women's lib meeting rather than a wedding." Interestingly, even as far back as August 1966 Marlo Thomas had proclaimed that "Ann Marie will never get married on the show."

Decades later, when asked by *TV Guide* what happened to the *That Girl* lovebirds, Ted Bessell, who then was contemplating a *That Girl* reunion telefilm, said he believed that the two never would have made it down the aisle.

"They would have remained friends," said Bessell, "and I think they would have gotten back together again. He probably would have married, and she might have done well as an actress."

That last episode contained flashbacks from earlier seasons while Ann and Donald were stuck in an elevator on their way to a women's lib meeting.

Thomas thought long and hard about the decision that the characters not marry on camera. And in doing so, she defined what the show was really about: "The *That Girl* show is about this young woman *wanting something*, being in that transition of her life, between her family and what she may commit to as her definition of life. But this is the period, the transition time, and I didn't think that we should say how that ends."

Thus, at 9:30 P.M. eastern standard time on Friday, March 19, 1971, *That Girl* was *that*.

Ann Marie's Boyfriends, Dates, and Male Admirers

From the very first episode aired, Ann Marie is dating Donald Hollinger, but throughout the five seasons of the series, Ann either dates or is pursued by the following characters, proving that That Girl sure had it:

Harry Banner (episode #35: "The Apartment")
Giuseppe Casanetti (episode #24: "A Tenor's Loving Care")
Buzzy Cavanaugh (episode #47: "Fur All We Know")
Major Culpepper (episode #90: "Nobody Here But Us Chickens")
Freddy Dunlap (episode #17: "Among My Souvenirs")
Federico Gente *(also one of Ann's neighbors; saw her naked in the shower)* (episode #67: "The Face in the Shower Room Door")
Frank Gilder (episode #23: "What Are Your Intentions?")
Captain Gooney (episode #115: "I Ain't Got Nobody")
Eduardo Guzman (episode #30: "The Mating Game")
Marty Haines (episodes #98 and #99: "She Didn't Have the Vegas Notion, Parts One and Two")
Clinton Hayworth (episode #50: "Call of the Wild")
Buddy Hobard *(just a rumor)* (episode #57: "Just Spell the Name Right")
Major Brian James *(after ignoring her for the whole episode, he finally made a play)* (episode #83: "Fly Me to the Moon")
Dr. Rex Kennedy *(played by Ted Bessell)* (episode #56: "If You Were Almost the Only Man in the World")
Kowali, The King of *(eleven years old!)* (episode #132: "That King")
John MacKenzie (episode #72: "Decision Before Dawn")
Detective Sergeant Ray Mandel (episode #55: "The Detective Story")
Bobby Miller *(ex-boyfriend and current landlord)* (episode #96: "Fix My Screen and Bug Out")
Harvey Miller (episode #37: "The Philadelphia Story")
Marty Nickels (episode #59: "The Drunkard")

Hobart Niles (episode #15: "Beware of Actors Bearing Gifts")

Jack Packard *(fellow juror of Ann's)* (episode #63: "Eleven Angry Men and That Girl")

Noel Prince (episodes #43 and #44: "It's a Mod Mod World, Parts One and Two," and #52: "He and She and He")

Dick Shawn *(as himself)* (episode #42: "The Mailman Cometh")

Chris Talley *(fellow juror of Ann's)* (episode #63: "Eleven Angry Men and That Girl")

Andrew Washington *(the oldest of Ann's admirers)* (episode #60: "Old Man's Darling")

Roddy Waxman (episode #6: "Rich Little Rich Kid")

Chapter 11

Life after *That Girl*

"People have a love for it [That Girl].*"*
—TED BESSELL, TO *TV GUIDE*, 1996

"I was happy to let it go. It was what it was. That was it."
—BILL PERSKY, 1998

That Girl *belonged to the new generation. It was the seedling that led all the way to* Murphy Brown.

—MARLO THOMAS, 1998

SYNDICATION, CARTOONS, AND PAPER DOLLS

And the very next week, *That Girl* was back! Well, in reruns, anyway.

Viewers who missed it, or wanted to relive it, could start Ann and Don's engagement period all over again on March 26, 1971. And if they had a mind to, they could also catch earlier episodes of the series during the day, where it had been syndicated by ABC since mid-1969. And in 1971, Metromedia acquired the syndication rights to all 136 episodes, meaning that conceivably one could watch *That Girl* around the clock on different local stations. (In Germany, under the translated title *Sweet But a Little Crazy*, *That Girl* was a number-one TV hit.) Even in the heat of August's summer reruns, *That Girl* was number four in the top twenty shows. As she had hoped, Marlo Thomas went out on top.

Actual production ended on *That Girl* on November 10, 1970, when Thomas and company filmed the last of episode #132: "That

King." Appearing in thousands of dollars worth of jewels, including a tiara that belonged to actress Marion Davies, Thomas went out in a sparkling way.

On November 28, 1970, at 7:30 P.M. Hollywood time, Marlo Thomas threw a huge farewell party for the cast and crew, and mixed emotions abounded. The invitation read "Miss Marlo Thomas invites you to help celebrate five wonderful years of *That Girl!* . . . Wear What Yez Want."

But although *That Girl* may have stopped production, the series was still very much around. And, in the decades to come, *That Girl* could always be seen somewhere around the world. It even became a novel by Paul W. Fainman in 1971. In the book, which has a photograph of Marlo Thomas on the cover, Ann Marie is trapped in a haunted mansion in the windy Maine wilderness. The paperback book is a collector's item now and sells for as much as sixty dollars. It joins the list of expensive *That Girl* collectibles including the *That Girl* board game (one of the five most difficult such games to find), several coloring books, and cutout paper dolls.

Surprisingly, Ann Marie resurfaced in a Saturday morning television one-shot animated hour-long feature called *That Girl in Wonderland*. This 1973 cartoon featured Marlo Thomas as the voice of Ann Marie in a spin-off of the series. Ann, as an editor for a children's book publisher, daydreamed while preparing a book of fairytales. She imagines herself as the various heroines of *The Wizard of Oz, Snow White, Sleeping Beauty, Cinderella,* and *Goldilocks.* All the stories become interwoven (this would later be a plot device of the Stephen Sondheim/James Lapine musical *Into the Woods*) and end, unlike the musical, happily. This was originally seen on *The ABC Saturday Superstar Movie* and was a Rankin-Bass Production, written by Stu Hample, with music by Maury Law and Jules Bass.

For years after it left the air, *That Girl*'s impact continued to be felt. In the 1970s, the very popular *Saturday Night Live* TV series (NBC, 1975–) did a recurring sketch called "That Black Girl" featuring Danitra Vance as an African-American Ann Marie. In the 1990s, the sitcom *Roseanne* (1988–97) did two episodes that tapped into the *That Girl* lover's sensibility: one in which Roseanne actually fantasizes that she and her husband, Dan Conner (John Goodman), are Ann and Donald (Roseanne/Ann: "But I can't marry you. Don't you know that I'm television's first feminist . . . well, television's first *pretty* feminist?"), the other a Halloween fantasy with Roseanne and other TV icons dressed as the witches from Shakespeare's *Macbeth.*

"In this show I was in this little tiny scene where I was one of these witches around a caldron," remembered Thomas at the Museum of Television and Radio's *That Girl* seminar in 1996. "It's a nightmare she's having. The other two witches are the women from the AbFab *[Absolutely Fabulous]* series. We're all mixing this brew and one of the witches tells Roseanne, 'You must drink this brew.' Roseanne pulls away and is afraid, and she keeps forcing it on her. Roseanne says, 'I'll only drink it if I get it from . . . That Witch!' The camera pushes in in that familiar way to [my] face . . . as a hag-like Ann Marie. It was really funny."

Even little children, who could only know of *That Girl* from reruns, got an animated taste of Ann Marie when Steven Spielberg's 1990s cartoon TV series, *Animaniacs*, did their version of *That Girl*'s opening credit sequence.

With the advent of cable TV, and especially Nick at Nite and TV Land which specialize in classic television, *That Girl* once again has come into vogue.

"When the show went on Nick at Nite they had a party in New York," recalls Bill Persky, "and they ran the original pilot . . . that was never on the air because we did have a cast change. In New York there is a group of very attractive [people] who go someplace every night for hors d'oeuvres. . . . And I was amazed . . . it was a large audience . . . and those young women loved that show. They were attracted to it like a whole breath of fresh air had come into their lives. It was so rewarding to see. It was all about a girl who wanted to change her name, and her father's pain that she would change her name, and the two of them fighting it out and coming together. These sophisticated kids loved it. And they were just so moved. It was great to see this hip group of kids loving that."

But, although Ann and Don and Lou and Helen and the rest would live on in syndication, Marlo Thomas, Ted Bessell, Lew Parker, and Rosemary DeCamp would move on to other projects. Still, many of the associations and friendships that the five-year run had wrought would remain strong. Thomas and Persky are friends to this day, and she and Bessell were close until his untimely death in 1996. The following is what happened to the principal players after the show went off the air.

THE CAST

Lew Parker
(Lou Marie; 1966–1971)

The first of the *That Girl* alumni to leave this earth was Lew Parker.

During the period that he was playing Lou Marie, Parker also appeared on *F-Troop* (1965–67), *Gidget* (1965–66), and several episodes of *The Lucy Show* (1962–68). After *That Girl* went off the air, Parker returned to the stage.

"He just loved me and I loved him," reflects Thomas today. "When he was dying, he was appearing in *A Funny Thing Happened on the Way to the Forum* [the 1972 revival with Phil Silvers; Parker played the role of Senex, which was originated on Broadway by comic actor David Burns], and I went to see him in that and he didn't look well. His wife [Betty Kean of the Kean Sisters; she also appeared on *That Girl*] called me and . . . told me he had collapsed [on stage]. He was in a hospital [St. Claire's] and I went to see him. And he said to me, 'You know, you're the daughter I never had.'"

"And I went to see him every day and brought him ice cream and we really sat. And I said, 'What would you like to do?' He said, 'Bring me the show, the birthday show' [episode #22: "Paper Hats and Everything," February 9, 1967]. He loved that show, where I said, 'If I were a boy would you love me more?' and he said . . .'"

Thomas's voice sadly trails off here, but then she continues.

"We watched it together and we cried and he asked me if I would do his eulogy. I had never done a eulogy in my life. I said yes, because how could I say no? He said, 'That's what I want. I want you to say my eulogy.'"

"So I called my father after Lew died and I said, 'How do you do a eulogy? I don't know what you do.' And he said, 'You just tell all the wonderful stories about him.' He said, 'Just talk about his life and what you loved about him and what your relationship was. That's all there is. You're not a rabbi or a priest. You're not going to get up and give blessings or say Sermons from the Mount. You just talk about the person.' So I did, but it was very hard. I cried though the whole thing."

Lew Parker died on October 27, 1972. His last *That Girl* episode was #133: "Stag Party," February 26, 1971.

"I really . . . I still miss him because he was just a darling, innocent, sweet man. Just a sweet man. Teddy had that too. Teddy was a very innocent person."

Ted Bessell
(Don Blue Sky; 1965) (Don Hollinger; 1966–71)

How ironic that, after five seasons, Ted Bessell was finally recognized by the Emmys and nominated for Outstanding Continued Performance by an Actor in a Leading Role in a Comedy Series. Critics and the Emmys had tended to ignore Bessell's contribution to the show, but not Marlo Thomas. She understood why Bessell had such appeal.

"Teddy was a sexy guy. Girls liked him. Guys could identify with him. He wasn't a dope. A lot of guys were dopes on shows with girls. That kind of was the way they did it. Either the woman was like Lucy, afraid of him, or, on my father's show *[Make Room for Daddy]*, he was this guy who was a toothless lion who made a lot of noise, but in the end the children-knew-best kind of thing."

In fact, it was the audience who appreciated Bessell the most.

"When they did the testing, I think I remember, Teddy had the highest rating of any second banana. Very, very strong . . . the audience really liked him. And he tested very high. There's no two ways about it. Ted Bessell was half that show."

But the Don Hollinger role had typecast Ted Bessell and he later found it difficult to escape the role.

"Donald Hollinger made me a name but took away what was the heart of me," he told *People* magazine in 1989, dismissing the role as "an imposition on my creative needs."

Bessell's success on *That Girl* got him cast in a series of television films, such as *Two on a Beach* (ABC, 1971), *Your Money or Your Wife* (CBS, 1972), *Scream Pretty Peggy* (ABC, 1973), *What Are Best Friends For?* (ABC, 1973), *Breaking Up Is Hard to Do* (ABC, 1979), and *The Acorn People* (NBC, 1981).

One year after *That Girl*, Bessell starred in *Me and the Chimp*, a CBS-TV mid-season replacement that barely lasted out the season. It was created by Garry Marshall and Tom Miller (who later worked together on *Happy Days*, 1974–84, and *Laverne & Shirley*, 1976–83).

Bessell costarred with Broadway actress Anita Gillette and Jackie, a three-and-a-half-year-old chimp.

He did two unsuccessful pilots for CBS in 1973 and 1974: *The Ted Bessell Show* and *Bobby Parker and Company*. He became a recurring character on *The Mary Tyler Moore Show* in 1975.

In an attempt to leave Don Hollinger behind, Bessell went back to the stage, including starring on Broadway in *Same Time, Next Year* in 1976.

But the lure of the sitcom brought Bessell back to television in 1980 with his starring role in *Good Time Harry*. The series, an NBC summer replacement, lasted from July until September of that year. Bessell unsuccessfully tried sitcoms one more time in 1985 when he appeared opposite Patty Duke on ABC's *Hail to the Chief*.

Bessell had cut his directorial teeth on several *That Girl* episodes and it was in that capacity that he finally had comparable success. *The Tracey Ullman Show* (1987–90), which coincidentally was co-created by the same Jim Brooks who wrote his first script for *That Girl*, ran on the fledgling Fox network. Bessell became the show's director and producer, winning two Emmy Awards in 1989 for his efforts.

"He never let me fake a move," Tracey Ullman says. "He was truly an actor's director."

Bessell, the director, was soon in demand and he helmed episodes of *The Naked Truth*, *Good Advice*, and *Sibs*. In 1996, Bessell began working on a big-screen version of *Bewitched*. Bessell began talking to Thomas about a possible *That Girl* reunion TV movie which would star Thomas and himself. It seems that Bessell was coming to terms with his past and making peace with *That Girl*.

"People have a love for it," Bessell told *TV Guide* in the mid-1990s. "It's remarkable through the years that you get that kind of response."

Bill Persky recalls, "They [Bessell and Thomas] were talking about a film about them meeting up with each other. I guess I would have been involved. They wanted me to be. . . . I was happy to let it go. I figured it was what it was. That was it. I don't have any need to do a reunion of any of the shows."

This was not the first attempt to relive the past.

"We have been asked over the years to do another *That Girl*," says Sam Denoff. "[In 1996] I got a call from an agent. . . . They wanted to know if they could secure the rights . . . to do a feature on *That Girl*. We said no, because this is a trend now, people trying to make films of old TV shows. Anyway, before his [Bessell's] death, Billy and I learned that Marlo and Teddy were really talking about it, because he was involved with Penny Marshall's company, and they actually had an idea of Ann Marie and Donald meeting in later life, which would have been a very nice movie. I think a feature. It would have been terrific. She was very serious about doing it then."

"I was considering that because Teddy was so high on it," concurs Thomas. "He wanted [it to be] a television movie of us meeting years later, with one of us being widowed and one of us being divorced, and we fall in love and finally consummate our relationship. I wasn't for it when he first started talking about it and he kind of wore me down. I thought, 'Well maybe there is something here.'"

Having left the end of the series up in the air, the field was wide open to what might have happened to Ann and Donald. For instance, did they marry and live happily ever after?

"We just figured that they didn't, since we left it so open-ended," Thomas continues, "that we didn't choose to get married. Maybe they didn't. It seemed like a romantic and interesting idea, like those Christopher Isherwood stories where people happen to meet on the street twenty years later and they realize they never forgot each other. So it had kind of that to it. I never wanted to do a *That Girl* reunion. We turned it down several times. This was different. Billy [Persky] and I talked about it and thought this would be different. This would be a love story. Not a *That Girl* reunion, not a replay of *That Girl*, but something that would actually happen twenty-five years later. So it did kind of touch my interest."

But early in October 1996, Bessell began having chest pains, which his doctor thought were discomfort from anxiety. On October 4, Bessell's pain got worse and he was rushed to the emergency room at St. John's Hospital in Santa Monica, California. He was once again diagnosed as having anxiety and sent home. This happened yet again, on Saturday, October 6, and he again went home. Late that evening, after tucking his daughters into bed, Ted Bessell collapsed on the floor of his bedroom. His wife rushed him to nearby UCLA Medical Center, where he died on the operating table of a ruptured main heart artery. Bessell died just five days before the Museum of Television and Radio's *That Girl* seminar, which he was to co-host with Marlo Thomas. At the seminar, Thomas devoted the first part of the evening to Bessell's career and showed many clips from his non-*That Girl* shows.

For Marlo Thomas, Ted Bessell was a very special friend who would be sorely missed. "When my father died [in 1991]," recalled Thomas at the Museum's retrospective, "a few days after the funeral, [when] everything had quieted down, Teddy called me up and he said, 'You want to go for a ride?' And I said, 'Yeah, I really do.' He picked me up and we drove back and forth from Beverly Hills to the beach for hours and we cried and we talked and, of course, even on that darkest day he was able to make me laugh. I worked with Ted every day for five years," Thomas told the audience that night. "I loved him and I will miss him for the rest of my life."

Rosemary DeCamp
(Helen Marie; 1966–70)

After her stint as Helen Marie, *That Girl*'s mother, in 1972 Rosemary DeCamp played yet another mother, on TV's *The Partridge Family* (which was *That Girl*'s lead-in during its last season in 1970–71, in which DeCamp did not appear.) This time DeCamp not only had Shirley Jones as a daughter, but Shirley's whole singing brood as grandchildren. DeCamp also appeared on *The Brady Bunch* (1969–74), *The Love Boat* (1977–86), *We've Got Each Other* (1977–78), and the miniseries *Blind Ambition* (1979). She also was in the 1978 TV remake of *The Time Machine*.

In 1979, DeCamp joined the cast of the long-running daytime drama *Days of Our Lives* in the recurring role of the mother superior of a convent (well, once a mother, always a mother!). A few years ago she suffered a stroke and she is now deaf, but she is otherwise doing well. DeCamp currently resides in Redondo Beach, California, with her husband of six decades, and is thrilled about the book you are reading. Her last *That Girl* episode was episode #107: "The Night They Raided Daddy's," which originally aired on February 19, 1970.

THE CREATORS/EXECUTIVE PRODUCERS

Sam Denoff and Bill Persky
(1965–71)

Denoff and Persky stayed with *That Girl* from its inception to the very last episode. However, during this period they kept themselves very busy with other projects as well. Besides overseeing everything on the home front, they created and produced *Good Morning, World* (a one-season work in 1968), wrote material for *The Sid Caesar Special* in 1967 (winning an Emmy in the process), *The Bill Cosby Special* in 1968 (another Emmy), and two Dick Van Dyke specials (*Dick Van Dyke and Other Women* and *Confessions of Dick Van Dyke*) in 1969 and 1970.

Once *That Girl* stopped production, the team went on to produce *The Funny Side* (an hour-long comedy series for NBC hosted by Gene Kelly, which ran from September 14 to December 7, 1971). They created the short-lived *Don Rickles Show* (January 14 to May 26) in 1972 and, with co-creator Carl Reiner, *Lotsa Luck* (1973–74).

Persky's desire to branch out into directing led the team to split up, amicably, and Persky went on to helm episodes of such sitcoms as *The Montefuscoes*, *The Betty White Show*, *Joe and Valerie*, *Bustin' Loose*, *The Practice*, *Big Eddie*, and *The McLean Stevenson Show*. And then Persky really hit pay dirt by creating and directing *Kate & Allie* (1984–89), another descendant of *That Girl*.

Looking back on his career, Bill Persky is justifiably proud.

"In a way . . . if I did nothing else ever, I did really interesting bookends on women, from the first emergence to these contemporary, eighties-type women. What happened to women in television is on *That Girl*, if Marlo had a problem with her plumbing, she would call her father. Mary [Tyler Moore], on her show, would have called a plumber. Kate and Allie fixed it themselves. That really says it all."

Persky was nominated for several Emmys and won the Award for Outstanding Directing in a Comedy Series in 1984 for *Kate & Allie*. He was recently given the Lifetime Achievement Award by the Writers Guild of America East. The award was presented to him by Marlo Thomas, who sang a special song parody to Persky in which she sang that the show "came at just the right time, now we live on Nick at Nite time."

Denoff went on to produce CBS's *On Our Own* (1977–78), and executive produce NBC's *Turnabout* in 1979 and NBC's *Harper Valley P.T.A.* (1981–82).

Separately and together, both men have claimed four Emmy Awards and received twelve nominations.

Sam Denoff resides in Beverly Hills, where he teaches comedy writing, and Bill Persky lives in New York City. Both men remain active in television today.

THE PRODUCERS

Jerry Davis
(1966–67)

After one season, Jerry Davis left *That Girl*. He went on to create *The Cop and The Kid* (1975–76) for NBC, a series that starred Charles Durning, and produce *Rosetti and Ryan* (1977), an hour-long crime show featuring Tony Roberts. His last *That Girl* episode was episode #30: "The Mating Game," which originally aired on April 6, 1967.

Jerry Davis died in April 1991. He was seventy-three years old.

Danny Arnold
(1967–69)

Danny Arnold left his two-year stint on *That Girl* to create and produce *My World and Welcome to It* (1969–70). Although the program lasted only one season, it won the Emmy Award as Best Comedy Show. In 1975, he created and produced *Barney Miller*. The sitcom, about a New York City precinct captain and his multiethnic band of officers, ran until 1982 and won the Emmy Award for Outstanding Comedy Series in 1982. (It was nominated every year from 1976 to 1982, with Arnold nominated for writing the show in 1977.) In 1977, Arnold was the executive producer of a spin-off of *Barney Miller*, called *Fish* (1977–78).

In 1978, Arnold produced another TV show that resembled *Barney Miller*, called *A.E.S. Hudson Street* (starring Gregory Sierra of *Barney Miller*), which lasted for only one month. His final *That Girl* episode was episode #86: "Sue Me, Sue Me, What Can You Do Me?" which he also co-wrote. It originally aired on March 27, 1969.

Danny Arnold died in August 1991. He was seventy years old.

Bernie Orenstein and Saul Turteltaub
(1969–71)

Bernie Orenstein and Saul Turteltaub were primarily writers when they were tapped by Bill Persky and Sam Denoff to produce the last two seasons of *That Girl*. (They also wrote nineteen episodes, the most of any of the writers.) After *That Girl* went off the air in 1971, they were in demand. Shows they wrote and/or produced included ABC's *A Touch of Grace* (1972–73, starring Shirley Booth), and *Grady* (an NBC 1975–76 spin-off of the popular *Sanford and Son*, 1972–77). Along with Bud Yorkin, they were the executive producers of ABC's *What's Happening!!* (1976–79) and *Carter Country* (1977–79). Also in 1979, along with Yorkin, Orenstein and Turteltaub developed *13 Queens Blvd.*, a short-lived sitcom with Jerry Van Dyke and Eileen Brennan. Throughout the 1980s, Orenstein and Turteltaub worked on such sitcoms as *One in a Million* (writers/producers), *Condo*, *One of the Boys*, *Foley Square*, and *You Again*, as well as writing the pilot for *E/R* (1984–85, with Elliott Gould).

Both men are alive and well today and active in television.

Edgar J. Scherick
(Former vice president in charge of programming at ABC)

The man who told Marlo Thomas that she could be a television star went into independent production in 1967. Always a Marlo Thomas fan, the first film he produced under the banner of ABC Pictures was *Jenny* (1970), in which Thomas costarred with Alan Alda. Over the years, he produced *Take The Money and Run* (1969), *Sleuth* (1972), *The Heartbreak Kid* (1972), *The Stepford Wives* (1975), and *I Never*

Promised You a Rose Garden (1977). On television he packaged *Raid on Entebbe* (1977) and *Little Gloria . . . Happy At Last* (1982).

Scherick appeared at the Museum of Television and Radio's *That Girl* seminar in 1996. He is now retired.

THAT STAR

And, of course, there has been a lot of life after *That Girl* for That Girl herself . . .

Marlo Thomas
(Ann Marie, 1965–71; voice of Ann Marie, 1973)

Marlo Thomas started branching out before *That Girl* shut down production. During the hiatus in 1969, she began shooting her first feature film, *Jenny* (originally entitled *And Jenny Makes Three*), in New York City. The movie was released in 1970 and Thomas could be seen on both the small and big screens.

After *That Girl* went off the air, Thomas chose her next professional steps carefully. Never one to repeat herself, Thomas conceived, produced, and appeared in a revolutionary television special: *Free to Be . . . You and Me* (March 11, 1974). (This was also a book and a record, and was followed up by *Free to Be . . . A Family* on December 14, 1988). She was rewarded for her efforts with her first Emmy Award. The production also won a Peabody Award, as well as a Christopher and a Maxi Award. She followed that with an Emmy in 1981 as Best Performer in a Children's Program for *The Body Human: Facts for Girls* and another for Best Actress in a Special for *Nobody's Child* in 1986.

In 1977, Marlo starred in an ABC holiday movie called *It Happened One Christmas* (playing a female version of Jimmy Stewart's character in the 1946 movie classic, *It's a Wonderful Life*).

Meanwhile, in 1974, Marlo made her Broadway debut in the Herb Gardner play *Thieves*, and repeated that role in the 1977 movie version opposite Charles Grodin. In 1986, she made a splash in Mike Nichols' stage production of *Social Security* and, more recently, appeared in an acclaimed revival of *The Shadow Box*.

Thomas frequently appears on the stage around the country in such plays as *Six Degrees of Separation*, *The Effect of Gamma Rays on Man in the Moon Marigolds*, and *Who's Afraid of Virginia Woolf?*

In recent years, Thomas has played leading roles in big- and small-screen movies such as the TV film *The Lost Honor of Kathryn Beck* (1984), *Consenting Adults* (a 1985 TV film), *In the Spirit* (1990), the TV movie *Held Hostage: The Sis and Jerry Levin Story* (1991), *Ultimate Betrayal* (a 1994 TV film), *Reunion* (a 1994 TV film), and *The Real Blonde* (1997), with Matthew Modine and Kathleen Turner. Marlo continues to produce in both television and film.

Thomas has been married since 1980, to former talk-show legend Phil Donahue. She has guest-starred on sitcoms such as *Roseanne* and, most recently, on the very popular *Friends* as Rachel's mom, for which she received an Emmy nomination. Above all, she carries on her father's, Danny Thomas, lifework for St. Jude Children's Research Hospital, the institution he founded, which specializes in catastrophic diseases in children and which spearheaded the battle against childhood leukemia. Marlo serves as the National Outreach Director.

THAT KITE

And the *That Girl* kite that Ann Marie flew so proudly in the opening credits of the TV series? It now resides at New York City's Planet Hollywood restaurant.

"They asked for something from the series," Marlo told *TV Guide* on June 6, 1996, "and I thought the kite would be a wonderful thing to have somewhere where it could be appreciated."

The show itself lives on in syndication all over the world—at the Museum of Television and Radio, on America Online Chats, on the Internet at the unofficial *That Girl* Web site which can be found at http://www.thatgirltv.com/ and in the hearts and memories of the fans of the series.

Ann Marie's Survival Jobs

Like all actresses, Ann Marie had to supplement her showbusiness income with what are known to actors as survival jobs. Here are some of the positions that she accepts during the five years of trying to make it on Broadway (and elsewhere) as an actress:

* **Assistant at a travel agency** (see episode #38: "There's Nothing to Be Afreud of But Freud Himself")
* **Babysitter** (see episodes #3: "Never Change a Diaper on Opening Night" and #112: "All's Well That Ends")
* **Candy-counter salesperson** (see episode #1: "Don't Just Do Something, Stand There")
* **Christmas elf at a department store** (see episode #16: "Christmas and the Hard Luck Kid")
* **Cosmetics salesperson at Best & Co.** (see episode #20: "Gone with the Breeze")
* **Don Hollinger's secretary** (see episode #7: "Help Wanted")
* **Door-to-door shoe salesperson** (see episode #18: "These Boots Weren't Made for Walking")
* **Flight attendant** (see episode #62: "The Hi-Jack and The Mighty")
* **Interviewer for *Newsview* magazine** (see episode #24: "A Tenor's Loving Care")
* **Magazine writer** (see episode #122: "Stop the Presses, I Want to Get Off")
* **Meter maid** (see episode #103: "That Meter Maid")
* **Miss Chicken Big** (see episode #90: "Nobody Here But Us Chickens")
* **Model:** At Sardi's restaurant (see episode #42: "The Mailman Cometh") At the auto show (see episode #40: "When in Rome") At the race track (see episode #134: "Two for the Money") For a furrier (see episode #47: "Fur All We Know") For a high-fashion photographer (see episodes #43 and #44: "It's a Mod Mod World, Parts One and Two")
* **Playwright** (see episode #39: "The Collaborators")

* **Public relations person for the U. S. Air Force** (see episode #83: "Fly Me to the Moon")
* **Restaurant staff, including maitre d', waitress, cook, busboy** (see episode #131: "Chef's Night Out")
* **Sales announcer in a department store** (see episode #130: "That Shoplifter")
* **Seamstress and industrial spy** (see episodes #87 and #88: "Mission Improbable," Parts One and Two")
* **Teacher** (see episode #16: "Christmas and the Hard Luck Kid")
* **Telemarketer** (see episode #35: "The Apartment")
* **Waitress** (see episodes #2: "Good-bye, Hello, Good-bye," #9: "Time for Arrest," #11: "What's in a Name?", and the untill recently unaired pilot: "What's in a Name?")

Chapter 12

That Last Word

There was Betty Freidan, Gloria Steinem, and Marlo Thomas. She was so smart. The message of the show is still fresh today. Fresher than we know. It isn't just for the retro-sixties look that people watch it today. It's for the deep underlying message of the show. A woman can be on her own, remain unmarried, have a wonderful life, and laugh and have the love of her parents, and still have her own apartment. And she made it gentle, funny and easy to take.

—SUSAN L. DWORKIN, FEMINIST, AUTHOR, AND ACTIVIST

A WHOLE NEW ERA

That Girl. She was new, she was fresh, she was innovative. She stood on her own. But let's let Marlo Thomas, the woman who first dreamed it, have the last word about the show:

It was apparent that the chemistry was really between me and Teddy [Bessell]. We knew that's where the gold was. And he was phenomenal. He had the ability to be funny and charming and he was so male. A lot of guys who played the boyfriends or the husbands to the strong females on television were kind of buffoons for the women. It never was really an equal thing. [But] Teddy had the ability to stand up to a very strong female character.

I think it's been very rewarding, having people come up to me, women of all ages, and say, 'If it hadn't been for That Girl *I wouldn't have gone to New York, if it hadn't been for* That Girl *I would have gotten married right out of college. . . .'*

It's a whole new era. It's brand new. And it is the seedling then that gets all the way to Murphy Brown *[1988–98]. People often say to me, 'If you did* That Girl *today, what would you do different?' If I did* That Girl *today, I'd be* Kate & Allie. *I'd be a divorced single woman raising a kid. Or I'd be* Cagney & Lacey *or* Murphy Brown, *women with real jobs. You couldn't just do* That Girl *again. You'd have to do* That Girl *today . . . because, for her time, she was a revolutionary figure. I want to keep it historically of its time. If you look back at* That Girl *you could say, 'Well, she didn't call the plumber, she called her father.' But that's not the point of that time, the important thing of that time is she had the key to her own apartment and she wasn't beholden to anybody. Her parents tried to make her beholden to them. They tried to make her answer to them. I don't know how many shows we did where I said to my mother or father in the show, 'You did a wonderful job of raising me and helping me grow up, but now I'm up!' That was a very sweet line that Billy and Sam wrote. And they really got it.*

—MARLO THOMAS

So did we, Marlo. We still do!

THE CAST SEEMED TO HAVE FUN WHEN SILLY COSTUMES WERE USED IN A NUMBER OF EPISODES.

Ann (Thomas) is amused when Don (Bessell) appears in drag in Episode #68, "A Muggy Day in Central Park"; In Episode #123, "Super Reporter"—a fifth-season episode inspired by real life—Don (Ted Bessell) appears on television wearing a SuperDon costume; Ann as Miss Chicken Big does the mating dance of the chicken at a local takeout store in Episode #90, "Nobody Here but Us Chickens."

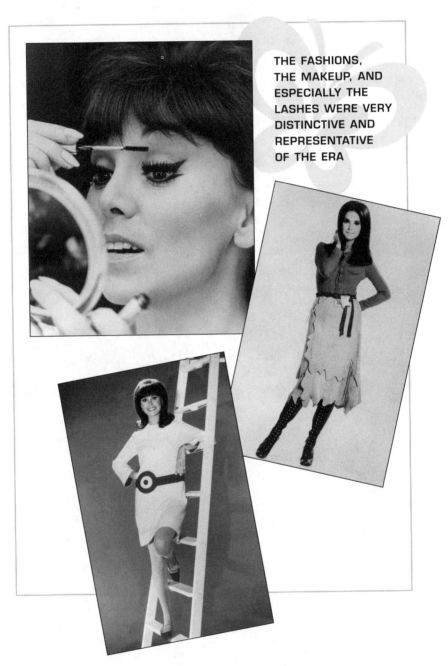

THE FASHIONS, THE MAKEUP, AND ESPECIALLY THE LASHES WERE VERY DISTINCTIVE AND REPRESENTATIVE OF THE ERA

CLOCKWISE FROM TOP:
The lashes and liner were quintessentially *That Girl* and the times; Marlo Thomas in a very '70s buckskin skirt in the fifth season; There was a definite "London-mod" style to much of the wardrobe worn by Thomas as Ann Marie.

THAT GIRL BEHIND
THE CAMERAS

CLOCKWISE FROM TOP:
Producer/director Danny Arnold gives some last-minute direction to Thomas and Bessell on a New York City location shoot; Marlo and co-creator/executive producer Bill Persky during a typical production meeting; Marlo Thomas applying the makeup that so many young girls would copy. Note the bumper sticker on her mirror.

ABC called Thursday night "Ladies Night," with Elizabeth Montgomery (*Bewitched*), Judy Carne (*Love on a Rooftop*), and Marlo Thomas (*That Girl*) each starring in their own shows; In its fifth and final season ABC moved *That Girl* from Thursdays at 9:30 P.M. to Fridays at 9:00 P.M.

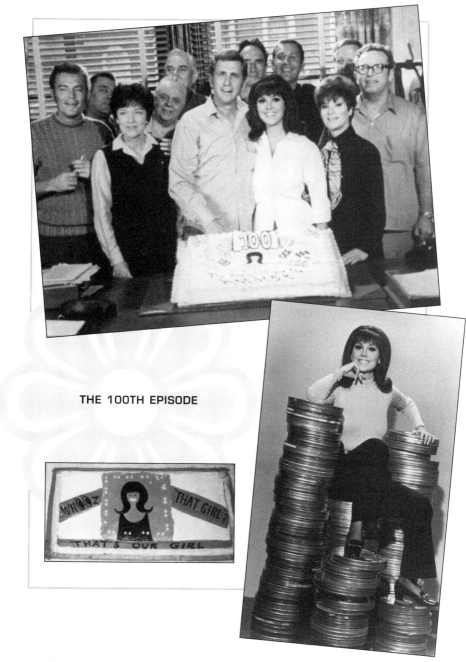

THE 100TH EPISODE

CLOCKWISE FROM TOP:

Thomas and Bessell celebrate with the staff the first one hundred episodes in the can; Marlo Thomas sits on one hundred cans of *That Girl* episodes; A closeup of the celebratory cake.

MISS MARLO THOMAS

INVITES YOU TO HELP CELEBRATE

FIVE WONDERFUL YEARS OF "THAT GIRL!"

SATURDAY, NOVEMBER 28, AT 7:30 O'CLOCK

811 LILLIAN WAY, HOLLYWOOD

RSVP
469-7058

WEAR WHAT YEZ WANT

THE SERIES' FINAL WRAP PARTY

The invitation to the final wrap party that Marlo Thomas threw for the cast and crew; A cocktail napkin from the wrap party.

Episode Guide

What follows is the most complete episode guide of *That Girl*, including the until recently unaired pilot. The shows are arranged in the order they originally aired (please note that syndication order is different) and by seasons one through five. Each season contains an overview of the season and a list of the crew for that year. At the end of each season is a list of the awards and honors associated with *That Girl* that season.

Each installment is listed with its original title, airdate, writer, director, and guest cast. This is followed by a brief synopsis of the plot, the highlights (as seen by the author), notes compiled by the author (including trivia facts), and who said "that girl" in that episode.

Production Team for All Episodes
Executive Producers and Series Creators: Bill Persky and Sam Denoff

Regular Cast for All Episodes
Marlo Thomas (Ann Marie), Ted Bessell (Donald Hollinger)

PILOT EPISODE: WHAT'S IN A NAME?
ORIGINALLY UNAIRED
Writers: Sam Denoff and Bill Persky; Director: Jerry Paris; Producer: Jack Ellinson; Fashions by Mr. Mort; Guest Cast: Harold Gould (Lou Marie), Penny Santone (Helen Marie), Walter Sande (Max), Michael Hoffer (Jimmy, the waiter), Cliff Norton (Chef), Shirley Bonne (Charlotte), Jackie Joseph (Sharon), Ann Whitfield (Linda), David Azar (Actor), Douglas McCairn (Customer), Rance Howard (Customer), Owen Bush (Customer), Mary Foran (Customer)

We meet Ann Marie, aspiring actress, who is working as a waitress to survive. In this pilot episode we find out that she has just left home to make it on her own in New York City, has an agent (Don Blue Sky) who is also her boyfriend, and is about to undertake her first substantial TV role. The dilemma becomes what to do about her name. Everyone thinks she should change it, except her parents (especially her father). In the end, Ann does the right thing and remains true to her family and herself.

Highlights
This is a model pilot episode, with the highlight being the fully formed character of Ann Marie and the fully realized performance of Marlo Thomas. Although much about the show would change, Ann/Marlo was there from the start. The scene where Ann and her father argue while trying to step around sweaters drying all over the living room floor is a gem and remains a favorite of co-creator and co-writer Bill Persky.

Notes
The character of Don Blue Sky, Ann's Native American talent agent, so upset the ABC network bosses that they tried to fire Ted Bessell. It was the creators who realized that they'd made a big mistake with the character and that Ann should have both a boyfriend *and* an agent, but that they should not be the same person. After much argument, the network agreed and kept Ted Bessell on in the new role of Donald Hollinger, *Newsview* magazine reporter and boyfriend to Ann Marie. The other big changes from the pilot to the series entailed recasting the two actors playing Ann's parents, Lou and Helen Marie. Ann also moved from the East End Hotel (a women's residence on 70th Street on the East River in New York) to a nice little East Side (or West Side, depending on the episode) apartment. In this show we are told that Ann has siblings, which she clearly does not have in the series. This whole script was later revamped (but not much) and used as episode #11. The scenes with Donald and her parents were reshot with the changes in cast and characters, but several scenes and shots are taken right from the pilot.

Who Gets to Say "That Girl!"
The honors go to Ted Bessell, as Don Blue Sky, and Michael Hoffer as Jimmy the waiter. They speak the title line in scenes that establish

key facts: that her agent represents her and that she is a waitress waiting for that big break in show business. When co-creators and executive producers Sam Denoff and Bill Persky invented the trademark device on the show of saying "that girl!," they thought they would never be able to keep it up past the pilot or first episodes. Happily, they were wrong and it became the show's signature.

SEASON ONE

SEPTEMBER 1966–APRIL 1967

Season One Overview

Debut seasons of situation comedies are about meeting the characters and establishing their relationships. Ann Marie is a young actress who is leaving her suburban Brewster, New York, home for the first time to live on her own. Brewster is a real town, about forty miles due north of New York City and about eight miles from the Connecticut border. Ann Marie has taught in a private school at the elementary level, and now has decided to go for broke and become an actress in New York City. As soon as she departs from home, she gets an apartment (where her next-door neighbors, Judy and Leon Bessamer, become her best friends) and temporary survival jobs. She also meets Donald Hollinger, a magazine reporter and the man who will be her steady boyfriend for all five seasons, eventually becoming her fiancé. As a journalist, Donald covers a wide range of news stories, from hard news to puff pieces. When Don meets Ann's parents for the first time, a relationship of hostility is established between the young man and Lou Marie, Ann's very protective father. Ann's mother likes Don, but defers to her husband.

In the course of carving out a theatrical career, Ann auditions for Jules Benedict, a drama coach, and wins a spot in his acting workshop. She gets a role as a mop on a children's TV show, acts in an experimental production off-off-off Broadway entitled *A Preponderance of Artichokes*, wins a role as understudy to a Broadway star, gets her first bit part on television, plays a recurring role on a soap opera, does a play called *Honor's Stain*, has an article written about her in *Newsview* magazine, and does a standup comedy routine.

To supplement her income as a performer, Ann takes jobs as a candy-counter salesperson, a waitress, a salesclerk at Macy's, an elf at Christmastime, secretary to Don, a door-to-door shoe salesperson, and substitute reporter for *Newsview* magazine.

Early in the season, Ann is faced with the decision of dating a very rich suitor or the more modestly paid Don and she chooses Don, setting the course for the whole series. Their relationship deepens and becomes second nature.

In short, in 1966–67 Ann Marie's life consists of career, family, boyfriend, and survival . . . not to mention getting a bowling ball stuck on her toe for good measure!

Production Team for Season One
Executive Producers and Series Creators: Bill Persky and Sam Denoff; Producer and Script Consultant: Jerry Davis; Director of Photography: Jack Marquette; Art Directors: Pato Guzman and Ken Reid; Film Editor: Bob Moore; Music: Walter Scharf with theme by Earle Hagen; Fashions: Werle; Hair: Lynn Masters; Makeup: Tom Case; Origination: Filmed at Desilu-Cahuenga Studios by Daisy Productions; Executive in Charge of Production: Ronald Jacobs; Agencies and Sponsors: Armstrong Cork Company through Batten, Barton, Durstine & Osborn, Inc., Bristol-Myers Company through Grey Advertising Inc., and Liggett & Myers Tobacco Co. through J. Walter Thompson Company

EPISODE 1: DON'T JUST DO SOMETHING, STAND THERE
ORIGINAL AIR DATE: SEPTEMBER 8, 1966
Writers: Jim Parker and Arnold Margolin; Director: Bob Sweeney; Guest Cast: Bonnie Scott (Judy), Jack Goode (Mr. Rudolph), Ed Peck (Sam), Jerry Fogel (Ernie), Luana Anders (Shirley), Burt Taylor (Waiter)

Ann Marie, a New York actress who is working behind the candy counter to make ends meet, lands a role in a perfume commercial in which the character she plays is abducted by two hoods. Donald Hollinger, a reporter who works in the same office building, sees the abduction and, thinking it's real, goes to her rescue—nearly spoiling the commercial. In the process, the two meet and find they are mutually attracted.

Highlights

The scene where Donald whisks Ann away in the elevator is delightful. Another high point has perky Ann evading the amorous advances of an antiques salesman by trapping his busy fingers in his own antique roll-top desk.

Notes

This is not only the first-aired episode, but also the one in which Ann and Donald first meet. We find out that *Newsview* magazine, where Donald is a writer, is located at 1330 Sixth Avenue between 52nd and 53rd Streets in New York. We see Ann at one of her many jobs taken to survive (this time selling gum and candy in the lobby of the building) and we discover that Don's and Ann's favorite restaurant is Nino's. Oddly enough, this preview episode (at the end of the show Marlo Thomas thanks the audience for tuning in and calls it, not the first show, but the "preview") is actually the second, chronologically, since in the next entry we see Ann leaving her parents' home for the big city. The slogan for the perfume Ann is advertising is "Jungle Madness brings out the beast in a man." Jerry Fogel (Ernie) also appears in episode #116: "No Man Is a Manhattan Island" and in episode #133: "Stag Party." Luana Anders (Shirley), who is seen in this segment as a redhead, also appears in episode #25: "Leaving the Nest Is for the Birds," but as a blonde.

Who Gets to Say "That Girl!"

Ed Peck as Sam, the director of the commercial, has the distinction of being the first to say "that girl!" on the air. He says it as he decides that he can use any girl for his commercial. Even *"that girl!"*

EPISODE 2: GOOD-BYE, HELLO, GOOD-BYE

ORIGINAL AIR DATE: SEPTEMBER 15, 1966

Writers: Bill Persky and Sam Denoff; Director: Bob Sweeney; Guest Cast: Lew Parker (Lou Marie), Rosemary DeCamp (Helen Marie), Bonnie Scott (Judy Bessamer), Ronnie Schell (Harvey Peck), Byron Morrow (Doorman), J. B. Larson (Studio Usher), Carol Worthington (Janet, a waitress), Ogden

Talbot (Customer), Joan Granville (Woman Customer), Aileen Carlyle (Woman Customer), Ivy Bethune (Woman Customer), Duke Stroud (Man)

Ann Marie leaves her home in Brewster, New York, and moves forty miles south to New York City to live on her own and become an actress. She says goodbye to her parents, moves into her new apartment, gets her first acting role (as a mop on a kids' TV show) and meets her next-door neighbor Judy. Soon thereafter, her mother knocks on the door and declares that she is coming to live with Ann! After finding out that her mother has just fought with her father about his overprotective nature, Ann tells them that she is ready to leave the nest and puts her parents on the next train back to Brewster.

Highlights
This installment is full of solid moments, beginning with the unique drawings at the top of the show, depicting birds leaving their nests and Eskimo children leaving their igloos. The scenes with Ann dressed as a mop (she's a guest mop on TV's *Merry Mop-a-teers* and makes fifty dollars) are adorable. Classic Lou Marie line: "You send a girl to college for four years and watch her end up as a mop!" The dramatic linchpin of the entire series, though, comes when Ann tells her parents that they did a great job bringing her up, but now she is "up."

Notes
This entry marks the first official appearance of Ann's parents, Lou and Helen Marie, and really is the start, chronologically, of the series. We are also introduced to Ann's agent, Harvey Peck, who has replaced Don Blue Sky of the pilot episode, and Ann's next-door neighbor, Judy Bessamer (who has black hair at this time, but will reappear as a redhead after a few segments). Episode #1 is really the second filmed in the series, and since it introduces Don Hollinger, episode #2 is one of the few episodes *not* to include Ted Bessell. In this installment, Ann's building has a doorman. He is never seen again. We also find out that Helen Marie conveniently gets headaches when she wants to avoid subjects.

Who Gets to Say "That Girl!"
After Ann's mother, Helen, tells her worrying husband that thousands of girls leave home every year, Lew Parker as Lou Marie says, "I'm not interested in thousands of girls, I'm only interested in *that girl!*"

EPISODE 3: NEVER CHANGE A DIAPER ON OPENING NIGHT
ORIGINAL AIR DATE: SEPTEMBER 22, 1966
Writer: Milton Pascal; Director: Bob Sweeney; Guest Cast: Bonnie Scott (Judy Bessamer), Billy DeWolfe (Jules Benedict), Dabney Coleman (Dr. Leon Bessamer)

Ann survives an interview with the demanding and prissy drama coach Jules Benedict. She is invited to return that evening to audition, but is soon commandeered by neighbor Judy Bessamer to babysit. Having no choice, Ann takes the baby with her to the audition, where, although the infant keeps interrupting her, she impresses Benedict enough to rate a second chance. She is invited to become a member of the workshop.

Highlights
Ann's attempt at auditioning while Judy's baby wails in the next room is memorable, as is her tirade directed at fussy Mr. Benedict. Billy DeWolfe's entire performance is a joy to watch.

Notes
This marks the first appearances of two recurring characters, Dr. Leon Bessamer (Judy's obstetrician husband, played by Dabney Coleman), and Jules Benedict (Ann's drama coach and the head of her acting workshop, played by the hilariously fussbudgety Billy DeWolfe). Note the sign on Benedict's office door: Never Enter Here. The next time we see Judy Bessamer (in episode #6) she is a redhead and we seldom hear about her baby, Stanley, again. We find out that Ann's actual acting credits are meager but that she did win the acting prize at Camp Winipoo. Note the classic Billy DeWolfe witticism directed to Ann when she says that she wants to be in his class: "a pupil possibly, but never in my class."

Who Gets to Say "That Girl!"
Billy DeWolfe as Jules Benedict does the honors. After berating a potential student and scaring all the other applicants (including Ann) half to death, he says, "Who here thinks he is fit? Come, come! All right! *That girl!*"

EPISODE 4: "I'LL BE SUING YOU"
ORIGINAL AIR DATE: SEPTEMBER 29, 1966
Writers: Peggy Elliott and Ed Scharlach; Director: Bob Sweeney; Guest Cast: Carl Ballantine (Mr. Lemming), Robert Emhardt (Judge), James O'Rear (Bailiff), Rupert Crosse (Cop), A. G. Vitanza (Shoemaker), Ruth Perrott (Antiques Lady), Don Diamond (Singing Butcher), Sammy Reese (Father John Moore)

In civil court, where she is being sued by a pedestrian who ran into Donald's car with a sewing machine, Ann tells her side of the story in flashback while awaiting the arrival of her star witness. When the witness turns out to be a priest, Ann wins the case.

Highlights
The linking scenes with comedian Carl Ballantine as Mr. Lemming, bantering with Ann and the judge, provide most of the comedy here. Ann is delightful as she tries to pull out all the stops defending herself. Any resemblance to Perry Mason is purely intentional.

Notes
In this show we see Donald's new car for the first time (although the vehicle is shown in the unaired pilot); it is a red Mustang with the license plate number 4G82H9. Evidently the dent that has been put into Donald's car by Mr. Lemming's "Deluxe Superflyer" sewing machine will be fixed—at a cost of $46.53 (my, how times have changed!)—by the next installment (episode #5: "Anatomy of a Blunder"), when Donald and Ann use the car to drive upstate to visit Ann's parents in Brewster. We wonder what has happened to the sewing machine, which Ann accepts at the end of the episode in lieu of payment for the damages. She claims that with her new acquisition she will make her own clothes and save money. If this is true, considering Ann's incredible wardrobe, she is a sewing whiz! Guest star Carl Ballantine had just finished a very successful run as Seaman Lester Gruber on *McHale's Navy* (1962–66), also an ABC sitcom.

Who Gets to Say "That Girl!"
Carl Ballantine as Mr. Lemming venomously spits out *"that girl!"* as Ann is called before the judge.

EPISODE 5: ANATOMY OF A BLUNDER

ORIGINAL AIR DATE: OCTOBER 6, 1966

Writers: Dale McRaven and Carl Kleinschmidt; Director: Bob Sweeney; Guest Cast: Lew Parker (Lou Marie), Rosemary DeCamp (Helen Marie)

Ann brings new boyfriend Donald home to meet her parents in Brewster. On the way, they stop for a picnic and everything that can go wrong for Don does.

Highlights

The whole episode is a comic gem, showcasing Ted Bessell's talent for physical comedy. The scene where he becomes, as he calls himself, a "blotchy, limping, one-eyed man" in a ditch with mud all over him, is worthy of *I Love Lucy*.

Notes

It is not often in the series that Donald is the put-upon character (it is usually Ann) and it is very endearing to see Don coping with such a bad day. First we see him stepping on a bee, which makes his foot swell. We find out that he is allergic to the horseradish in the chopped liver that Ann has made and that he wears contact lenses (which of course get knocked out). We also witness an annoying side to Ann which seldom resurfaces. She makes fun of Don's attire. He is dressed in a jacket and tie for a picnic because he wants to make a good impression on her parents.

Who Gets to Say "That Girl!"

Lew Parker as Lou Marie (Ann's father) when she phones to tell him that she is bringing Donald to meet him. His response when she hangs up is to look at her picture and proclaim: "There isn't a guy in the world who's good enough for *that girl!*"

EPISODE 6: RICH LITTLE RICH KID

ORIGINAL AIR DATE: OCTOBER 13, 1966

Writer: Joseph Bonaduce; Director: Sidney Miller; Guest Cast: Bonnie Scott (Judy Bessamer), Sam Melville (Roddy Waxman), Larry Hankin (Gus), Ed Tontini (Maitre d'), Paul Bryar (Clerk), Pat O'Hara (Butler)

While paying a traffic fine, Ann Marie meets a handsome and wealthy suitor who dazzles her with flowers, gourmet foods, and a ride in a Rolls-Royce. The rich bachelor even buys out the house for a stage performance of Ann in *A Preponderance of Artichokes*. Donald tries to compete and, in the end, Ann realizes that there are more important things than money. As she says, "I guess I like root beer better than champagne."

Highlights
The peak of the episode is Ann's one-woman performance (playing all the roles) in the simply awful experimental play, *A Preponderance of Artichokes*. Wearing an artichoke around her neck, she intones lines (in her best Katharine Hepburn voice) that are paraphrased from the film *Stage Door* (1937): "The artichokes are in bloom again. I wore them on my wedding day and now I wear them in remembrance of something that is dead." Simply hilarious!

Notes
This is the episode in which Ann realizes that she really loves Donald and from now on, although there might be other men in her life, it is clear that none really have an effect on their relationship. From now until she departs the series, Judy Bessamer will have red hair, presumably because there could only be one brunette on the program. Trivia note: Ann only drives a car with an automatic transmission.

Who Gets to Say "That Girl!"
Sam Melville as Roddy Waxman tells the clerk collecting money for traffic tickets, "Don't look at me, I'm with *that girl!*"

EPISODE 7: HELP WANTED
ORIGINAL AIR DATE: OCTOBER 20, 1966
Writers: Tom and Helen August; Director: Bob Sweeney; Guest Cast: Bonnie Scott (Judy Bessamer), Bernie Kopell (Jerry Bauman), Ogden Talbot (Messenger Boy), Yuki Tani (Japanese Waitress), Bob Lindquist (Terry Doby)

Donald's secretary, Shirley, is pregnant. Against his better judgment, he hires Ann for the job. They decide to separate their personal and professional lives, but find it impossible. Although she is very efficient,

Ann makes Don very uncomfortable all day long. The things he'd normally do, like lie on the couch or flirt on the telephone, suddenly become inhibited by Ann's presence. And when Ann doesn't correct one of Don's stories and Don sends it to the editor, all hell breaks loose. In the end, they realize that what they want is the personal relationship, rather than a professional one, and she is happily fired.

Highlights
The scene in which Ann drives Don crazy with her efficiency is the high point of this installment.

Notes
In this episode we find out that Ann types very well. We also hear about the first in a long line of Don's secretaries (he was the Murphy Brown of his day). In one entry we learn about Shirley leaving and, after Ann is fired, Terry Doby (a man) takes over. Yuki Tani, who plays the waitress in this episode, also appears in episode #19: "Kimono My House."

Who Gets to Say "That Girl!"
After Don wonders who could possibly be his new secretary, Bonnie Scott as Judy points to Ann and yells, *"That girl!"*

EPISODE 8: LITTLE AUCTION ANNIE
ORIGINAL AIR DATE: OCTOBER 27, 1966
Writer: Rick Mittleman; Director: Sidney Miller; Guest Cast: Bonnie Scott (Judy Bessamer), Dabney Coleman (Dr. Leon Bessamer), Michael Conrad (Mr. Johnson), Steve Nisbet (Auctioneer), Dodo Denney (Mrs. Morrisey), Teddy Quinn (Patrick), Arlene Anderson (Woman), Ken Lynch (Police Officer)

Ann, Don, and the Bessamers attend an auction, where Ann bids $7.50 for a box of junk which contains a mounted baseball. A strange man who arrives late to the auction pursues Ann, and it's soon evident that he's after the baseball. Ann thinks that the man is a spy. It turns out that he is a former baseball star who now works for the FBI and wants the ball only for sentimental reasons.

Highlights

Ann and Donald's comic terror when they notice that the stranger has a gun is the big moment of this show, and it is excerpted in the series finale to demonstrate how foolish Ann can be when she jumps to conclusions.

Notes

In this outing we meet two of Ann's other neighbors, Mrs. Morrisey and her little boy who likes to lock himself in the bathroom. They never reappear.

Who Gets to Say "That Girl!"

Arlene Anderson, as a woman at the auction, points out to Michael Conrad (as Mr. Johnson) the person who bought the box of junk: "Over there! *That girl!*"

EPISODE 9: TIME FOR ARREST

ORIGINAL AIR DATE: NOVEMBER 3, 1966

Writer: Jack Winter; Director: David McDearmon; Guest Cast: Milton Selzer (Al Morganthaler), Richard X. Slattery (Lieutenant Sylvestri), Herb Edelman (Eddie Parell), Dick Balduzzi (Sergeant), Johnny Silver (Joey), Bella Bruck (Martha), Roxanne Arlen (Miss Friendship), Bernie Allen (Lou), Jackie Joseph (Margie), Jeanette O'Connor (Girl), Kenny Washington (Yorkey), Tom McDonough (Policeman)

When Don comes to bail Ann out of jail, he finds her dressed in a skimpy leopard-skin cave-girl outfit. She explains what happened the night before to Don and the police: Ann's friend Margie has Ann substitute for her as a waitress in a nightclub called "The Cave." On the job, Ann finds herself serving two rival factions of the underworld. The club is raided by the police and now Ann is in jail telling the story.

Highlights

Bella Bruck as Martha, showing Ann the ropes as a hatcheck girl, makes this entry memorable.

Notes

This episode is not very connected to the series, and although Ann is in every scene, she is not really part of the story. Except for being a good friend to Margie (who doesn't show up much in the show), we learn very little about Ann.

Who Gets to Say "That Girl!"
With Ann behind bars in her cave-woman outfit, Dick Balduzzi as the sergeant asks who is next. Kenny Washington as Yorkey says, "Over there, Sergeant! *That girl!*"

EPISODE 10: BREAK A LEG
ORIGINAL AIR DATE: NOVEMBER 10, 1966
Writers: Jim Parker and Arnold Margolin; Director: Jerry Davis; Guest Cast: Bonnie Scott (Judy Bessamer), Dabney Coleman (Dr. Leon Bessamer), Sally Kellerman (Sandy Stafford), George Carlin (George Lester), David Fresco (Wesley), Robert Sampson (Jim Perryman, the company manager)

Ann's school friend Sandy wins a role in a Broadway play and becomes Ann's houseguest. When Sandy needs an understudy, Ann is hired. Despite her efforts to keep Sandy healthy, everything goes wrong and it looks as if Ann is pulling an *All About Eve* (1950) ploy and undermining her friend in order to take over her stage role. When Sandy gets chicken pox after opening night, it seems Ann might go on, but the show is a flop and closes after only one performance.

Highlights
Sally Kellerman's sparkling performance as the star of a new Broadway offering who is frightened of her understudy—who also happens to be a friend—is a gem. The last moments of the episode, in which Ann walks onto the stage, are both breathtakingly sad *and* hopeful. A wonderful moment!

Notes
This episode was the first filmed and became the first in the package when the show was aired for syndication. It is also comic George Carlin's one appearance as George Lester, Ann's agent. We get to see several nice shots of West 45th Street, including the Majestic and the St. James theatres where *Funny Girl* and *Hello, Dolly!* were playing at the time. This is also one of the few non-Donald shows. Ann doesn't even refer to him. This is also the only *That Girl* entry directed by its producer, Jerry Davis.

Who Gets to Say "That Girl!"
Marlo Thomas as Ann speaks it when she is showing Judy her school yearbook. Judy looks at the wrong picture and asks, "This girl?" "No,"

says Ann, pointing to a photo of herself wearing a headdress out of a German opera, *"that girl!"*

EPISODE 11: WHAT'S IN A NAME?
ORIGINAL AIR DATE: NOVEMBER 17, 1966
Writers: Bill Persky and Sam Denoff; Director: Henry Falk; Guest Cast: Lew Parker (Lou Marie), Rosemary DeCamp (Helen Marie), Ronny Schell (Harvey Peck), Bonnie Scott (Judy Bessamer), Dabney Coleman (Dr. Leon Bessamer), Walter Sande (Max Cochran, the desk clerk), Cliff Norton (Charlie, the chef), Michael Hoffer (Jimmy, the waiter)

When Ann earns her first TV acting job, her agent convinces her to change her name. Donald comes up with the name Marie Brewster and Ann tries it on her parents. They are very unhappy about it. In the end, she keeps her given name.

Highlights
The scene where Ann and her father fight over the proposed name-change—with all of Ann's sweaters drying on the living room floor— is the high point. This sequence (as it was written for the pilot) is one of creator/writer/executive producer Bill Persky's favorites.

Notes
This is a revised version of the unaired pilot episode, but with several of the shots taken directly from the pilot. The change of actors and characters (Ann's parents; Donald no longer being her agent or a Native American) necessitated some reshoots. In an early scene it is clear that Ann's lips are asking for Mr. Blue Sky (Donald's original surname on the pilot), but the sound has been dubbed to say "Mr. Peck, please." (What happened to George Lester, her other agent?) It is also interesting to note that Ann lives in Manhattan at the East End Hotel on FDR Drive at East 70th Street. She has obviously not gotten her apartment yet, although we have seen it before. It is also odd that Judy and Leon Bessamer live next door to her in the hotel as well as at her real apartment. We find out about two of Ann's temporary jobs: waitress and a salesperson at Macy's. We also get to hear her father call her "Miss Independence," the original title of the show. The warmth between father and daughter is very well established during this installment. Don says that he is from Toledo, Ohio, which later

will be amended to Shelton, Ohio, and then to St. Louis, Missouri, for the rest of the series. Interesting note: the original pilot scenes were directed by the unbilled Jerry Paris (*The Dick Van Dyke Show*).

Who Gets to Say "That Girl!"
Michael Hoffer as a busboy, when a customer asks who his waitress is. This takes place after we have seen Ronnie Schell as Ann's agent promoting her as a great actress.

EPISODE 12: SOAP GETS IN YOUR EYES
ORIGINAL AIR DATE: NOVEMBER 24, 1966
Writers: Tom and Helen August; Director: Seymour Robbie; Guest Cast: Kurt Kaszner (Dr. Randall), Mabel Albertson (Mildred Hollinger, Don's mother), Bonnie Scott (Judy Bessamer), Steve Franken (Dr. Bruce Alden), George Cisar (Mr. Hollinger), Stevenson Philips (Director), Geoff Edwards (Announcer), Joe Mell (Sol), Marjorie Bennett (Rose from Yonkers)

Ann's success as a vampy villain on a daytime soap opera coincides with her first meeting with Donald's parents. To Ann's dismay, Mrs. Hollinger, thinking that Ann is just like the evil character she plays on television, immediately dislikes her.

Highlights
The high spot is Kurt Kaszner as the actor playing kindly Dr. Randall, getting drunk at the dinner party at Ann's apartment. She invites him over to put in a good word for her with Donald's mother, but the actor proceeds to drink everything in sight. Instead of ruining the evening though, it makes Mrs. Hollinger realize that if the besotted Randall is nothing like the character he plays, then Ann could be different too. Thus, it takes the actor playing her favorite character, Dr. Randall, to convince Mrs. Hollinger that life and art are not necessarily the same.

Notes
This was the first appearance of Mabel Albertson as Mrs. Hollinger. She specialized in playing snooty, disapproving, small-town mothers, and this character was not so different from her role as Darren Stephen's headache-ridden mom on *Bewitched*. When at their first dinner at Rocky's (a supposedly chic actors' hangout, but Mrs. Hollinger sees no one she has ever heard of, as they are all "stage" actors), Ann tries to explain that she, too, is from a small town—Brewster, New

York. But she is rewarded with a withering response: "Yes, but it's in New York!" Primo Mabel! It is in this segment that Rose from Yonkers, who knew Mrs. Marie, relates that Ann was "fat and round as a cantaloupe" as a small child. We also learn that Donald drinks milk with his corned beef sandwiches!

Who Gets to Say "That Girl!"

Steve Franken, as Dr. Bruce Alden on Ann's untitled soap opera, has the honors. With the proper genre histrionics, he proclaims about Sheila (Ann's character), "I can't live without *that girl!*" Steve Franken is a familiar face from his role as Chatsworth Osborn Jr., the spoiled rich kid on *The Adventures of Dobie Gillis* (1959–63).

EPISODE 13: ALL ABOUT ANN
ORIGINAL AIR DATE: DECEMBER 1, 1966
Writer: Milton Pascal; Director: Jon Erman; Guest Cast: Bonnie Scott (Judy Bessamer), E. J. Peaker (Sheila Harmon), Howard Morton (Slocum, director of Ann's workshop), Bernie Kopell (Jerry), Marti Litis (Miss Cleary, Don's secretary), Rob Reiner (Acting Student in Ann's workshop)

When Judy tells Ann that she has seen Donald with fellow actress Sheila Harmon, Ann suspects the worst. In actuality, Donald is writing a story about Ann for *Newsview* magazine and Sheila is supplying candid photos.

Highlights

The best scene is the climax where Ann decides that she can take the deception no more. She has overheard Don on the phone with Sheila and is sure he doesn't love her (Ann) anymore. After feeding the birds in Central Park (a lovely location shot), Ann shows up late to her workshop (followed by Don) where she proceeds to do an improvisation scene with Sheila. The two actresses play nurses and Ann makes it very clear that she knows that Sheila is fooling around with Don. The director and the class (including a very young Rob Reiner) are confused, but Don and Sheila get the point and only when Don shows Ann the *Newsview* story is she convinced that he still loves her.

Notes

Not only does this episode reveal the depth of Ann's feelings for Don, but it also shows her serious approach to her career. We see her polishing her craft in an acting workshop, even if it isn't the one run by Jules Benedict (where she was accepted in episode #3: "Never Change a Diaper on Opening Night").

Who Gets to Say "That Girl!"

Bonnie Scott as Judy Bessamer, wife of Dr. Leon Bessamer (who, in this episode, we learn has just delivered triplets). As the camera finds Ann's image in a mirror, Judy tells her that she has seen Donald going into a restaurant and "there was a girl and it was not *that girl!*"

EPISODE 14: PHANTOM OF THE HORSE OPERA
ORIGINAL AIR DATE: DECEMBER 8, 1966
Writers: Peggy Elliott and Ed Scharlach; Director: John Erman; Guest Cast: Bonnie Scott (Judy Bessamer), Dabney Coleman (Dr. Leon Bessamer), Bill Sargent (Vernon Lyons), Sterling Holloway (Everett Valentine), Maxine Stuart (Manager), Reta Shaw (Saleslady), Phil Arnold (Tobacco Shop Man)

Ann is awakened at night by organ music. She and Don track down the culprit and he turns out to be a sweet old man who used to accompany silent films. Ann tries to find him a job by encouraging Donald to write a human interest story about him. Unfortunately, when the story is published, the man disappears. He doesn't want publicity because he is wanted by the police in seven states as a bigamist and a thief!

Highlights

Sterling Holloway's sweet performance as the silent cinema buff is the strong point of this installment.

Notes

The issues of *Newsview* magazine (front and back covers) that we see in this episode are identical to the *Newsview* seen in episode #13: "All About Ann." The end credits for this segment list several characters who don't appear in this installment, and Holloway's character is listed as Mr. Farnaey instead of Everett Valentine. We also find out that Don lives on West 54th Street in Manhattan.

Who Gets to Say "That Girl!"
Marlo Thomas as Ann says it while recalling her bad dream: ". . . who is my next victim? And Dracula pointed at me and said, 'That girl!'"

EPISODE 15: BEWARE OF ACTORS BEARING GIFTS

ORIGINAL AIR DATE: DECEMBER 15, 1966

Writer: Richard Baer; Director: Bob Sweeney; Guest Cast: Billy DeWolfe (Jules Benedict), Bruce Hyde (Hobart Niles), Carol O'Leary (Jane), Burt Taylor (Frank), James Millhollin (Clerk), Billy Gray (Stanley Zip), Lloyd King (Houseboy), Ben Lessey (Waiter)

When Hobart Niles, one of Ann's acting class colleagues, keeps giving her presents, Ann and Don assume he is stealing them. After they return gift after gift, including a new TV, they find out that the actor is very wealthy.

Highlights
One of the perks of viewing this funny episode is Billy DeWolfe's acerbic performance as Jules Benedict, Ann's acting coach, who tells Ann to "squeeze the audience like a frightened orange!" (Ethel Merman gives her similar advice on episode #31: "Pass the Potatoes, Ethel Merman.") When Ann asks Benedict how to interpret the scene she is playing, he responds, "Much, much better!" The other highlight is the scene with Billy Gray as Stanley Zipp, of Zipp's Discount Emporium, where Ann finds out that Hobart acquired the television set "wholesale."

Notes
One of the funnier props on *That Girl* is the sign on Benedict's door: "Never Enter Here."

Who Gets to Say "That Girl!"
Bruce Hyde as Hobart Niles, poor little rich kid, as he explains to Ann why he had to buy her a watch: "If that wristwatch belongs on anyone it belongs on the pretty wrist of *that girl!*"

EPISODE 16: CHRISTMAS AND THE HARD LUCK KID
ORIGINAL AIR DATE: DECEMBER 22, 1966
Writer: Jim Brooks; Director: John Erman; Guest Cast: Lew Parker (Lou Marie), Chris Shea (Tommy), John Fiedler (Mr. Merriman), June Vincent (Tommy's Mother), Gerald Michanaut (Roger Green), Don Keefer (Mr. Carson)

On a break from one of her necessary jobs—this time as a department store elf at Christmas—Ann tells Donald a story about three Christmases ago, when she was still a teacher in her hometown of Brewster. The flashback shows Ann giving up her holiday to stay at the boarding school with a little boy whose parents are working and can't come to get him.

Highlights
Finding out about a character's past is always interesting. The flashback to Ann as a teacher shows what a compassionate woman she was and what a good teacher she must have been.

Notes
This is the first *That Girl* episode written by Jim Brooks, who would later go on to co-create *The Mary Tyler Moore Show* (1970–77) and write and direct such films as the Oscar-winning *As Good as It Gets* (1997). This segment contains the seeds of a future Christmas on a *Mary Tyler Moore Show* episode, in which Mary is forced to work alone on the holiday. It is the first of very few flashbacks to Ann's past. It takes place three Christmases before she decided to become an actress and shows her as a teacher (in real life Marlo Thomas was also going to be a teacher, before turning to acting). We also find out that Ann is the best snowball thrower in Putnam County (where Brewster is located).

Who Gets to Say "That Girl!"
June Vincent, as Tommy's mother, tells Donald that she is waiting on line to see Santa in a department store so Mary can thank one of Santa's helpers. He asks which one and she answers, "*That girl!*"

Donald Hollinger's Secretaries

Throughout Donald Hollinger's five years as a reporter for Manhattan-based *Newsview* magazine, we hear about and/or see a long line of his secretaries. Although he is no Murphy Brown, Don goes through many an assistant. Here are some of them:

* Ann Marie (she didn't work out, although she was a great typist)
* Dora Holman
* Elaine (played by both Elaine Princi and Barbara Minkus)
* Gloria
* Margie
* Miss Cleary
* Mrs. LaConk
* Nancy
* Pat Crawford
* Shirley
* Terry Doby (a man)

EPISODE 17: AMONG MY SOUVENIRS
ORIGINAL AIR DATE: JANUARY 5, 1967
Writers: Peggy Elliott and Ed Scharlach; Director: Seymour Robbie; Guest Cast: Bonnie Scott (Judy Bessamer), Steve Harmon (Freddy Dunlap)

While cleaning out the garage at Ann's parents' home in Brewster, Ann and Donald find souvenirs reminiscent of her childhood boyfriend Freddy Dunlap. Ann downplays Donald's jealousy and arranges a meeting with Freddy to return a valuable ring he'd once given her. Freddy turns out to have designs on Ann, just as Don has said he would.

Highlights
A noteworthy scene in this entry has Ann Marie's old boyfriend Freddy show his true colors and try to seduce her with lies. Her surprised reaction is delightful.

Notes

Besides finding out about Freddy, we are informed that Don's old girlfriend was named Loretta Fitch and that Ann was a very orderly child (she organized her dolls by name), an avid fan of Dean Martin and Jerry Lewis, and does not like anchovies on her pizza.

Who Gets to Say "That Girl!"

When Don finds a wishbone among Ann's souvenirs, she points to a picture of herself as a child and tells him that it is "an engagement present for *that girl!*"

EPISODE 18: THESE BOOTS WEREN'T MADE FOR WALKING

ORIGINAL AIR DATE: JANUARY 12, 1967

Writers: Peggy Elliott and Ed Scharlach; Director: John Erman; Guest Cast: Paul Lynde (Nate Caswell), Bonnie Scott (Judy Bessamer), Kelly Jean Peters (Margie, Don's secretary), Art Lewis (Customer), Patty Regan (Customer), Doreen McLean (Dissatisfied Customer), Charles Lampkin (Janitor), Digby Wolfe (Mr. Flushing), Len Lesser (Guard)

To supplement her income, Ann takes a job as a door-to-door shoe salesperson. She does very well until all the shoes she sells begin to fall apart.

Highlights

The scenes involving Paul Lynde as Mr. Caswell, the owner of the Smart and Stunning Shoe Service, are gems. He gets all his stock from "the most reputable bankrupt companies," thus the Norman's Rent-a-Shoe shoehorns ("Norman had a good idea but it just didn't catch on with the public") and the mysteriously disintegrating shoes that Ann sells. The scene where he discovers that the reason the shoes are falling apart is because they came from a funeral supply house and were only meant for corpses is priceless. Ann trying to be a jolly, pushy saleswoman is very also amusing.

Notes

In this offering we find out that Don's secretary is Margie. (He has a new one, it seems. In episode #7: "Help Wanted," he went through three, including Ann, and in episode #13: "All About Ann," he employed Miss Cleary.) Margie is sweet on Jerry (we do not see him, but she orders slippers for him from Ann). Is this Jerry Myer (played by Bernie

Kopell, whose wife Margie was later played by Arlene Golonka) or Jerry Bauman (also played by Bernie Kopell, whose wife Ruth was played by both Carolan Daniels and Alice Borden)? Either way, Margie was a favorite name on the show. (See episode #21: "Rain, Snow, and Rice" for the only other appearance of Margie before she "turns into Ruth.") Paul Lynde was to have been a regular on *Two's Company*, Marlo Thomas's unsold pilot of the year before.

Who Gets to Say "That Girl!"
Judy, who has been doing Ann's hair, tells her, "It's perfect, it's you!" Ann looks at her silly hairdo in the mirror and laughs delightfully as she asks, "I'm *that girl?*"

EPISODE 19: KIMONO MY HOUSE
ORIGINAL AIR DATE: JANUARY 12, 1967
Writers: Peggy Elliott and Ed Scharlach; Director: John Erman; Guest Cast: Caroline Kido (Miko Yamagata), Bill Saito (Toshiro Takahaski), Yuki Tani (Japanese Hostess)

Thinking Don's apartment is a disaster, Ann hires a maid for him—sight unseen. But when he opens the door, Don finds a beautiful Japanese girl who assumes it's a live-in position. Ann steps in and takes the girl back to her own apartment. Soon the maid is doing everything for Donald, which *he* likes, but Ann gets jealous.

Highlights
Yuki Tani's sweet and restrained performance as Don's maid makes this a very special episode.

Notes
This is the first time we see Donald's apartment. We find out that he is a slob. This segment also contains the one and only reference to Don's brother. We meet Don's parents and his sister, but never hear about his brother again.

Who Gets to Say "That Girl!"
Don says it to Jerry, while looking at a picture of Ann and thinking about getting a girl to clean his apartment: "What would my other girl say?" Jerry: "What other girl?" Don: *"That girl!"*

EPISODE 20: GONE WITH THE BREEZE
ORIGINAL AIR DATE: JANUARY 26, 1967

Writers: Tom and Helen August; Director: John Erman; Guest Cast: Bonnie Scott (Judy Bessamer), Bernie Kopell (Jerry Bauman), Audrey Christie (Miss Daley), Richard Schaal (Lost and Found Man), Mitzi Hoag (Salesgirl), Harriet MacGibbon (Middle-Aged Lady), Lela Bliss (Irate Woman), Maxine Semon (Lost and Found Woman)

Don finishes his novel and gives Ann what she thinks is the only copy of the manuscript. When she gets home and wants to read it she can't find it. When Donald presses her for a critique, Ann stalls for time by pretending to be a slow reader. Meanwhile, Donald finds the manuscript and teases Ann into confessing she lost it.

Highlights
The scenes at the Best and Co. department store, where Ann is a part-time cosmetics salesperson are very funny. Ann is only interested in finding the lost novel, but has to wait on snooty customers like Harriet MacGibbon (Mrs. Drysdale of *The Beverly Hillbillies*) who demand her full attention.

Notes
This is the first mention of Don's novel, *City of Strangers*, which will figure in episode #33: "Black, White and Read All Over." Unfortunately, the book is rejected by several publishers at the end of the segment.

Who Gets to Say "That Girl!"
Ted Bessell as Don reads the dedication of the book to Ann: "I dedicate this book to the laughter and loveliness of *that girl!*"

EPISODE 21: RAIN, SNOW, AND RICE
ORIGINAL AIR DATE: FEBRUARY 2, 1967

Writer: James L. Brooks; Director: John Erman; Guest Cast: Lew Parker (Lou Marie), Rosemary DeCamp (Helen Marie), Bernie Kopell (Jerry Bauman), Arlene Golonka (Margie), J. Pat O'Malley (Judge Hardy), Nydia Westman (Old Lady), James O'Reare (Hotel Clerk)

Jerry and Margie decide to get married at a cozy inn in Connecticut, and invite Ann and Donald to be their witnesses. When bad weather forces Don and Ann to stay the night, they discover that there are only two rooms available, so the boys stay in one room and the girls in the other. Finally, it becomes so painful for the newlyweds that Ann and Donald decide to share a room for the night. The usual complications ensue, including having her parents, Lou and Helen, catch Don and Ann "together."

Highlights

Ann and Don trying to be nonchalant about sleeping in the same room is charmingly naïve, but also one of the cornerstones of what this series was all about: Ann's innocence being threatened by outside forces. She and Donald never succumb because they have too much respect for each other. However, the outside world, including her parents, always tend to think the worst.

Notes

This is one of Marlo Thomas's favorite episodes. The first mention and appearance of "Margie" is in episode #18: "These Boots Weren't Made for Walking," where she is played by Kelly Jean Peters and works at *Newsview*. Later in the series, Jerry is married to Ruthie (played by Carolan Daniels and later Alice Borden), and no mention of Margie is ever made again! Even more bizarre is that, for the first and only time, Jerry is referred to as Jerry Myer (in the wedding ceremony), but is billed at the end of the show as Bauman. Arlene Golonka appears in episode #60: "Old Man's Darling" as Bonita La Salle and again as a stewardess in episode #62: "The Hi-Jack and the Mighty," but never again as Jerry's wife.

Who Gets to Say "That Girl!"

Before they leave for the wedding, Margie happily proclaims "and my maid of honor will be . . ." and her husband-to-be finishes her sentence, "You guessed it. *That girl!*"

EPISODE 22: PAPER HATS AND EVERYTHING

ORIGINAL AIR DATE: FEBRUARY 9, 1967

Writer: Sydney R. Zelinka; Director: John Erman; Guest Cast: Lew Parker (Lou Marie), Richard Dreyfuss (Actor/Waiter), Bonnie Scott (Judy Bessamer), Dabney Coleman (Dr. Leon Bessamer), Amanda Randolph (Harriet), Mitzi

Hoag (Patty), Bob Duggan (Waiter), Armin Hoffman (Paul), Laurie Main (Maitre d'), Joe Corey (Marvin, the cabbie), Alan Dexter (Bartender)

When her father invites her out to dinner for her birthday, Ann thinks that she is being given a surprise party. When Judy realizes there is not going to be one, she plans one for Ann herself. After several mishaps Donald gets the word to Mr. Marie and Ann gets her party.

Highlights

This show has several fun scenes, including the appearance of a very young Richard Dreyfuss (this is one of his first breaks) as an actor/waiter who quotes from the play *Tea and Sympathy* (which Ann and he performed in acting school*)* to Ann and her father. Another "moment" occurs in front of Ann's apartment door after her lovely evening out with her father. In this scene she asks if he was very disappointed that she was a girl. Lou replies that he was thrilled to have a healthy baby and is glad she is not a boy. This sequence, and others in the show between the two actors, under-scores the sweet and sometimes complex father-daughter relation-ship. It is one of the dramatic underpinnings of the series.

Notes

In this episode Ann mentions several of her relatives names. We find that her mother has gone to visit Aunt Gladys in Baltimore (she is on her mother's side of the family) because Uncle Oscar has gone to Chicago on business. We also hear about relatives who must live closer, because Ann expects them at her party: Aunt Rosie and Uncle Henry. We also find out what each of the principals drinks. Ann orders a vermouth Cassis, her father a scotch on the rocks, and when Donald despairs of ever getting Ann to her party, he orders a double scotch. During the course of Ann's date with her father, we learn that Lou wanted Ann to be a dental assistant, not an actress, and that his father wanted him to be a chiropodist, rather than a restaurateur. We also find that Lou is a good dancer and once had a sandwich named for him at Roseland (a popular dancehall in New York City). This was Lew Parker's favorite episode (also Marlo Thomas's). See Parker's entry in Chapter 11: Life after *That Girl*, for the importance of this installment.

Who Gets to Say "That Girl!"
Lou Marie's maid tells him to call Ann and invite her out for her birthday. Lou is hesitant, thinking she will have other plans. The maid thinks that a grown man should be able to stand a little rejection. Lou picks up Ann's picture and answers, "I can, but not from *that girl!*"

EPISODE 23: WHAT ARE YOUR INTENTIONS?
ORIGINAL AIR DATE: FEBRUARY 16, 1967
Writer: Milton Pascal; Director: John Erman; Guest Cast: Lew Parker (Lou Marie), Rosemary DeCamp (Helen Marie), Paul Carr (Frank Gilder)

Since Ann and Don have been dating steadily for eight months, Lou decides it is time to find out if Don really wants to marry his daughter. Ann and Donald, in an attempt to avoid the issue, explain that they also date others. Neither knew the other had outside interests, and an argument ensues. The situation is complicated when Lou gives Ann's phone number to a prospective suitor who takes her on a date. However, Ann can only think of Donald and, by the end of the episode, they reconcile and decide to only date each other.

Highlights
As usual, whenever he appears as Ann's father, Lew Parker is the highlight of the episode. He steals every show in which he appears. Having Rosemary DeCamp along for the ride here makes this one even better.

Notes
This is an uncharacteristic installment because in most of Lou's other appearances he is not very fond of Donald and only addresses him as "Hollinger." Here he wants him to marry his daughter and he calls him Don. It is also one of the only times we see Lou Marie smoke. In this episode, Donald brings Ann roses and she seems to have no allergic reaction, as she will in episode #77: "The Earrings."

Who Gets to Say "That Girl!"
Lew Parker as Lou Marie wants to know, "What goes on with that boy when he goes out with *that girl?*"

EPISODE 24: A TENOR'S LOVING CARE
ORIGINAL AIR DATE: FEBRUARY 23, 1967

Writer: Joseph Bonaduce; Director: John Erman; Guest Cast: Carroll O'Connor (Giuseppe Casanetti), Peter Madsen (Reporter), Jim Begg (Tommy), Herb Ellis (Detective), James McCallion (Cooper)

It seems that the only way to get an interview with a famous opera star is to send Ann, who knows something about the subject. But the singer has more on his mind than vocalizing or giving Ann a story. Fortunately for Ann, she keeps the tape recorder going as the married singer makes a romantic play for her.

Highlights
The seduction scene where Ann is chased around the couch by the amorous opera star is the comedic highlight. She finally gets away by pretending to have a cold, which terrifies the singer.

Notes
This entry is memorable chiefly for the early comic TV performance of Carroll O'Connor (who would go on to play the role of the bigoted Archie Bunker on *All in the Family*, 1971–83). O'Connor's little bit of singing is his own.

Who Gets to Say "That Girl!"
The title phrase is memorably spoken by Carroll O'Connor as he chooses one reporter to interview him. This is the only time it is uttered in Italian: *Quella Ragazza!* We even get to see the title in Italian, with *That Girl* in parentheses underneath.

EPISODE 25: LEAVING THE NEST IS FOR THE BIRDS
ORIGINAL AIR DATE: MARCH 2, 1967

Writer: Barbara Avedon; Director: Hal Cooper; Guest Cast: Lew Parker (Lou Marie), Rosemary DeCamp (Helen Marie), Jerry Van Dyke (Howie Frankel), Hazel Shermet (Aunt Harriet), Luana Anders (Girl), Britt Lumano (Man)

Ann has her parents and her disapproving Aunt Harriet to dinner. She sees this get-together as a chance to demonstrate how living in the city is not as hazardous as they all believe. However, the appearance of a stranger on the ledge outside Ann's window does not help to prove her point. He threatens to jump, robs them, and generally disrupts the whole dinner, until he and his girlfriend across the street are reconciled.

Highlights
The highlight scene has Ann coaxing the jumper in from her apartment's window ledge. A classic moment shows Ann as a corpse on the TV show *The Ladykiller*. Just as the camera comes in for a closeup, she opens her eyes.

Notes
This half-hour puts Ann's father on her career side for the first time in the series. He tries to convince Aunt Harriet that Ann is all right living on her own and unmarried. (Harriet's daughter, Ann's cousin, has always been the competitive perfect child.) Ann states her thesis about marriage in this show, "I promised myself a year at least and no wedding."

Who Gets to Say "That Girl!"
On the TV show within the show, the actor playing the killer asks, "Who did I kill?" and the voice-over says, *"That girl!"*

EPISODE 26: YOU HAVE TO KNOW SOMEONE TO BE UNKNOWN
ORIGINAL AIR DATE: MARCH 9, 1967
Writers: Saul Turteltaub and Bernie Orenstein; Director: Jerrold Bernstein; Guest Cast: Bonnie Scott (Judy Bessamer), Bernie Kopell (Jerry Bauman), Herbert Rudley (Harold J. Davis), A. G. Vitanza (Herbie), Dee J. Thompson (Harriet), Art Lewis (Mover), Paul Sykes (Bearded Man), Eddie Carroll (Sheldon), Harvey Jason (Bruce), Ogden Talbot (Marv)

When Ann reads in *Variety* that a producer is looking for a total unknown for his new Broadway venture, Ann sets out to prove to him that she's the unknown face he's seeking. Although he had interviewed the producer the year before, Don at first refuses to put in a good word for Ann, so she tries every trick in the book to meet the producer. When Don finally does phone on her behalf, he learns that the part was cast long ago. He tries to warn Ann, but she doesn't believe him and she humiliates herself. Typically, in the end, although rejected she is still hopeful.

Highlights

Ann's tirade on the elevator to Herbert Rudley as the producer is the essence of her on-camera character.

Notes

This was the first episode written by Turteltaub and Orenstein, who would go on to produce the series in its last two seasons (1969–71). The character of the producer, known as the prince of publicity, was patterned after Broadway legend David Merrick.

Who Gets to Say "That Girl!"

Marlo Thomas as Ann does. It seems that Harold J. Davis is looking for an unknown, talented, and bright new face: "Oh, Donald, that girl is this girl. I'm *that girl!*"

EPISODE 27: THE HONEYMOON APARTMENT

ORIGINAL AIR DATE: MARCH 16, 1967

Writers: Austin and Irma Kalish; Director: Hal Cooper; Guest Cast: Warren Berlinger (Harold Turner), Bonnie Scott (Judy Bessamer), Dabney Coleman (Dr. Leon Bessamer), Judee Morton (Edith Turner), Dick Wilson (Desk Clerk), Warren Parker (Manager)

Ann gets a visit from her cheap cousin, Harold Turner, and his new bride. When Harold (supposedly) can't find a hotel good enough for them, he and Edith stay at Ann's apartment, while she bunks with the Bessamers. When Harold won't leave, Ann and Edith move into the bridal suite of a hotel. Finally, Ann kicks him out and tells him that he's a cheapskate.

Highlights

The best sequence in this episode is the hotel scene where Donald tries to register both Ann and Edith into the bridal suite. The reaction of the desk clerk is a small comic masterpiece.

Notes

Dick Wilson, who plays the desk clerk, is well-known to viewers as Mr. Whipple in the Charmin commercials and as a drunk on *Bewitched* (1964–72). In this episode, we find out that Ann's childhood nickname, at least according to her cousin Harold, is "Punky Puss."

Who Gets to Say "That Girl!"

Warren Berlinger as Ann's cousin Harold yells as he enters her apartment, "Is Punky Puss here?" Don says, "Who?" Harold points to *"That girl!"*

EPISODE 28: THIS LITTLE PIGGY HAD A BALL

ORIGINAL AIR DATE: MARCH 23, 1967

Writers: Arnold Margolin and Jim Parker; Director: Hal Cooper; Guest Cast: Bonnie Scott (Judy Bessamer), Dabney Coleman (Dr. Leon Bessamer), Murray Roman (Manager of Bowling Alley), Jerry Fogel (Fireman), Jane Dulo (Nurse), Marc London (Dr. Wisnicki), Shirley Bonne (Sharon Hackett), Gene Tyburn (Man), Diane Quinn (Girl), Rob Reiner (Carl), Terry [Teri] Garr (Estelle)

Ann gets a bowling ball stuck on her toe just hours before she is to accept an award for a friend who is out of town. All efforts to either find a substitute recipient or to get the ball off her foot fail. She attends the banquet with the ball still attached to her toe.

Highlights

This is a classic *Lucy*-like segment which keeps escalating, from the moment we see Ann trying to toe-bowl ("Donald, I think I figured out what's so tough about toe-bowling—letting go of the ball.") to the moment when the ball (which has been cut in half so that she can walk up to accept the award) comes off her foot ("My toe relaxed"). In between, there are visits to the emergency room and the fire department. The climax is when Ann takes too many muscle relaxants and seems to be intoxicated.

Notes

We learn that Ann got her elbow stuck in a peanut butter jar when she was five years old. Here we see Ann actually working in a play (albeit only backstage). The production is called *Honor's Stain* and its poster hangs in the star's dressing room. Also note the early appearances of Rob Reiner and Terry (soon to be Teri) Garr as Ann's friends and colleagues. Reiner has appeared already, in episode #13: "All About Ann," as a fellow acting student. Now we know his name is Carl. Jane Dulo appears in episode #61: "Sock It to Me" as a passenger on a plane. Co-creator Denoff explains how the installment came to be: "Remember the episode of *[The Dick] Van Dyke [Show]* where she [Mary Tyler Moore] gets her toe stuck in the [bathtub] faucet?" Denoff adds that he once ". . . got my thumb stuck in a bowling ball." This is the last appearance of Dabney Coleman as Dr. Leon Bessamer.

Who Gets to Say "That Girl!"

Shirley Bonne as Sharon Hackett, the star of the play in which Ann is appearing, needs to choose someone to accept her award for Most Promising Young Actress at the Annual Drama Guild Awards banquet. By virtue of an "eenie, meenie, minie, moe" procedure, she proclaims that "my mother says to choose *that girl!*" Also note that at the end of the show, after Ann has clomped with pride and poise to the podium with a half of a bowling ball on her foot, Donald lovingly proclaims "Oh! *That girl!*"

EPISODE 29: AUTHOR, AUTHOR

ORIGINAL AIR DATE: MARCH 30, 1967

Writers: Ronald Axe and Howard Harris; Director: Danny Arnold; Guest Cast: Bonnie Scott (Judy Bessamer), Bernie Kopell (Jerry Bauman), Sidney Gould (Ernie Bernie), Jack Goode (Mr. Hanley), Fay DeWitt (Betsy), Sang Werris (Waiter), J. B. Larson (Assistant Producer), Kay Cole (Girl in dance team), Skip Marin (Boy in dance team)

Ann needs original comedy material for her audition. After trying Jerry's unfunny cousin, Ernie Bernie, Ann begs Donald, who in college apparently wrote funny songs, to write some amusing dialogue. When the jokes don't prove humorous to Ann, or to anyone else, she and Donald argue. In the end, Don comes to his senses and Ann doesn't use the material.

Highlights

The scenes with Sidney Gould as an inept, unfunny comedy writer are delightful.

Notes

Kay Cole, who is seen briefly dancing with Skip Marin, went on to create a role in the 1975 Broadway hit *A Chorus Line* and introduce the song "At the Ballet." Fay DeWitt, who plays another auditioning actress, is also a musical theater favorite, appearing most recently in *Nite Club Confidential* (1992). This was the first *That Girl* installment directed by Danny Arnold, who would go on to produce the second and third seasons of the series, and the last time Bonnie Scott would play Judy Bessamer. (Guess the Bessamers moved.) It is interesting to note that the songs that Donald plays and sings for Ann ("In Love with Atilla the Hun" and "The Only Girl I Ever Loved") were taken from *The Dick Van Dyke Show* (episode #118: "Bupkiss"), written by none other than Bill Persky and Sam Denoff. In this installment there is a poster of *Honor's Stain* (the play Ann did in episode #28: "This Little Piggy Had a Ball") outside the door of the rehearsal.

Who Gets to Say "That Girl!"
Fay Dewitt as Betsy doesn't want to be next at the audition. When the director asks who is next, "This girl?" she responds, "No, *that girl!*"

EPISODE 30: THE MATING GAME
ORIGINAL AIR DATE: APRIL 6, 1967
Writers: Treva Silverman and Peter Meyerson; Director: Hal Cooper; Guest Cast: Bernie Kopell (Jerry Bauman), Alejandro Rey (Eduardo Guzman), Dan Tobin (Eddie Turner), Steve Dunne (Bob Williams), Bobo Lewis (Louise Lewis), Dorothy Rice (Ellen), Linda Meiklejohn (Nancy), Bob Lussier (Peter Blake)

When Donald is assigned to do a story on the TV show *The Mating Game*, he gets Ann to be a contestant. Unbeknownst to her, Don decides to be one of the bachelors from which she will have to choose. When Ann selects another man instead, Donald goes along on the date in his capacity as a reporter. He gets very jealous and leaves his tape recorder so he can hear the rest of the date for his pending article. Ann teaches him a lesson by staging a very romantic scene with her "date."

Highlights
Don's reaction to Ann's "staging" of her date with Alejandro Rey is the high point of this last show of the first season.

Notes: Treva Silverman went on to write some of the best *Mary Tyler Moore Show*s and won an Emmy in the process. We learn in this episode that Ann is a Scorpio and Don, whose birthday is September 26, is a Libra. Alejandro Rey, who costarred in *The Flying Nun*

(1967–70), also appears in episode #124: "That Senorita." This is the first time viewers see Bobo Lewis, who is cast as different characters every time she appears on the series. We also learn about Nancy, another of Don's ever-changing secretaries. This was Jerry Davis's last assignment as *That Girl* producer.

Who Gets to Say "That Girl!"
Ted Bessell as Donald speaks it after Jerry asks who Donald is going to get to be on *The Mating Game* when he does his story.

Awards and Honors for the First Season

Marlo Thomas won a Golden Globe Award for Most Promising New Actress.

Marlo Thomas was named the Most Promising New Female Star by *Television Today, Motion Picture Daily,* and *Fame* magazines.

Marlo Thomas won Photoplay's Gold Medal Award as Most Promising New Star.

Marlo Thomas received an Emmy nomination for Outstanding Continued Performance by an Actress in a Leading Role in a Comedy for Season #1.

Marlo Thomas was signed to a multi-picture deal by Paramount Pictures in April 1967.

SEASON TWO
SEPTEMBER 1967–APRIL 1968

Season Two Overview

There were many changes between the first and second seasons of *That Girl.* The next-door neighbors, the Bessamers, disappear from Ann Marie's life. Ann's apartment, wardrobe, and makeup seem different. With a new producer in place (Danny Arnold), there are other staff changes. Ruth Brooks Flippen is brought on board to balance out the men/women quotient and she contributes many great scripts with and without Arnold.

Ann's career seems to be going well this second season. Right off the bat, she gets to act on the same stage as musical-comedy legend Ethel Merman, gets cast in a Broadway show (a comedy/mystery called *And Everything Nice*) that tries out in Philadelphia (unfortunately, it closes there too), does several commercials, tries to write a play with Donald about her life, almost gets the lead in an Italian movie by Vittorio Barini (she turns it down because there is a nude scene), gets signed by the Gillian and Norris Talent Agency, and wins her first long-term agent, Seymour Schwimmer. He maneuvers her into several commercials, including a job as the Creamy Soap Girl, as well as a part in the Broadway hit *The Knights of Queen Mary*. Ann also becomes a high-fashion model and gets her face on the cover of a magazine. Donald is now well-established as her steady boyfriend and their relationship continues to deepen, while Ann's father persists in objecting to it. Don's novel gets rejected twelve times before one publisher expresses an interest—on the condition that Don raise the smut quotient. He refuses.

Production Team for Season Two
Executive Producers and Series Creators: Bill Persky and Sam Denoff; Producer: Danny Arnold; Script Consultant: Ruth Brooks Flippen; Director of Photography: Jack Marquette; Art Directors: Pato Guzman and Arnold Margolin; Film Editor: Bob Moore; Music: Dominic Frontiere with theme by Earle Hagen; Miss Thomas's wardrobe by Cardinelli, Inc.; Hair: Lynn Masters; Makeup: Tom Case; Origination: Filmed at Desilu-Cahuenga Studios and on location in New York City, Philadelphia, and elsewhere by Daisy Productions; Executive in Charge of Production: Ronald Jacobs; Agencies and Sponsors: Bristol-Myers Company through Grey Advertising Inc., and Brown & Williamson Tobacco Corp. through Ted Bates and Company

EPISODE 31: "PASS THE POTATOES, ETHEL MERMAN"
ORIGINAL AIR DATE: SEPTEMBER 7, 1967
Writer: Jim Brooks; Director: James Frawley; Guest Cast: Ethel Merman (as Herself), Lew Parker (Lou Marie), Carolan Daniels (Ruth Bauman), Sandy Kenyon (Ed Burns, the director), Renata Vanni (Mrs. Brandano), Joy Harmon (Mrs. Bridges), Allan Emerson (Assistant Director)

When Ann gets a one-line role in a short-term revival of *Gypsy*, she invites its star, Ethel Merman, to her apartment for a home-cooked meal. Merman and Ann's father argue over stuffed cabbage recipes, and Ann gets a lesson in singing from "The Merm."

Highlights

The scene where Merman and restaurateur Lou Marie debate over how to make the best stuffed cabbage is hysterical. (In real life, Merman was proud of the fact that she never cooked. When living in her last apartment at the Surrey Hotel in New York City, she would brag that she had the stove removed from the kitchen.) This scene was also a reunion of sorts for Merman and Lew Parker. They had appeared on the stage together in Merman's first Broadway show, *Girl Crazy* (1930), and again in 1936 in *Red, Hot and Blue*. Another special scene shows Ethel in the kitchen teaching Ann how to belt out a number. (Merman sings a little bit of "After You've Gone," a song she sang in vaudeville and filmed in a 1932 short subject entitled *Be Like Me*.) Special mention should go to Renata Vanni as Mrs. Brandano (Ann's landlady) for her uninhibited excitement at seeing a great star in her building and letting everyone know that she has seen "The one! The one!" A classic line is uttered by Ann: "One day you're nobody and the next Ethel Merman's stuffing your cabbage."

Notes

This is the first time that Ann has a job in a big-time stage show. It is nice to see her succeed. We witness her happiness at getting the role and her anxiety over keeping it. The line that she is given to speak, directly after Merman sings "Small World," is "Hey everybody, here comes the picnic wagon!" There is no such line in *Gypsy*, and the actual scene in which the song is sung is in a backstage setting as she tries to seduce Herbie (the male lead), not at a picnic surrounded by the ensemble. Merman is also seen singing "Everything's Coming Up Roses" at the end of the show (in a very 1960s sequined miniskirt, in front of a curtain, which looks more like a concert or TV special than *Gypsy*).

This episode marked the second *That Girl* script (see episode #21: "Rain, Snow, and Rice") written by future filmmaker/director/

screenwriter Jim Brooks. Brooks captures the Merman persona perfectly (despite the fact that Merman never cooked) and taps into the loneliness of being a performer, which is pointed up by the interaction of the star (Ethel) and the bit player (Ann). It is made clear at the end of the entry that Ann is lucky because, besides her career, she has Donald and she has her father. The chemistry between Thomas, Parker, and Merman is so special that Merman is hired to do a follow-up segment (see episode # 51: "The Other Woman"). This debut of the second season also marks the first time we see the credit for Ruth Brooks Flippen as Script Consultant, and Marlo Thomas's clothes are now by Cardinelli. We also find out that Ann won the Drama Award at Brewster College. This is the first appearance of Carolan Daniels as Ruth Bauman.

Who Gets to Say "That Girl!"
Ethel Merman, says it, of course. She states it emphatically when she is asked to choose which of a line of girls (all toothy and buxom, except for perky Ann) she thinks would be right for the walk-on in scene three. "I do see someone. Let's use *that girl!*"

EPISODE 32: THE GOOD SKATE
ORIGINAL AIR DATE: SEPTEMBER 14, 1967
Writers: Tom and Helen August; Director: Jeff Hayden; Guest Cast: Mark Harris (Advertising Man), Paul Smith (Director), Rob Reiner (Makeup Man/Hairdresser), Kerry MacLane (Boy), Joan Johnson (Stunt Girl), Janet Hamil (Twinkie Girl), David Allen Saber (Twinkie Boy), Richard Jury (Businessman)

Ann is in the running for a television commercial for Twinkie, a new soda pop. She is the perfect Twinkie Girl, except that the Twinkie Girl is expected to perform on roller skates and Ann cannot roller-skate. Don tries to teach her, but in the end they settle for him holding her up for the screen test. Unfortunately, if he is to be her partner, Don must act! And that is one thing that Ann cannot teach him.

Highlights
Ann teaching Don how to act using the sense-memory method is a delightful scene.

Notes

The slogan that Ann and Don have to utter after skating to the camera is: "Twinkie is the drinkie for young people on the move. If you dig action, you'll love Twinkie and you'll be in the groove." We find out that Ann would get $1,200 for the commercial and, of course, that Ann cannot roller-skate at all (although in episode #25: "Leaving the Nest Is for the Birds" she refers to her childhood of skating with her cousin and how she always lost her skate key).

Who Gets to Say "That Girl!"

Paul Smith as the director of the commercial. He describes the Twinkie Girl as young, alive, sleek as a deer, and graceful as a fawn. He then summons the applicants: ". . . and *that girl!*" And Ann very ungracefully gets up on her skates and falls.

EPISODE 33: BLACK, WHITE AND READ ALL OVER

ORIGINAL AIR DATE: SEPTEMBER 21, 1967
Writer: Richard Baer; Director: Jeff Hayden; Guest Cast: Lew Parker (Lou Marie), Rosemary DeCamp (Helen Marie), Henry Jones (T. L. Harrison)

Donald is a little down because of his unpublished novel and needs cheering when he gets his twelfth rejection slip. Ann boosts his morale with a home-cooked dinner. Donald is cheered even more when an unexpected visitor—Ann's father—drops by and promises to show the book to famous publisher T. L. Harrison, whom he knows as a customer of his restaurant. However, after reading the book, Mr. Marie thinks it is obscene and that it is a veiled portrait of Don and Ann. He refuses to submit it, but Ann is determined to get it to the publisher. She succeeds, and Harrison says that if Don raises the smut quotient and changes the title, it will be a bestseller. Don turns down his offer, gaining the respect of the Marie family.

Highlights

Ann's attempt to find Mr. Harrison among her father's customers at La Parisianne Restaurant is the highlight of this episode.

Notes

Don's novel, *City of Strangers*, is first mentioned in episode #20: "Gone with the Breeze." In this installment the publisher wants to change the title to *City of Sin*. And Lou admits that he realizes Don might eventually marry Ann.

Who Gets to Say "That Girl!"
Marlo Thomas as Ann refers to her photograph and says, "The only person who hasn't read Don Hollinger's book is *that girl!*"

EPISODE 34: TO EACH HER OWN
ORIGINAL AIR DATE: SEPTEMBER 28, 1967
Writer: Stanley Ralph Ross; Director: James Sheldon; Guest Cast: Bernie Kopell (Jerry Bauman), Ruth Buzzi (Marge "Pete" Peterson), Rich Little (Andrew Marshall), Susan Charney (Lisa Stevens)

Donald is assigned to write an article about computer dating. Ann is jealous when Donald's Compu-date match turns out to be attractive model Lisa Stevens, so she fills out a Compu-date card herself, listing all of Don's good points. Her date is very much like Donald, but, in the end, Ann finds that he lacks Don's talent for kissing.

Highlights
The bonus here is Rich Little as Ann's computer date, doing what he does best: imitating John Wayne, Ed Sullivan, Humphrey Bogart, and Clark Gable.

Notes
In this segment we find out that Ann is 5 feet 5½ inches tall, weighs one hundred pounds in the morning and one hundred four at other times, wears a size six dress, and a size 6A shoe. This is the first appearance of Ruth Buzzi as Ann's friend Marge "Pete" Peterson. We don't know it yet, but "Pete" is an actress too and will appear in *And Everything Nice* with Ann in Philadelphia (episode #37: "The Philadelphia Story").

Who Gets to Say "That Girl!"
Ted Bessell as Donald says it while looking at a photo of Ann and wondering where the computer would "ever find another one like *that girl!*"

EPISODE 35: THE APARTMENT
ORIGINAL AIR DATE: OCTOBER 5, 1967
Writer: Ruth Brooks Flippen; Director: Danny Arnold; Guest Cast: Lew
Parker (Lou Marie), Bill Bixby (Harry Banner), Florence Halop (Clerk),
Hollis Morrison (Guy), Louise Lorimer (Interviewer), Leon Colker (Man)

Ann gets a telemarketing job just as her apartment must be vacated
for fumigation. Don solves her problem by lending her his apartment
while he is out of town. Unbeknownst to either of them, Don's old
friend Harry Banner (who has a key) arrives from St. Louis to stay
with Don. The usual complications ensue with Ann sleeping on the
couch, Harry nailing himself into the bedroom, and Ann's suspicious
father showing up at just the wrong moment in the morning.

Highlights
Bill Bixby's wonderful performance as Harry Banner stands out in
this excursion. He is attracted to Ann, but is so gallant that he nails
shut the door between them so she will feel safe during the night.

Notes
This is the first *That Girl* episode written by Ruth Brooks Flippen,
who is now billed as script consultant on every episode. Also note
that, according to Marlo Thomas, Bill Bixby was one of several candidates to play Don, but lost out, of course, to Ted Bessell. Danny
Arnold received an Emmy nomination for Outstanding Directorial
Achievement for Comedy for this episode. It was the only nomination
in this category that the series received.

Who Gets to Say "That Girl!"
Ted Bessell as Donald gets to speak it at the employment office. A
clerk looking for Ann (who is on the phone) asks if Don is Ann Marie.
He points to Ann and says, "No, *that girl!*"

**EPISODE 36: ABSENCE MAKES THE HEART GROW NERVOUS
(PART ONE)**
ORIGINAL AIR DATE: OCTOBER 12, 1967
Writers: Jim Parker and Arnold Margolin; Director: Danny Arnold; Guest
Cast: Lew Parker (Lou Marie), Richmond Shepard (Sam), Willie Switkes
(Joe), Terry [Teri] Garr (April), Kitty Malone (Dodie), Phil Arnold (Busboy)

Ann's elation at winning a role in her first Broadway show fades when she realizes that the out-of-town tryouts will mean a long separation (twelve weeks in all) from Donald. To cheer Ann up, Don takes a week off from his job to escort her on a sightseeing trip of New York.

Highlights
The show has lots of wonderful location shots and a great montage of Ann and Donald enjoying the sights of New York City. They try to take in everything in the week before she leaves for Philadelphia. They see Broadway shows *(Funny Girl, Mame)* and all the usual tourist attractions, such as the Statue of Liberty, the Empire State Building, the Staten Island Ferry, Grant's Tomb, and so on.

Notes
This is the first half of a two-part segment. Part Two is episode #37: "The Philadelphia Story." We find out that this is the first time Ann and Don go dancing together.

Who Gets to Say "That Girl!"
In a voice-over provided by Ted Bessell as Donald, we observe Ann's elation at getting the role in the play. Don's voice-over wonders who it could be . . . "Perhaps it's *that girl!*"

EPISODE 37: THE PHILADELPHIA STORY (PART TWO)
ORIGINAL AIR DATE: OCTOBER 19, 1967
Writers: Jim Parker and Arnold Margolin; Director: Danny Arnold; Guest Cast: Lew Parker (Lou Marie), Bernie Kopell (Jerry Bauman), Ruth Buzzi (Marge "Pete" Anderson), Jim Connell (Harvey Miller), Ken Greenwald (Bellboy), Tony Ballen (Waiter), Dallas Smith (Actor), Mark Baker (Stagehand #1), Ralph Montgomery (Stagehand #2), Leon Colker (Man)

Despite attention from a fellow castmate, Ann misses Donald while she is in Philadelphia to do a play. Equally lonely, Donald wangles an assignment from his editor to do a feature story about the birth of an actress (Ann) and the birth of a play. Unfortunately, the show turns out to be a bomb and Don must review it. Ann returns home to Brewster in defeat (the show closes on the road), until she reads that *Variety* liked her "socko comedy performance." She and Don reconcile and life goes on.

Highlights

Don and Ann do a whirlwind tour of Philadelphia (all shot on location), where they see the Liberty Bell and other tourist attractions.

Notes

This is one of those unusual episodes in which we see the real anguish that goes along with a career in show business. Marlo brings such a reality to the scenes of theatrical disaster in this segment that it is actually painful to watch.

Who Gets to Say "That Girl!"

In a similar voice-over to the previous episode, Bessell as Don points out, "My girl is *that girl!*"

EPISODE 38: THERE'S NOTHING TO BE AFREUD OF BUT FREUD HIMSELF

ORIGINAL AIR DATE: OCTOBER 26, 1967

Writer: Milton Pascal; Director: Hal Cooper; Guest Cast: Bernie Kopell (Jerry Bauman), Carolan Daniels (Ruth Bauman), Renzo Cesana (Dr. Enrici Cesana), Dub Taylor (Horace Chatsworth), Amzie Strickland (Mrs. Chatsworth), Ben Wright (Manager)

Donald is writing an article on Dr. Enrici Cesana, whose studies with inkblots may revolutionize the study of Sigmund Freud. Showing off his knowledge, Donald administers the inkblot test to Ann and evaluates her as stubborn, aggressive, argumentative, and opinionated. Jerry and Ruth Bauman don't fare well either. It is only when the doctor himself shows up and tells them that these qualities are in every healthy person, that Ann and Don make up.

Highlights

Jerry and Ruth Bauman's scenes, as Donald analyzes the results of their inkblot test, are the comic highlights of this entry.

Notes

At the beginning of the show Ann has one of her many survival jobs, this time working for a travel agency.

Who Gets to Say "That Girl!"

When Ann puts the decimal point in the wrong place on the ad board at the travel agency, a trip that should cost $3,598 is advertised as costing $35.98! The infuriated manager asks who put those erroneous numbers on the board. Dub Taylor as a country bumpkin customer answers, "I think it was *that girl!*"

EPISODE 39: THE COLLABORATORS

ORIGINAL AIR DATE: NOVEMBER 2, 1967

Writer: Ruth Brooks Flippen; Director: Bruce Bilson; Guest Cast: Bernie Kopell (Jerry Bauman), Carolan Daniels (Ruth Bauman)

Don and Ann collaborate on a play about Ann's life. They fight and Ann throws the play (which she thinks is splitting them apart) down the incinerator. Don is very upset and disappears. He recreates his lost work but, unfortunately, the play is ultimately rejected by three agents.

Highlights

The realistic scene that shows Donald's anger when Ann throws his play down the incinerator shows us a side of Don, the writer, that we have never seen.

Notes

In this episode we learn that Ann was known as "Twinkle-Fingers Marie, the speedy steno" at Brewster College. We also learn that Ann's phone number is PLaza 3-0598 and that Donald's is BRyant 9-9978.

Who Gets to Say "That Girl!"

Donald doesn't quite say it. He says, "Collaborating is hard, especially collaborating with. . . ." The screen freezes on Ann Marie and he doesn't have to say it. We know it is *that girl!*

EPISODE 40: WHEN IN ROME

ORIGINAL AIR DATE: NOVEMBER 9, 1967

Writers: Saul Turteltaub and Bernie Orenstein; Director: Hal Cooper; Guest Cast: Bernie Kopell (Jerry Bauman), Carolan Daniels (Ruth Bauman), Francis Lederer (Vittorio Barrini), David Mauro (Antonio Ricci), Anna Lisa (Rosanna Barrini), Frank Puglia (Restaurant Owner), Renata Vanni (Momma)

Famed Italian director Vittorio Barrini (read Federico Fellini) sees Ann modeling at an auto show and offers her the lead in his new movie. Ann is overjoyed at a chance to work with the renowned film-maker, until she realizes that the movie will require a nude scene. Her modesty makes her turn down the chance of a lifetime.

Highlights

The restaurant scene in which Ann reads the script to the entire staff comes to a wonderful climax when she gets to the part that says her character will have to appear nude!

Notes

Frank Puglia and Renata Vanni appear as restaurant owners. We, of course, also know them as Ann's landlords. Either they are moon-lighting or Daisy Productions just wanted to give these splendid actors a double role.

Who Gets to Say "That Girl!"

Veteran film star Francis Lederer as Vittorio Barrini sees Ann model-ing at the car show and proclaims that his film heroine, Angelica, "is *that girl!*"

EPISODE 41: THANKSGIVING COMES BUT ONCE A YEAR, HOPEFULLY

ORIGINAL AIR DATE: NOVEMBER 23, 1967

Writer: Peggy Elliott; Director: James Sheldon; Guest Cast: Lew Parker (Lou Marie), Rosemary DeCamp (Helen Marie), Mabel Albertson (Lillian Hollinger), George Cisar (Harold Hollinger), Joseph Perry (Mailman), Nick Parisi (Fireman)

It is Thanksgiving and Don's parents want him to come home to St. Louis (even if it means bringing Ann along) and Ann's parents want her to come to Brewster (even if she must bring Donald). Ann solves the problem by having both families to her apartment for the holiday. Trying to cook everyone's favorite dishes, Ann takes over the Baumans' kitchen. As the four parents bicker, Ann smells smoke and discovers she has locked herself out of the neighbors' apartment with the cooking turkey still inside! The holiday ends with the two fami-lies eating the food that Ann cooks in her own kitchen.

Highlights
The fun begins with Ann running back and forth between apartments, trying to cook a goose and a turkey simultaneously. It gets better when she realizes that she has put the wrong stuffing in each bird.

Notes
We find out that Don's father (named Harold for this episode) owns a hardware store and that both sets of parents fear impending nuptials between their offspring.

Who Gets to Say "That Girl!"
George Cisar, as Mr. Hollinger, can't seem to remember who Ann is until his wife pulls out a picture of Don, with Ann's face bent to the back. He looks at it and exclaims, "Oh, *that girl!*"

EPISODE 42: THE MAILMAN COMETH
Original air date: November 30, 1967
Writers: Danny Arnold and Ruth Brooks Flippen; Director: James Sheldon; Guest Cast: Dick Shawn (as Himself), Ruth Buzzi (Marge "Pete" Peterson), Don Penny (Seymour Schwimmer), George Neise (Norman Kramer), Paul Dubov (Maitre d'), Patti Gilbert (Receptionist)

Ann's idea of doing little dramatic monologues while working as a roving clothes-model at Sardi's restaurant pays off when she gets signed by a big theatrical talent agency. The only caveat is that she will be assigned to agent-in-training Seymour Schwimmer as his first client. To win Ann over, Seymour tells her that she has a publicity date with comic Dick Shawn. Only Shawn doesn't know about it.

Highlights
Don Penny's performance as Seymour. His desperation and Ann's realistic reaction to him make for great comic chemistry—desperate as she is to have an agent, she realizes that this guy knows nothing. The other highlight is Ann's reaction to Donald when he voices concern over her going out with Dick Shawn: "Donald, comedians belong to everybody. No one in their right mind would want one for their very own." Also hilarious is Ann alternating between smiling and wetting her lips for the photographers.

Notes

Although Sardi's, New York's famous theatrical restaurant, is mentioned and used as a setting several times, this is not a location shoot. The restaurant, with its prized caricatures on the walls, is vaguely recreated. None of the drawings are authentic and there is even dancing in a restaurant that never had any. On the other hand, Ann's reading of a scene from *The Anniversary Waltz* (as acted originally by Kitty Carlisle to Macdonald Carey in 1954) rings with authenticity. We find out that the Gillian and Norris Talent Agency is at 1330 Sixth Avenue. However, we never learn how Seymour knows Donald. Ann meets Seymour that afternoon, gives him twenty-four hours to make good, and when he shows up at her apartment he seems to be old friends with her boyfriend. Very odd! Also note that George Neise will be demoted from head of Ann's agency, in this episode, to a hotel manager in Hollywood in episode #64: "7¼." That's show biz. Danny Arnold and Ruth Brooks Flippen earned an Emmy nomination for Outstanding Writing Achievement in Comedy for this episode. It was the only nomination in this category that the series received.

Who Gets to Say "That Girl!"

Donald says it as he enters Sardi's where Ann is modeling/acting. Maitre d': "Are you waiting for someone?" Donald: "Yes, *that girl!*"

**EPISODE 43: IT'S A MOD MOD WORLD
(PART ONE)**

ORIGINAL AIR DATE: DECEMBER 7, 1967

Writers: Tom and Helen August; Director: James Frawley; Guest Cast: Lew Parker (Lou Marie), Garry Marshall (Noel Prince), Laurie Main (Grimsley), James Millhollin (Clerk), Lea Marmer (Woman), Richard Ramos (Man), Patrick Hawley (Man), Sally Marr (Model)

During an encounter at an automat, a flippant young Englishman slips his card into Ann's purse as she brushes him off. Later, Donald recognizes the name on the card as that of famous fashion photographer Noel Prince. Ann goes to Prince's hotel to apologize and emerges with a job offer for a shoot in California. Ann becomes one of his models and Prince falls for her. By the end of Part One, he tells Don that it is "war."

Highlights
The scene in the automat in which the scruffy, childlike Ann is pursued by the worldly photographer is very cute. Her part about making ketchup soup is adorable.

Notes
For those too young to know, the automat was a Depression-era, self-service restaurant that lasted into the 1960s in New York City. In an automat there would be an entire wall full of doors, each containing different types of food. One would put coins into a particular slot, then open the door to remove one's choice of food. It was a way of eating by the course and saving money.

Who Gets to Say "That Girl!"
Richard Ramos as a man in line with Ann at the automat says it. Someone asks what is holding things up and he replies, *"That girl!"*

EPISODE 44: IT'S A MOD MOD WORLD
(PART TWO)
ORIGINAL AIR DATE: DECEMBER 14, 1967
Writers: Tom and Helen August; Director: James Frawley; Guest Cast: Garry Marshall (Noel Prince), Laurie Main (Grimsley), Sidney Clute (Policeman), Bill Callaway (Lab Man)

Ann's Hollywood modeling assignment gets complicated when Noel Prince actively woos her and Don gets very jealous. When he spots a newspaper photo of Ann and Noel being arrested for frolicking in a fountain, Don is on the next plane to California. Ann finds out the truth about randy Noel, but not before Don punches him in the jaw.

Highlights
The fashion montage that shows Ann being photographed all over Los Angeles in mod clothes is wonderful. She looks gorgeous.

Notes
Garry Marshall would reappear as Noel Prince in episode #52: "He and She and He."

Who Gets to Say "That Girl!"
Ted Bessell as Don does a voice-over telling viewers what happened

on last week's show, ending with, "That new face and the third side of the triangle is *that girl!*"

EPISODE 45: 'TWAS THE NIGHT BEFORE CHRISTMAS, YOU'RE UNDER ARREST

Original air date: December 21, 1967
Writer: Ruth Brooks Flippen; Director: James Sheldon; Guest Cast: Lew Parker (Lou Marie), Bernie Kopell (Jerry Bauman), Carolan Daniels (Ruth Bauman), Jay C. Flippen (Sergeant Fitzgerald), Herbie Faye (Milton), Ed Peck (Bart), Paul Bryar (Eppie), William Bramley (Tim)

Ann buys hard-to-get theater tickets from a scalper as a Christmas gift for the Baumans. She gives the scalper a check with her address on it and tells him that the tickets are for her neighbors. That night, before Ann and Don go to Brewster for Christmas, Don tells her about thieves who give theater tickets to unsuspecting victims and rob the apartment when they are gone. Ann is sure that is what is about to happen. So, she and Donald move all the Baumans' valuables (including their Christmas gifts) to her apartment. Unfortunately, they are observed by a neighbor and soon are arrested for robbery. Somehow, Ann's father gets arrested too and it takes the Baumans to explain it all to the police.

Highlights
Herbie Faye gives a flavorful performance as the ticket scalper.

Notes
This is the second holiday episode and is always included in the syndication package. By this time, television certainly had come a long way since the exclusion of the "Christmas Episode" from the *I Love Lucy* (1951–57) package, when the executives decided that viewers wouldn't be interested in a holiday episode out of season.

Who Gets to Say "That Girl!"
No one says it. The title comes on after Herbie Faye as the scalper says, "Beg your pardon, young lady," and an old lady looks at him questioningly.

EPISODE 46: A FRIEND IN NEED
ORIGINAL AIR DATE: DECEMBER 28, 1967
Writer: Richard Baer; Director: Hal Cooper; Guest Cast: Rosemary DeCamp (Helen Marie), Bernie Kopell (Jerry Bauman), Carolan Daniels (Ruth Bauman), Danny Arnold (Producer), Benny Rubin (Dr. Ferguson), Sally Richards (Secretary)

When Ann sprains her ankle while playing a guerrilla in a war movie, her mother comes to stay with her. Understanding Donald comes to the rescue, saying he will devote his weekend to Ann so that Mrs. Marie can return home. While Ann convalesces, Don cooks, defrosts her refrigerator, cleans her oven, and changes the shelf paper in her kitchen cabinets. He does such a good job that Ann begins to resent it. Ann and Don fight because she is convinced that he is challenging her femininity. When she hobbles over to his apartment, she finds it a horrible mess and realizes that he only did the cleaning and cooking to impress her.

Highlights
Donald's fussbudget act while taking care of Ann is delightful.

Notes
Producer Danny Arnold plays the unbilled part of the movie producer in the opening sequence. This is the only episode of *That Girl* in which Rosemary DeCamp appears without Lew Parker. Although veteran performer Benny Rubin is billed as the doctor in this installment, he never appears in the final print.

Who Gets to Say "That Girl!"
Sally Richards, as the secretary to the film producer, says, when they find out that one of their actor/guerrilla fighters is hurt and ask which one, "It was *that* guerrilla!"

EPISODE 47: FUR ALL WE KNOW
ORIGINAL AIR DATE: JANUARY 4, 1968
Writers: Peggy Elliott and Ed Scharlach; Director: Hal Cooper; Furs courtesy of Edwards-Lowell; Guest Cast: Quinn Redeker (Buzzy Cavanaugh), Benny Rubin (Mr. Mellinger), Judy Cassmore (Girl), Edward Guardino (Cabbie)

While working as a model at a Manhattan furrier, Ann is asked by Don to accompany him to a jet-set party which his magazine is covering. Fearing she has nothing proper to wear, Ann borrows a chinchilla stole from her employer. Looking every bit the rich girl, Ann catches the eye of dashing jet-setter Buzzy Cavanaugh. He presses Ann for a lunch date, where she discovers that he is a fortune hunter with no money of his own. When he finds out that Ann is also poor, he quickly disappears.

Highlights
Ann, in her chinchilla stole, trying to mingle with the rich, hits the entertainment high-water mark in this episode. She approaches clusters of people and mutters to herself, "Mingle, mingle . . ." Marlo Thomas says that this is one of the things that people who love the series quote to her the most.

Notes
We learn that Ann's apartment rent is $88.43 a month and that she has saved $219.73 (that is, until she lends it to Buzzy).

Who Gets to Say "That Girl!"
Ted Bessell as Don tries to find Ann in a crowd of fur models: "I think she's *that girl!*"

EPISODE 48: THE RIVALS
ORIGINAL AIR DATE: JANUARY 11, 1968
Writer: Richard Baer; Director: Hal Cooper; Guest Cast: Lew Parker (Lou Marie), Rosemary DeCamp (Helen Marie), Byron Morrow (Officer Cooper)

A weekend in Brewster with Ann's parents turns out to be a competition between Don and Lou Marie. Lou sees Don as a rival for his "little girl's" affections. Things go from bad to worse when Don and Lou have a car accident and neither will take the blame.

Highlights
The scenes in the Marie home where Lou tries to beat Don at ping-pong are very funny. Mr. Marie loses every serve. There is also a lovely sequence between DeCamp as Helen and Thomas as Ann. (It is one

of DeCamp's only long scenes in the series.) They are washing dishes and Helen explains how Lou feels about Ann and why he is so competitive with Don.

Notes
We learn that Lou Marie has never gotten a traffic ticket in thirty years of driving. In fact, the Brewster Boosters gave him the Safest Driver of 1947 award. (The award was discontinued in 1950 because the winner was arrested for drunk driving!) We also are told that Lou never went to college and observe that he mispronounces many words.

Who Gets to Say "That Girl!"
Lew Parker as Ann's dad, Lou, to Donald: "You're just her boyfriend. How would you like to be the father of *that girl?*"

EPISODE 49: SIXTY-FIVE ON THE AISLE
ORIGINAL AIR DATE: JANUARY 18, 1968
Writer: Ruth Brooks Flippen; Director: James Frawley; Guest Cast: Lew Parker (Lou Marie), Don Penny (Seymour Schwimmer), Norman Fell (Bernie), Buddy Lester (Barney), Clinton Sundberg (Manager), Donald Foster (Mr. Merral), Lorna Thayer (Queen)

Ann finally gets a job on Broadway, in the long-running hit *The Knights of Queen Mary*. Her father invites a huge theater party to her opening to surprise her. Because the management is afraid that the group from Brewster will leave before the final curtain, they want to shorten the play by cutting some of the dialogue, specifically Ann's lines. A farcical situation follows where every time Ann's dialogue gets cut, her father changes the reservation, until someone gets the good idea to bring the theater party down on a charter bus. When she finally gets to go on, Ann, Don, and Seymour (her agent) get stuck in an elevator and she barely makes her entrance in time.

Highlights
The scene in the elevator with Ann, Don, and Seymour fighting the clock and trying to escape to make Ann's Broadway debut is both funny and frightening.

Notes

Ann makes $130 a week for her Broadway debut at the Empire Theatre (now torn down) in a show that has been running for one and a half years. This is the first time that Seymour gets her a great acting job.

Who Gets to Say "That Girl!"

Clinton Sundberg says it as he fires "that girl" from her survival job demonstrating the Famaker Shamaker (a device to lose weight).

How Many Times Each Character Says "That Girl!"

Ted Bessell as Donald Hollinger is the champion. He introduces the show with the famous catch phrase on thirty-one episodes. Marlo Thomas as Ann Marie comes in second, introducing herself twenty-one times. Lew Parker as Lou Marie utters the special phrase eight times. Jesse White, as three different characters, gets to say it a total of four times. Bernie Kopell as Jerry Bauman, Bonnie Scott as Judy Bessamer, Jules Munshin as both Rudy Clarn and Harry Fields, Gino Conforti as Nino, and Ethel Merman as Ethel Merman all tie with two "that girls" each. In all her appearances on *That Girl,* Rosemary DeCamp never gets to say it.

Ted Bessell:	31 that girls
Marlo Thomas:	21 that girls
Lew Parker:	8 that girls
Jesse White:	4 that girls
Bernie Kopell:	2 that girls
Bonnie Scott:	2 that girls
Jules Munshin:	2 that girls
Gino Conforti:	2 that girls
Ethel Merman:	2 that girls
Rosemary DeCamp:	0 that girls

EPISODE 50: CALL OF THE WILD
ORIGINAL AIR DATE: JANUARY 25, 1968
Writer: Milton Pascal; Director: Hal Cooper; Guest Cast: Lew Parker (Lou
Marie), Bernie Kopell (Jerry Bauman), Jesse White (Clinton Hayworth)

Ann wins the assignment as the Creamy Soap Girl on a commercial
because the producer sees her as a fresh-scrubbed face whose whole-
some looks no housewife could resent. Ann is distraught by her lack
of sex appeal and takes a good hard look at herself . . . stripping in
front of the mirror. Unfortunately, that is the very moment her father
drops by. After she shoots the commercials (in which we never see
her face), the producer, Clinton Hayworth, makes a play for her,
proving to Ann that she does indeed have sex appeal.

Highlights
Ann's fantasy striptease in front of the mirror is a peak moment in
this episode, as is Jesse White's attempted seduction of Ann.

Notes
Ann's street address is given on this episode as 344 West 78th Street.
In addition, viewers find out that Don has passion for her (tempered
with respect). Jesse White will also appear on episodes #57: "Just
Spell the Name Right" and #60: "Old Man's Darling" as Eddie Edwards
(a press agent), #65: "7¼ (Part Two)" as Phil Bender (a producer),
and #80: "There Was a Time Ann Met a Pie Man" as Hal Grissom
(a producer).

Who Gets to Say "That Girl!"
Jesse White as Clinton Hayworth dismisses all the beautiful, glam-
orous creatures and chooses *"that girl!"* for the part of the Creamy
Soap Girl.

EPISODE 51: THE OTHER WOMAN
ORIGINAL AIR DATE: FEBRUARY 1, 1968
Writer: Richard Baer; Director: Andrew McCullough; Guest Cast: Lew Parker
(Lou Marie), Rosemary DeCamp (Helen Marie), Ethel Merman (as Herself),
Arthur Julian (Waiter), Peter Leeds (Director)

After Ann, Don, and Mr. Marie encounter Ethel Merman at a restaurant, Ann suggests that her father escort Ms. Merman to her rehearsal.

In no time, newspaper reporters see the two together and publish an article insinuating they are now an "item." When Ann's mother reads the article, she believes she's lost her husband to a glamorous star, and promptly leaves her spouse. Don and Ann must get Merman to convince Mrs. Marie that it's not true—which gets even more difficult when they find Mr. Marie hiding in Ethel's dressing room during the taping of a TV show!

Highlights
The dressing room scene is a gem, with Lou (who has a bad back) hiding behind a screen (Merman: "It worked in all my shows") while his wife confronts her rival. Classic Merman line to Helen: "Uh . . . Mrs. Marie, I don't know how to tell you this, but . . . you're out of your bird!"

Notes
This is the follow-up show to episode #31: "Pass the Potatoes, Ethel Merman." The star remembers Ann and Donald, but thinks that Lou's name is Max. She also recalls teaching him how to make stuffed cabbage!

Who Gets to Say "That Girl!"
Again, The Merm says it, of course. Across a crowded deli, she informs her director, "I'd never forget *that girl!*"

EPISODE 52: HE AND SHE AND HE
ORIGINAL AIR DATE: FEBRUARY 15, 1968
Writers: Saul Turteltaub and Bernie Orenstein; Director: Norman Hall; Guest Cast: Lew Parker (Noah), Garry Marshall (Noel Prince)

Donald is stunned when Ann receives a marriage proposal from persistent Noel Prince, the British fashion photographer. Noel expects his answer in the morning, despite Ann's protestations that she loves Donald. However, when Don insists that she keep to the deadline, Ann falls asleep and dreams she's married to them both. Because it has been raining for forty days and forty nights, Ann must choose which husband to take on the ark! When she awakens she turns down Prince's proposal.

Highlights
What could be better than the hilarious dream sequence where Ann is married to two men and her father shows up at the door as Noah to tell her that he only has room for her and one husband?

Notes
This is a follow-up to episodes #43 and #44: "It's a Mod Mod World, Parts One and Two." We see the fruits of Ann's modeling labors at the beginning of the show. She is a cover girl.

Who Gets to Say "That Girl!"
When Don brings dozens of magazines to Ann, she emerges from the bedroom in a robe, with a scarf around her head. He looks at the glamorous magazine image and then at her and says, "Would you believe that this girl is *that girl?*"

EPISODE 53: ODPDYPAHIMCAIFSS
(TRANSLATION: "OH DON, POOR DON, YOUR PANTS ARE HANGING IN MY CLOSET AND I'M FEELING SO SAD")
ORIGINAL AIR DATE: FEBRUARY 22, 1968
Writer: Richard Baer; Director: Hal Cooper; Guest Cast: Lew Parker (Lou Marie), Mabel Albertson (Lillian Hollinger), Johnny Silver (Mr. Newman)

Don's mother comes for a visit from St. Louis. Ann invites her to stay overnight, but the overprotective and prudish Mrs. Hollinger is not amused when she sees a sexy peignoir that Don gave Ann and then finds Don's pants hanging in Ann's closet. When Ann's father finds out about the pants, all hell breaks loose. Of course, there is a good explanation and all ends well.

Highlights
The scene where Lillian Hollinger and Lou Marie square off against each other is worth the entire show.

Notes
This is the third time we have met Donald's mother. She previously appeared in episodes #12: "Soap Gets in Your Eyes" (where she was called Mabel, not Lillian) and #41: "Thanksgiving Comes But Once a Year, Hopefully." Later she will appear in episodes #118 and #119, "There Sure Are a Bunch of Cards in St. Louis" (a two-part installment).

Who Gets to Say "That Girl!"
Johnny Silver as Mr. Newman, Ann's cleaner (and the man who started this whole mess), utters the key words about the well-meaning but trouble-prone *"that girl!"*

EPISODE 54: GREAT GUY
ORIGINAL AIR DATE: MARCH 7, 1968
Writers: Bruce Howard (story by Ruth Brooks Flippen and Danny Arnold); Director: John Rich; Guest Cast: Ruth Buzzi (Marge "Pete" Peterson), Albert Salmi (George Lakonc), Dick Balduzzi (Glenn)

When her show unexpectedly closes in Washington, D.C., Ann's plain actress friend, "Pete," comes to stay with her until Pete's own apartment becomes available. Pete introduces Ann and Don to her new boyfriend, George. George likes Pete because she's a "great guy." She jogs, boxes, and kicks a football into the wind. Although Ann thinks a girl should be liked for being a girl, Pete is deliriously happy. In fact, she is so carried away that she proposes marriage to George. He runs away from her, and, at Ann's insistence, Don pays men to date Pete. After a few bad evenings, George returns and he and Pete depart.

Highlights
This is Ruth Buzzi's showcase and could have been a pilot for a TV series for her. She is marvelous, but would soon be a regular on *Rowan & Martin's Laugh-In* (1968–73).

Notes
One of Buzzi's dates is set at a disco called "Gay 'n' Frisky," which just goes to show how times have changed since this episode.

Who Gets to Say "That Girl!"
Marlo Thomas as Ann says it to her sneezing TV image in a commercial: "There I am! I'm *that girl!*"

EPISODE 55: THE DETECTIVE STORY
ORIGINAL AIR DATE: MARCH 14, 1968
Writer: Carl Kleinschmidt; Director: Hal Cooper; Guest Cast: Hal Buckley (Det. Sgt. Ray Mandel)

After Ann receives an obscene phone call, police detective Sergeant Ray Mandel stays overnight at her apartment, trying to catch the caller in the act. However, when Donald arrives at Ann's the next morning, Mandel emerges from Ann's bedroom—giving Donald the wrong impression. When the obscene calls persist, Mandel spends the night again, but this time Don insists on staying as well.

Notes
This is the first of the socially relevant *That Girl!* episodes. Taking on a subject such as obscene phone calls was something very new for TV sitcoms in the late 1960s.

Who Gets to Say "That Girl!"
After getting an obscene call, Ann says, "Who's afraid?" and the title comes on, silently but boldly, proclaiming, *"That girl!"*

EPISODE 56: IF YOU WERE ALMOST THE ONLY MAN IN THE WORLD
ORIGINAL AIR DATE: MARCH 21, 1968
Writers: Danny Arnold and Ruth Brooks Flippen; Director: Hal Cooper; Guest Cast: Lew Parker (Lou Marie), Ted Bessell (Dr. Rex Kennedy), Milton Seltzer (Dr. Corey)

While Don is out of town, Ann is knocked unconscious by a line drive at a baseball game, and attending physician, Dr. Rex Kennedy, looks just like Donald. Ann keeps calling him Donald, and the resident psychiatrist thinks she is hallucinating. In the meantime, Rex dyes his black hair light brown, and takes off his glasses, in order to fool Ann into thinking he is Donald so that he can romance her.

Highlights
The trick photography at the end, where we see two Ted Bessells—as Rex and Don—is brilliant.

Notes
This is the only time since the series pilot that Bessell plays a character on the show other than Don. Ann remembers that her first kiss with Donald occurred on their third date.

Who Gets to Say "That Girl!"
After Ann is injured at the ballgame, an unidentified actor playing a baseball spectator points out that it was *"dat goil!"*

EPISODE 57: JUST SPELL THE NAME RIGHT
ORIGINAL AIR DATE: MARCH 28, 1968
Writer: Richard Baer; Director: John Rich; Guest Cast: Lew Parker (Lou Marie), Joan Blondell (Marjorie Hobart), Robert Alda (Buddy Hobart), Jesse White (Eddie Edwards), Johnny Silver (Mr. Newman)

Ann hires a fly-by-night press agent on a trial basis and the next day her name is in the papers. Unfortunately, it is as a corespondent in a divorce scandal between actor Buddy Hobart and his wife, Marjorie. This causes a fight between Ann and Don, who remembers that Ann once worked with Hobart on a soap opera. While Ann and Buddy commiserate over his crumbling marriage and Ann's tiff with Donald, Mrs. Hobart stops at Donald's apartment to get acquainted. Ann and Buddy arrive and the furniture starts to fly, until Ann points out that the older couple really do love one another.

Highlights
This is a very funny segment, with Jesse White making his first *That Girl* appearance as Eddie Edwards (a distant cousin to his *Private Secretary* [1953–57] character of talent agent Shifty Calhoun). The first scene, with Eddie using a phone booth as his office, is quite funny. Another highlight is Joan Blondell's attempted seduction of Donald.

Notes
We find out that Ann's answering service code number is 207. Ann's father, Lou, is very upset after reading the item about his daughter. One would think he would be more understanding about press agents, as this was exactly what happened to him in episode #51: "The Other Woman." Eddie Edwards reappears in episode #60: "Old Man's Darling." What a shame that Rosemary DeCamp wasn't in this episode. She could have been reunited with Robert Alda, whose mother she played in the feature film *Rhapsody in Blue* (1945).

Who Gets to Say "That Girl!"
As Ann is breaking open her piggy bank to pay her new press agent, Jesse White as Edwards says, "I wish I was as rich and famous as *that girl!*"

EPISODE 58: THE BEARD
ORIGINAL AIR DATE: APRIL 11, 1968
Writer: Richard Baer; Director: James Frawley; Guest Cast: Lew Parker (Lou Marie), Ruth Buzzi (Marge "Pete" Peterson), Gerald Saunderson-Peters (Headwaiter), Jackie Miller (Waitress)

Donald returns from a hunting trip with a beard, which Ann finds disconcerting. Believing that he's receiving special attention because of his new look, Don refuses to shave. After Ann pleads with Don to lose the beard and then pulls away from his kiss, Donald angrily leaves. To teach him a lesson, Ann shows up for their next date with short hair.

Notes
This episode is reminiscent of the 1950s *I Love Lucy* episode where Ricky grows a beard. Unlike Lucy, Ann doesn't put on a fake beard to teach Don a lesson, she just pretends to cut her hair. Interesting character note: When Lou sees Don's beard, his comment is that "all bearded men are commies."

Who Gets to Say "That Girl!"
When Ann asks what Don would say if she grew a beard, he answers: "I'd say, 'How about that? That's certainly a good-looking beard on *that girl!*'"

EPISODE 59: THE DRUNKARD
ORIGINAL AIR DATE: APRIL 18, 1968
Writers: Danny Arnold and Ruth Brooks Flippen; Director: Hal Cooper; Guest Cast: Sid Caesar (Marty Nickels), Audrey Christie (Ella Nickels), Buddy Lester (Bartender), Sid Melton (Assistant Director), Arthur Julian (Charlie)

Ann charitably lets Marty Nickels, a drunken comedian with whom she is working on a commercial, stay overnight at her apartment to sleep it off. When he wakes up the next morning he believes he is having a relationship with Ann. Soon Marty is showing up drunk at her door every night, until his mother, who thinks Ann is a gold-digging hussy, comes to take him away from her.

Highlights
Sid Caesar's drunken act is very funny, but hits a bit too close to home. According to Caesar's autobiography, *Where Have I Been?* (1982), this was right in the middle of his bad period of drinking: "There was more work for me in Hollywood. I took nearly every one-shot job that came along. . . . It didn't bother me when people would say, 'What's the great Sid Caesar doing in that piece of shit?'" Surely he wasn't talking about *That Girl!*

Notes
The characters of Nickels and his mother (minus the drinking) were loosely based on Milton Berle's relationship with his mother. Teri Garr makes her second appearance in the show as one of the actresses competing against Ann for the part in the commercial. However, she is not credited. (Her first appearance was in episode #28: "This Little Piggy Had a Ball.") In the "goof" department, it should be noted that Ann's stove is electric in this installment, but gas in episode #100: "I Am a Curious Lemon."

Who Gets to Say "That Girl!"
Sid Caesar as Nickels, when choosing Ann to do the commercial, takes a long look at her legs and says, "I want *that girl!*"

EPISODE 60: OLD MAN'S DARLING
ORIGINAL AIR DATE: APRIL 25, 1968
Writer: Richard Baer; Director: John Rich; Guest Cast: Lew Parker (Lou Marie), Cecil Kellaway (Andrew Washington), Arlene Golonka (Bonita La Salle), Jesse White (Eddie Edwards), Chet Stratton (Jeweler), Joe Besser (Messenger)

Ann meets an elderly man, Andrew Washington, at a party when he accidentally spills his shrimp cocktail on her new white crepe dress. Not realizing he's one of the ten richest men in the country, Ann refuses to accept his offer to buy her a new dress or at least pay for the cleaning. The next day, a bonded messenger arrives bearing a diamond bracelet from Mr. Washington. Because she can't accept it, Ann goes to dinner with the millionaire in order to return it. However, sleazy publicity agent Eddie Edwards spots Ann with her wealthy companion and hatches a scheme to finance a play. In the end, Ann accepts none of the gifts and keeps Mr. Washington as a friend.

Highlights
This is a very warm offering and Ann's scenes with Cecil Kellaway as Washington are quite sweet. The comic high point is the scene where all the characters converge on Ann in her apartment. All of them, of course, are drawing the wrong conclusions.

Notes
Arlene Golonka played Jerry Bauman's (or Myer's) wife in episode #21: "Rain, Snow, and Rice" and would go on to play a flight attendant in episode #62: "The Hi-Jack and the Mighty." We find out that Don's middle initial is "A."

Who Gets to Say "That Girl!"
Cecil Kellaway as Washington: "I dropped a shrimp cocktail on *that girl!*"

Awards and Honors for Season Two

Marlo Thomas received an Emmy nomination for Outstanding Continued Performance by an Actress in a Leading Role in a Comedy for Season #2

Danny Arnold received an Emmy nomination for Outstanding Directorial Achievement in Comedy for episode #35: "The Apartment."

Danny Arnold and Ruth Brooks Flippen received an Emmy nomination for Outstanding Writing Achievement in Comedy for episode #42: "The Mailman Cometh."

Marlo Thomas tied with Candice Bergen for the New Star in Fashion Award given by the Costume Designers Guild.

Marlo Thomas was presented with the Halo Award.

Marlo Thomas was named "Girl of the Year" by Yale University's Skull and Key Club.

SEASON THREE
SEPTEMBER 1968–MARCH 1969

Season Three Overview

The third season was again produced by Danny Arnold, thus providing good continuity with the second. As the ABC press release promised, Ann takes on many social issues in the next twenty-six episodes. Such front-page issues as Cuban hijackers, spousal abuse, violence in films, presidential elections, muggers, the IRS, race relations, and the space program are addressed by Ann and her cohorts in comical ways.

On the career front, Ann gets cast in a Broadway play called *The Revolutionary Heart* starring Barry Sullivan, makes a series of commercials for Action Soda, does another commercial for POP soft drink (aren't there rules about actors appearing in competing soda commercials?), undertakes a pie-in-the-face bit on a comedy TV show, and does promotion for the air force.

Ann and Donald remain the most devoted steadies, even though he punches Barry Sullivan in the face, loses Ann a lucrative commercial deal because of one of his articles, dresses as a woman, almost becomes the seventh husband of a seventy-year-old millionairess, sends Ann roses to which she is allergic, makes her father think he has rabies, and fights with that same father over a monopoly game.

Ann does her part to complicate the relationship by having a strange man see her naked, stands Donald up numerous times, does not appreciate Don's present of art, loses one of his gift earrings, tries to adopt a young African American boy, flies all over the world while *not* decorating Don's apartment (not to mention wallpapering his bathroom with valuable research clippings), and wakes him in the middle of the night because of a mouse in her house. However, through it all, there is always a kiss at the door before the episode's credits.

Production Team for Season Three
Executive Producers and Series Creators: Bill Persky and Sam Denoff; Producer: Danny Arnold; Associate Producer: Eddie Foy III; Script Consultant: Ruth Brooks Flippen; Director of Photography: Leonard J. South, A.S.C; Art Director: Gibson Holley; Film Editor: Hugh Chaloupka; Music: Warren Barker with theme by Earle

Hagen; Miss Thomas's wardrobe by Cardinelli, Inc.; Hair: Lynn Masters; Makeup: Tom Case; Casting: Fred Roos; Set Decorator: Don Webb; Production Manager: John Banse; Executive in Charge of Production: Ronald Jacobs; Origination: Filmed at Paramount, on location in New York City, and elsewhere by Daisy Productions; Sponsors: Bristol-Myers Company, Noxell Corporation, and Lever Brothers

EPISODE 61: SOCK IT TO ME

ORIGINAL AIR DATE: SEPTEMBER 26, 1968
Writers: Stan Cutler and Martin Donavan; Director: James Sheldon; Guest Cast: Lew Parker (Lou Marie), Barry Sullivan (as Himself), Milton Seltzer (Sidney Gold), Timothy Blake (Actor #1), Patricia Sullivan (Girl)

Ann gets a part in a long-running Broadway play entitled *The Revolutionary Heart,* starring Barry Sullivan. The only problem she has with the role is that she can't bring herself to slap the famous actor, as the script requires. But on opening night she overcomes her fear and knocks him out cold.

Highlights

The wonderful moment (all too rare) when Ann gets a role on Broadway is the obvious high point of this entry.

Notes

In this episode Don says that Ann weighs 108 pounds. That's four pounds more than she weighed last season.

Who Gets to Say "That Girl!"

Ann is nervous about being chosen for the stage role and Ted Bessell as Donald tells her that "If I were a leading man, it would take a half a second to decide I want *that girl!*"

EPISODE 62: THE HI-JACK AND THE MIGHTY

ORIGINAL AIR DATE: OCTOBER 3, 1968
Writer: Ruth Brooks Flippen; Director: John Rich; Guest Cast: Lew Parker (Lou Marie), Arlene Golonka (Terry), Valentin de Vargas (Manuel), Arthur Julian (Binswanger), David McLean (Pilot), Jane Dulo (Mrs. Stevenson), Leon Colker (Hoffman), Dick Wesson (Navigator)

To gain experience for an upcoming airline commercial, the company sets Ann up to work as a flight attendant. Donald joins Ann on her flight because she's scheduled to spend an extra day in Miami. Hearing Don will be there, Ann's father promptly buys a ticket and joins them. Once on the plane, Ann spots what she believes is a Cuban hijacker and, in no time, she and the other passengers tackle the man, grab his gun, and tie him up. Just about this time, the news comes that the man is a detective hired by the airlines to prevent hijackings. Ann loses the commercial.

Highlights

The scenes on the plane, when the passengers all get nervous about a possible skyjacking and Don and Lou keep popping out of their seats, are very funny.

Notes

Arlene Golonka, who plays Terry, the flight attendant who is attracted to Donald, had also appeared as Bonita La Salle in episode #60: "Old Man's Darling" and Margie (Jerry's first wife) in episode #21: "Rain, Snow, and Rice." Jane Dulo, the loud-mouthed passenger, also played a nurse in episode #28: "This Little Piggy Had a Ball." This installment could never be done today, with the advent of metal detectors.

Who Gets to Say "That Girl!"

As Ann practices serving passengers on a makeshift plane in her apartment, Ted Bessell as Don comments: "Out of seven million females in New York, I, Don Hollinger, had to pick *that girl!*"

EPISODE 63: ELEVEN ANGRY MEN AND THAT GIRL

ORIGINAL AIR DATE: OCTOBER 10, 1968
Writers: Stan Cutler and Martin Donavan; Director: Hal Cooper; Guest Cast: Lew Parker (Lou Marie), David Ketchum (Jack Packard), Stuart Margolin (Chris Talley), Hope Summers (Miss Marker), Bobo Lewis (Mrs. Franklin), Dick Wilson (Mr. Franklin), Joe Perry (Bailiff), Joe Besser (Foreman), Vinton Hayworth (Judge)

Ann has jury duty just when she and Donald are supposed to leave on a trip to visit his parents in St. Louis. When the jury is sequestered, Ann takes it very seriously and will not go along with the rest of the panel when they all want to vote "guilty" against a man accused of hitting his wife with an ashtray. Positive that the man couldn't have assaulted her with his right hand, Ann eventually convinces the others on the jury that the defendant is innocent. Just as he is about to be set free, the man picks up an ashtray from a courtroom table and belts his wife again, proving he has a great backhand.

Highlights
Ann, acting out the scene of the crime for the other jurors, is quite funny and the quality of her performance is appropriately representative of her chosen profession.

Notes
Hope Summers played Clara Edwards on *The Andy Griffith Show* (1960–68); Stuart Margolin will appear in episode #65: "7¼" as a film director; Bobo Lewis is Mrs. Clarn in episode #73: "Should All Our Old Acquaintance Be Forgot," and several other characters in episodes #30: "The Mating Game," #102: "Opening Night," #110: "They Shoot Pictures, Don't They?", #111: "Easy Faller," and #130: "That Shoplifter." Dick Wilson is best known as Mr. Whipple of the Charmin toilet tissue commercials and as the drunk on *Bewitched* (1964–72). Joe Besser was one of filmdom's Three Stooges.

Who Gets to Say "That Girl!"
Ted Bessell as Don: "There's nobody in the world I'd rather be convicted by than *that girl!*"

EPISODE 64: 7¼
(PART ONE)
ORIGINAL AIR DATE: OCTOBER 17, 1968
Writer: Arthur Julian; Director: Hal Cooper; Guest Cast: Lew Parker (Lou Marie), George Neise (Hotel Manager), Art Lewis (Bellboy), Buddy Lester (Waiter), Lea Marmer (Maid)

Ann accompanies Don on his new assignment to Los Angeles. He is doing a story on violence on TV and in film, and Ann wants to try her luck in Hollywood. This first segment of the two-part episode has the couple trying to keep a semblance of propriety as the hotel mixes up their room assignments and puts Ann's father's calls through to Donald's room.

Highlights

This episode plays like a funny Doris Day movie, with Ann desperately trying to convince the hotel staff and her father that nothing sexual is going on between Donald and herself. The first highlight is the scene back in New York when Donald tries to explain to Mr. Marie that Ann knows all about sex. The look on Lew Parker's face says it all. The second memorable scene comes from guest star, comedian Buddy Lester, who plays a waiter who must shuttle food back and forth between their rooms as Ann and Donald decide whose room to eat in. The solution in the last scene has the table sitting in the adjoining doorway between the two rooms, with Ann in hers and Donald in his.

Notes

Buddy Lester also played the bartender in episode #59: "The Drunkard" and George Neise (the hotel manager) played Norman Kramer, head of Gillian and Norris Talent, in episode #42: "The Mailman Cometh." This installment is noteworthy, not only for its comic elements, but also for once again showing the love that Ann and Donald have for each other, and Ann's integrity and her ambition to further her acting career.

Who Gets to Say "That Girl!"

Marlo Thomas as Ann says it when she is being brave about Donald going away for three whole weeks. Ann: "I've always wanted our friends to say Donald Hollinger doesn't have to worry about *that girl!*" After the credits, we see Ann in Donald's hallway, weeping, and this gives Donald the idea of taking her along on the trip. It is a very tender and real moment that pays off in Part Two.

EPISODE 65: 7¼
(PART TWO)

ORIGINAL AIR DATE: OCTOBER 24, 1968

Writer: Arthur Julian; Director: Hal Cooper; Guest Cast: Jesse White (Phil Bender), Peter Bonerz (Larry Yorkin), Frank Devol (Mr. Barber), Ken Lynch (Carl Sheldon, the TV producer), Stuart Margolin (Leonard Stanley, the film director), Barry Williams (Fan)

In this second part of Ann and Donald's Hollywood adventure, Ann gets cast in a series of commercials that have her doing death-defying stunts. Meanwhile, Donald proceeds to write his series of articles on violence in the media. Ironically, Don's articles put a stop to Ann's violent commercials.

Highlights
The whole show has a more cinematic feel than most *That Girl* episodes, with many crosscutting montages between Ann's commercials and Don's interviews. The highlight scene shows Ann so tired that she can hardly move and Donald tenderly putting her to bed. Ann caps the scene, drowsily and lovingly telling Don that she is "so lucky you're in love with me."

Notes
The product that Ann is advertising is called Action Soda. It is made from squash and Donald declares that it tastes like borscht. Ann makes reference to appearing with Ethel Merman in the Lincoln Center revival of *Gypsy* (see episode #31: "Pass the Potatoes, Ethel Merman") and the fact that it only ran two weeks. We get to see Ann filming at least ten commercials, which show her driving a car off a cliff, canoeing over a waterfall, being thrown off a mountain by an Indian, fighting a bull, getting blown up, and, finally, being tied to railroad tracks. After Donald's articles put a stop to the action commercials, Ann tries to take her career reversal with a stiff upper lip, but the show, uncharacteristically, ends, as Part One began, with Ann weeping about her missed opportunity. We really believe that she is heartbroken and that her career means a lot to her. Of interest to future sitcom watchers is the billed appearance of Peter Bonerz (*The Bob Newhart Show*, 1972–78) and the unbilled appearance of a very young Barry Williams (*The Brady Bunch*, 1969–74).

Who Gets to Say "That Girl!"
Jesse White as Phil Bender, when he sees Ann almost get hit by a golf cart on the Paramount lot and realizes that *that girl* is the sturdy type to do his daredevil commercials for Action Soda, that "pretty, perky, sweetie drink."

EPISODE 66: SECRET BALLOT

ORIGINAL AIR DATE: OCTOBER 31, 1968

Writer: Rich Baer; Director: John Rich; Guest Cast: Lew Parker (Lou Marie), Rosemary DeCamp (Helen Marie), Florence Halop (Librarian), Penny Marshall (Assistant Librarian), Richie Steel (Child)

Ann and her father get into an argument over ethics on the eve of Ann's first time voting in a presidential election. They fight, she and Donald leave, and when Ann returns for her forgotten purse, she literally ends up in a tree.

Highlights

The scene where Ann and Donald try to break into the Marie home in Brewster is vintage *I Love Lucy*. Ann climbs a ladder, it breaks, and she gets stuck in a tree.

Notes

In this installment we discover that Donald is not yet thirty-five, and Ann must be around twenty-one (this being her first time voting). Donald does not think that Ann is a very good driver. We also hear Lou Marie call Ann "Miss Independence" (the original title of the series): "Look Helen! Miss Independence is stuck in a tree!" Both Florence Halop (later a fixture on *Night Court*, 1984–92) and Penny Marshall make uncredited appearances in the opening sequence.

Who Gets to Say "That Girl!"

The unbilled Florence Halop as a librarian who is impressed with Ann's dedication. "There's someone with a head on her shoulders," she reflects. Penny Marshall utters "Who?" and the rest is history.

EPISODE 67: THE FACE IN THE SHOWER ROOM DOOR

ORIGINAL AIR DATE: NOVEMBER 7, 1968

Writers: Stan Cutler and Martin Donavan (story by Bill Idelson and Harvey Miller); Director: Danny Arnold; Guest Cast: Cesare Danova (Federico Gente), Renzo Cesana (Headwaiter), Jerry Riggio (Waiter #2), Leon Colker (Waiter #3)

When a prospective new building tenant shows up at her door while she is showering, Ann realizes that her shower door is stuck and she's trapped. Her visitor, a handsome Italian restaurateur, rescues her, but not without seeing her for a moment without her clothes. Taken with Ann, he stops by later to visit and finds her flustered by a burnt roast she's made for Donald. Swearing he can rescue her lost dinner, he keeps Ann and Don busy with kitchen tasks while he arranges to have their meal catered from his restaurant. Don is jealous and is not a happy diner. Somehow, he can't understand why Federico acts as though "he's seen Ann with her clothes off!" At the end of the episode, Ann gets stuck again and Federico tells Don how to get her out, thereby letting Don know that he was the one who helped her out before.

Highlights
Ann stuck in the shower as a handsome Italian attempts to get her out is the apex of the installment.

Notes
Although he moves into the building, we never see the continental Mr. Gente again.

Who Gets to Say "That Girl!"
No one says it. Ann, locked in the shower, says, "The first thing in the morning on a busy day, who gets locked in the shower?" The title comes on and reads "*That Girl!*"

EPISODE 68: A MUGGY DAY IN CENTRAL PARK
ORIGINAL AIR DATE: NOVEMBER 14, 1968
Writer: Arthur Julian; Director: Hal Cooper; Guest Cast: Lew Parker (Lou Marie), Dort Clark (Desk Sergeant), Bruce Mars (Schaffner), Roy Johnson (Man in the Park), Paul Sorenson (Bill Morgan), Dick Wesson (Charlie), Joe Perry (Foster), Norman Ransom (Woman), Noam Pitlik (Harry Walters), Danny Arnold (Mugger)

Ann is mugged in Central Park and her purse is stolen. She immediately goes to the police to report it and comes across a park detail of policemen dressed as women to catch muggers. When Don comes to pick her up, he decides that this would be a fascinating article for *Newsview*, so he dons a dress and goes undercover for the story. Once in drag, who should see him, but Ann's father! However, Ann doesn't want her dad to know she was mugged, so she won't let Donald explain the situation. When Lou sees Don cuddled up with a burly policeman, it's almost more than he can take. The whole thing is resolved when Don and the cop catch Ann's mugger and Lou finds out the truth.

Highlights
Don in a dress is a priceless scene, and Lou's incredulous reactions make it the highlight of the show.

Notes
Ann now gives her address as 344 West 78th Street in Manhattan.

Who Gets to Say "That Girl!"
Ann gets assaulted and, when his wife asks who got mugged, Roy Johnson as a man in the park yells, "Over there! *That girl!*"

EPISODE 69: JUST DONALD AND ME AND JERRY MAKES THREE
ORIGINAL AIR DATE: NOVEMBER 21, 1968
Writers: Stan Cutler and Martin Donavan; Director: James Sheldon; Guest Cast: Bernie Kopell (Jerry Bauman), Carolan Daniels (Ruth Bauman), Karen Arthur (Gloria), Hubert Noel (Waiter)

Neighbors Jerry and Ruth Bauman have an argument over Jerry adding sour cream to his baked potato and in no time they decide to divorce. Ruthie goes to Buffalo to be with her family and Jerry is left to spend all his time with Ann and Don. They scheme to make Jerry and Ruth each believe the other is having a wonderful time without the other. Finally, Ann and Donald trick the couple into meeting in Ann's apartment, and Jerry and Ruth's marriage is saved.

Highlights
Bernie Kopell's performance as a desperately lonely man is solid work. This really is *his* episode.

Notes
We find out that Ruthie is from Buffalo, New York.

Who Gets to Say "That Girl!"
Ted Bessell as Don says it after Jerry and Ruth tell him about their impending divorce, which Ann predicted: "I admit you had me fooled, but not *that girl!*"

How Many *That Girl*s Did They Direct?

In its five year history, *That Girl* was directed by many different talents. The director who holds the record number of *That Girl* episodes is Hal Cooper with twenty-three, followed by John Rich with nineteen, Richard Kinon with seventeen, John Erman and Russ Mayberry with ten each, James Sheldon and Bob Sweeney with seven each, producers Danny Arnold and Saul Turteltaub with six each, and James Frawley with five. Ted Bessell directed two episodes, creator and executive producer Bill Persky did one. It was once announced that Marlo Thomas was going to direct an episode of her own TV series but it never happened.

EPISODE 70: THE SEVENTH TIME AROUND
ORIGINAL AIR DATE: NOVEMBER 28, 1968
Writer: Carl Kleinschmidt; Director: Richard Kinon; Guest Cast: Bernie Kopell (Jerry Bauman), Benay Venuta (Margaret "Trixie" Weatherby), Ivor Barry (Earl), Frank Alesia (Messenger)

After Don does a story on multimillionairess Margaret "Trixie" Weatherby, he and Ann are invited to have dinner with her. Ann is immediately suspicious of the septuagenarian's intentions. Don only sees Trixie as a sweet little old lady, but Trixie views Don as her seventh husband. When Donald is promoted to foreign correspondent at *Newsview* magazine, with assignments in Spain, England, Switzerland, and Magumbi—each country where Trixie owns a castle—Ann learns that Trixie Weatherby is the owner of *Newsview!* The women square off, with Trixie trying to buy Don from Ann. But love wins out in the end and the old woman decides to marry her butler instead.

Highlights
This is a very funny entry, with a standout performance by Benay Venuta as Trixie (Venuta was far from the seventy years old that the

character was said to be). The moment when she shouts to Ann, "You wanna be a star! I'll buy it for you!" is one of the funniest bits on the show.

Notes
Benay Venuta was a Broadway pro who had replaced Ethel Merman in *Anything Goes* (1934) and appeared in *By Jupiter* (1942) and *Hazel Flagg* (1953) on Broadway and *Annie Get Your Gun* (1950) on film.

Who Gets to Say "That Girl!"
Ann says it while reading a love note from Trixie to Don: "'Thanks for everything, Love,' and it's signed *that girl!*"

EPISODE 71: ANN VS. SECRETARY
ORIGINAL AIR DATE: DECEMBER 5, 1968
Writer: Ruth Brooks Flippen; Director: Hal Cooper; Guest Cast: Carolan Daniels (Ruth Bauman), Jennifer Douglas (Pat Crawford), Queenie Smith (Mrs. LaConk, a secretary), George Dega (Captain), Leon Colker (Waiter)

Donald has a sexy new secretary who gets Ann's back up. She doesn't put her calls through and she makes her wait outside his office. When the secretary arranges to accompany Don on assignment to Washington, D.C., hoping to steal his heart from Ann, Ann decides to break up with him. She returns all borrowed items of hers and Donald's to their respective apartments. However, even though his secretary makes a pass, Don is true to Ann and returns to New York—just as Ann finishes hurriedly putting all the things back to where they were before he left.

Highlights
Jennifer Douglas's inspired performance as a predatory secretary is the highlight.

Notes
Jennifer Douglas later changed her name to Mary Frann and won fame as Bob Newhart's wife on TV's *Newhart* (1982–90).

Who Gets to Say "That Girl!"
Jennifer Douglas's [Mary Frann] disdainful voice on the other end of Ann's telephone asks Don if he wants to take this call: "It's *that girl!*"

EPISODE 72: DECISION BEFORE DAWN
ORIGINAL AIR DATE: DECEMBER 12, 1968
Writer: Jinx Kragen; Director: King Donovan; Guest Cast: Lew Parker (Lou Marie), Rosemary DeCamp (Helen Marie), Larry Storch (John MacKenzie), Woodrow Pefrey (Clerk), Vic Tayback (Max), Joe Higgins (Noel)

When Ann receives a $743.62 residual check from a TV appearance, everyone has an idea about what she should do with the money. Her mother wants her to buy a piano for culture's sake, her father suggests stocks for future security, and Donald mentions a trip to Hong Kong. Ann thinks she just needs a new bed. She compromises and rents a piano, buys stock, and invests in a travel club. The piano fills her living room, and she and Don and her parents are forced to eat their dinner on it. The real fun begins when the bed she ordered arrives during dinner and the salesman arrives with a bottle of wine.

Highlights
One highlight is Larry Storch as the Don Juan of mattress salesmen, suggestively selling Ann a bed. The scene during Ann's dinner party, with the bed being hauled over the piano, is also very funny. Lou: "My daughter came to New York and wound up living in a cocktail lounge." Another highlight is Ann and Don's very competent singing of Cole Porter's "I've Got You under My Skin."

Notes
We find out that Ann sells empty bottles to pay the rent. We know from episode #29: "Author, Author" that Don can play the piano. Amazingly, before this purchase, Ann was sleeping in her childhood bed.

Who Gets to Say "That Girl!"
Woodrow Pefrey as the clerk at the Screen Actors Guild, where Ann has picked up what she thought was a check for $1.62. When she realizes the actual amount, she screams. Someone asks who yelled, and Pefrey replies, "I think it was *that girl!*"

EPISODE 73: SHOULD ALL OUR OLD ACQUAINTANCE BE FORGOT

Original air date: December 26, 1968

Writers: Stan Cutler and Martin Donavan; Director: Hal Cooper; Guest Cast: Lew Parker (Lou Marie), Rosemary DeCamp (Helen Marie), Bernie Kopell (Jerry Bauman), Carolan Daniels (Ruth Bauman), Cliff Norton (Charlie), Renati Vanni (Mrs. Brentano), Franco Corsaro (Mr. Brentano), Alice Jubert (Mrs. Fern), Kenneth Washington (Mr. Fern), Patty Regan (Mabel Fitch), Miriam Elliot (Mrs. Batchelor), Michael Parson (Mr. Batchelor), Stefanianna Christoperson (Mrs. Haversham), Brett Dunham (Mr. Haversham), Timothy Blake (Terry Scott), Garry Goodrow (Fred Scott)

When Don has trouble getting reservations for New Year's Eve, Ann suggests they spend a quiet evening at her apartment and ring in the new year privately. It seems that Ann and Don's idea is a good one as all of their friends decide to stay home that night, especially the Baumans. Ann and Don's romantic night is immediately interrupted by her parents, who drop by for one quick drink. They are soon followed by most of Ann's neighbors and friends, and Ann and Don find themselves spending a fortune on champagne, serving hors d'oeuvres made of peanut butter and corn flakes, and using flower vases as glasses. All the while Ann keeps interrupting the Baumans, who are trying to be "alone." In the end, even the Baumans join the festivities.

Highlights

Lou Marie dancing on a table with a lampshade on his head. Don doesn't realize it's him and tries to stop the frivolity. Lou is *not* amused.

Notes

It is clear from this episode that Ann and Don have lots of friends.

Who Gets to Say "That Girl!"

No one says it. After Don tells Ann that he's going to spend New Year's Eve with a delightful, gorgeous, talented girl. Ann says, "No, you're not, you're gonna spend this New Year's Eve with . . ." And the title takes over.

EPISODE 74: THE HOMEWRECKER AND
THE WINDOW WASHER

ORIGINAL AIR DATE: JANUARY 2, 1969
Writers: Stan Cutler and Martin Donavan (story by Ken Englund); Director: Hal Cooper; Guest Cast: Jules Munshin (Rudy Clarn), Bobo Lewis (Ethel Clarn), Richard Elkins (Policeman), Oliver McGowan (Chairman), William Quinn (Priest)

When an aggressive bully collides with Ann in an office lobby, only nearby window washer Rudy Clarn comes to her aid. But while warning him off, the bully slugs Rudy and breaks his nose. Feeling terribly guilty, Ann accompanies the do-gooder to the doctor's and then home. Rudy's wife, Ethel—a terribly jealous woman— believes there is more to the relationship between Ann and Rudy, and threatens to leave him. Ann believes she must get word to Rudy so he can stop her, but how do you find a window washer somewhere in the city of New York? When she finally locates him, she ends up disrupting a corporate board meeting as she goes through the boardroom in order to lean out their window to speak to Rudy, who is on the ledge doing his job. Believing there's a jumper out there, the board chairman summons the police, who, in turn, bring in a priest. And where is Donald during all this? Getting stood up by Ann, over and over again!

Highlights
Bobo Lewis's brilliant performance as Mrs. Clarn is the highlight of this offering.

Notes
Bobo Lewis also appears in episodes #30: "The Mating Game," #63: "Eleven Angry Men and That Girl," #102: "Opening Night," #110: "They Shoot Pictures, Don't They?", #111: "Easy Faller," and #130: "That Shoplifter." Jules Munshin appears as Ann's agent in episode #81: "The Subject Was Rabies."

Who Gets to Say "That Girl!"
Jules Munshin as Rudy Clarn speaking to himself, "It looks like it's going to be up to you to go rescue *that girl!*"

EPISODE 75: THE EYE OF THE BEHOLDER
ORIGINAL AIR DATE: JANUARY 9, 1969
Writer: Paul Wayne; Director: James Sheldon; Guest Cast: Lew Parker (Lou Marie), Bernie Kopell (Jerry Bauman), Carolan Daniels (Ruth Bauman), Frank Puglia (Mr. Brentano), Renata Vanni (Mrs. Brentano)

Ann receives an art object as a gift from Donald and tells him how ridiculous she thinks it looks before she realizes it is from him. Before long, everyone who comes over to the apartment has a different opinion about it. Jerry thinks it's a spittoon and begins to clean his pipe on it. Ruth points out that it looks like a cow. Ann's father thinks it looks pornographic, and landlord Mr. Brentano props open a window with it believing it to be something broken. Ann refuses Don's offer to return it, believing she should keep it to remind her of her faults. Poor Donald has spent $97.50 on what Ann thinks looks like "brass mashed potatoes with fat hips."

Highlights
Mr. Brentano's reaction to the "work of art" is delightful. Anytime the Brentanos appear they lift the episode to greater comic heights.

Notes
We find out that Ann's landlord also does his own repairs. No super for the building?

Who Gets to Say "That Girl!"
Marlo Thomas as Ann says it as she looks at the art object that reminds Don of her: "Look at me . . . I'm *that girl!*"

EPISODE 76: DARK ON TOP OF EVERYTHING ELSE
ORIGINAL AIR DATE: JANUARY 16, 1969
Writer: Carl Kleinschmidt; Director: Ted Bessell; Guest Cast: Lew Parker (Lou Marie), Rosemary DeCamp (Helen Marie), George Fenneman (TV Announcer)

Although neither one really wants to, Ann thinks Don needs to spend the weekend alone and he believes that she does too. So, Ann goes to Brewster to be with her parents, only to find them leaving for a

New York restaurant convention. She decides to stay at their house and let her parents use her apartment. After looking through all her mementos and making phone calls to old friends, she tries to sleep. However, every little noise scares her and one finally leads her to the basement, where the door slams shut, locking her downstairs. While investigating the source of the noise, she jumps on a folding bed to close an out-of-reach window, but the bed suddenly folds back up and locks, trapping her inside. When her parents can't reach her on the telephone, they head back to Brewster. But Don arrives there first and rescues Ann. Of course, when the Maries arrive, Don and Ann are in a compromising position.

Highlights
The slapstick section showing Ann trying to get out of the locked basement is beautifully directed by Bessell and cleverly played by Thomas.

Notes
This is the first *That Girl* segment directed by Ted Bessell. He also would helm episode #103: "That Meter Maid."

Who Gets to Say "That Girl!"
Ted Bessell as Don makes a mental note to get together on Monday with . . . "what was her name? Oh yeah, *that girl!*"

EPISODE 77: THE EARRINGS
ORIGINAL AIR DATE: JANUARY 23, 1969
Writer: Howard Leeds; Director: Russ Mayberry; Guest Cast: Bernie Kopell (Jerry Bauman), Carolan Daniels (Ruth Bauman), Fabian Dean (Messenger), Albert Carrier (Waiter)

It's Valentine's Day, and after Ann makes Don a soufflé that sinks, and Don gives Ann roses to which she is allergic, they exchange more permanent gifts. She gives him a tie clasp and he presents her with genuine diamond earrings. Although Ann is scared to wear them, lest she lose them, she eventually does. And, of course, she is miserable after she misplaces one of them. Since she refuses a replacement, Don buys another earring and plants it in the apartment. Meanwhile, Ann also buys one to pretend to find it too. When the restaurant calls to say they have found her missing original, the secrets come out.

Highlights

Watching Ann trying not to lose an earring as she dances with Don is a delicious moment.

Notes

This is the last *That Girl* appearance of Carolan Daniels as Ruth Bauman. The next time we see Ruth, she will look very different. We find out in this episode that Ann is allergic to roses.

Who Gets to Say "That Girl!"

Fabian Dean as the messenger bringing roses to a sneezing Ann: "Some poor guy blew twenty bucks on *that girl!*"

EPISODE 78: MANY HAPPY RETURNS
ORIGINAL AIR DATE: JANUARY 30, 1969
Writer: John Whedon; Director: Jay Sandrich; Guest Cast: Lew Parker (Lou Marie), Jack Mullaney (Leon Cobb, the IRS Agent), Sam Javis (Taxpayer)

Just as Ann has an engagement with her father to go to a party, she gets a visit from an IRS agent with a bill for $2,600 in back taxes. She calls on Donald for help. While attempting to sift through Ann's unorthodox filing system, Don ends up covered in flour. When Mr. Marie arrives, he sees Don standing shirtless, holding a pillowcase stuffed with papers. Ann's explanation? She tells him that Don is there to sort her trash! Meanwhile, Don must convince the IRS that Ann did not make that much money.

Highlights

The ridiculous sight of Don trying to hide Ann's receipts from her father makes this show that much more special.

Notes

This is the first of only two *That Girl* episodes (the other was episode # 81: "The Subject Was Rabies") to be directed by Jay Sandrich, who went on to direct *The Mary Tyler Moore Show* (1970–77).

Who Gets to Say "That Girl!"

Jack Mullaney as Leon Cobb, tax agent, quotes the IRS: "Leon, you gotta go out and collect a whole lot of back taxes from *that girl!*"

EPISODE 79: MY SISTER'S KEEPER
ORIGINAL AIR DATE: FEBRUARY 6, 1969
Writers: Sam Denoff and Bill Persky; Director: John Rich; Guest Cast: McLean Stevenson (McKorkle), Terre Thomas (Rose Cassinetti), Tony Thomas (Tony Cassinetti), Judy Cassmore (Secretary), April Edie (Little Girl), John Nolan (Mr. Johnson, the director), Sam Denoff (Frank, the actor in the commercial), Eddie Foy III (Singer on the record), Danny Thomas (Priest)

Ann gets a commercial assignment for POP soft drink, but it requires that she sing. When she flunks the singing audition, the producer suggests that Ann's voice be dubbed. When Ann is introduced to her voice double, Rose Cassinetti, she feels she must do something to help accelerate Rose's career. However, Rose has to turn down the jobs because she is a nun—which no one, including Rose, has told Ann.

Highlights
Marlo Thomas, as Ann singing "Over Here" as her audition song, is delightful, as is her sister's beautiful rendition of "Turn Around."

Notes
This episode is very much a family affair. Terre Thomas, Marlo's sister, plays Rose; Tony Thomas, their brother, is cast as Terre's manager, Tony; and Danny Thomas, Marlo's real father, makes an uncredited cameo appearance as the priest Ann bumps into. She says, "Oh, excuse me, Father!" and he replies, "That's all right, my child." The only Thomas family member not involved in the outing is Marlo's mother. Co-creator and co-executive producer Sam Denoff plays the man in the POP commercial (Denoff: "I was motivated by a thirst to act and I'm the only one in town who will hire me. . . .") and associate producer Eddie Foy III voices the jingle, "Why Don't You Stop and Have a POP with Me?" This is one of the very few *That Girl* episodes written by Sam Denoff and Bill Persky.

Who Gets to Say "That Girl!"
McLean Stevenson as McKorkle looks at two photos of potential candidates for a commercial: "It's between this girl and *that girl!*"

EPISODE 80: THERE WAS A TIME ANN MET A PIE MAN
ORIGINAL AIR DATE: FEBRUARY 13, 1969
Writer: Milt Rosen; Director: Russ Mayberry; Guest Cast: Lew Parker (Lou Marie), Jesse White (Hal Grissom), Gene Baylos (Mort), Lea Marmer

(Wardrobe Lady), Renata Vanni (Mrs. Brentano), Maida Serven (Elderly Lady), Eddie Foy III (Man in TV blackout sketch)

Ann is offered a part in a comedy show (not unlike *Rowan & Martin's Laugh-In*, 1968–73) that sounds fabulous at first. She is to play a wealthy, beautiful woman who is dressed elegantly and covered in diamonds from Cartier's. She is to walk down a forty-step staircase very slowly and then pause demurely. And then she is to be hit in the face with a pie. At first, Ann is undecided about taking the job, but the $500 paycheck convinces her. After the scene is shown on national television, she is terribly embarrassed. She wears dark glasses, even in her apartment, because nearly everyone she knows has seen the skit, including her father (who's also wearing dark glasses). When her TV bit becomes a regular feature, Ann bites the bullet and does it again. However, the sponsor now wants big stars like Julie Andrews and Audrey Hepburn for the role.

Highlights
The backstage ambiance at ABC where, of course, the show is filmed is very effective and we get to see several of the short comedy sketches, one using the unbilled Eddie Foy III.

Notes
Jesse White appears as a producer. He has previously appeared as Eddie Edwards, a press agent, in episodes #57: "Just Spell the Name Right" and #60: "Old Man's Darling" and as Phil Bender in episode #65: "7¼ (Part Two)." This is the last appearance of Renata Vanni as Mrs. Brentano. Next season the Brentanos will sell the building and never be seen again on the series.

Who Gets to Say "That Girl!"
This is another of the few times that no one says *"that girl."* Jesse White sets it up with his dialogue line, "She's the one we hit in the face with a pie," and the title appears with no sound.

EPISODE 81: THE SUBJECT WAS RABIES
ORIGINAL AIR DATE: FEBRUARY 20, 1969
Writer: Skip Webster; Director: Jay Sandrich; Guest Cast: Lew Parker (Lou Marie), Jules Munshin (Harry Fields), Stuart Margolin (Dr. Priddy), Ed Peck (Ketchum), Dick Balduzzi (Messenger), Jack Colvin (Bounder), Keith Luckett (Little Boy with Dog)

A cute little dog follows Ann home, and when her father shows up at her apartment, the canine bites him. When Donald arrives and mentions the word "rabies," Lou is convinced he's feeling symptoms. The only way to know for sure that the animal is not rabid is to have it tested. However, the little pup has run off. So Donald offers neighborhood kids a dollar for every canine they bring to Ann's apartment. Then the health department and the media get into the act. All of this happens while Ann is scheduled for an important audition. In the end the dog is found and Lou realizes that he's fine.

Highlights
This is a very funny episode, highlighted by Lew Parker's overly dramatic performance when he thinks he has rabies. He is worried that he will "howl at people and eat out of trash cans."

Notes
Jules Munshin appears as one of Ann's many agents, Harry Fields (Munshin also played Rudy Clarne in episode #74: "The Homewrecker and the Window Washer"). He never again returns to the series. Stuart Margolin also appeared in episodes #63: "Eleven Angry Men and That Girl" and #65: "7¼ (Part Two)." This also is one of the few times on the series that we see the outside of Ann's apartment building.

Who Gets to Say "That Girl!"
Jules Munshin as Harry Fields looks at the manic Ann and says, "No interest, no drive, no ambition, that's what the matter is with *that girl!*"

EPISODE 82: THE DEFIANT ONE
ORIGINAL AIR DATE: FEBRUARY 27, 1969
Writers: Richard Baer (story by Gene Boland and Richard Baer); Director: Richard Kinon; Guest Cast: Terry Carter (Joey Johnson), Naomi Stevens (Shopper), Lillian Field (Lady), George Spell (David Johnson), Lewis Charles (Mr. Elkins), Sid Clute (Desk Sergeant), Ketty Lester (Mrs. Ellis)

While shopping in a neighborhood grocery store, Ann witnesses a young African American boy getting caught stealing a candy bar. When he insists his mother is in the store and will pay for it, he points out Ann as his mother. Ann protects him, pays for the candy, and then brings him home with her. When he tells her that he lives on Park Avenue, she does not believe him, so he tells her a sob story that she wants to believe. Ann feels so sorry for the boy that she considers adopting him. A more sensible Donald wants her to call the police. While they discuss it, the youth calls his wealthy father to say he's been kidnapped by a crazy white lady. When the father arrives it is clear that the family is very well off. Ann learns a lesson about her liberal attitude.

Highlights
The highlight is the scene on the crosstown bus going through Central Park. When a woman looks askance at Ann with a little black boy, Ann tells her that she's his governess and that her people have been with his people for generations.

Notes
Terry Carter, who plays the boy's father, was a well-known actor who had starred on Broadway in the musical *Kwamina* (1961).

Who Gets to Say "That Girl!"
George Spell as the little boy snitching candy says it. When the owner of the store asks him where his mother is, Spell points to the very white Ms. Marie and says, "She's right there—she's *that girl!*"

EPISODE 83: FLY ME TO THE MOON
ORIGINAL AIR DATE: MARCH 6, 1969
Writer: John McGreevey; Director: Richard Kinon; Guest Cast: Robert Colbert (Major Brian James), Noam Pitlik (Beaumont), Joe Perry (Fletcher), Joe Higgins (Staff Sergeant) Richard Jury (Airman), Ken Greenwald (Radioman)

Ann lands an assignment in public relations for the air force to promote women in the space program. Unfortunately, she has also taken on the job of redecorating Donald's apartment. Don, in the meantime, is trying to work from home on a major article. While Ann jets all over the world in private fighter planes, Don is stuck with questions about paint, wallpaper, and upholstery. During all this time, Ann cannot believe that her handsome but straight-laced boss, Major James, is not attracted to her!

Highlights
Ann whirling around in a centrifuge while, at the same time, answering Don's questions about his apartment is the show's highlight.

Notes
In this episode Ann seems to have no trouble flying all over the world in a very small plane, but in episodes #104: "Fly by Night" and #105: "Ugh Wilderness," she tells us she is, and always was, terrified of flying.

Who Gets to Say "That Girl!"
Joe Higgins tells Richard Jury as an airman, "She may be the one to help put the first woman on the moon." Jury responds incredulously with the famous question: *"That girl?"*

EPISODE 84: IT'S SO NICE TO HAVE A MOUSE AROUND THE HOUSE
ORIGINAL AIR DATE: MARCH 13, 1969
Writer: Ruth Brooks Flippen; Director: Russ Mayberry; Guest Cast: Lew Parker (Lou Marie), William Bramley (Bert Weevle)

Don is awakened by a call from Ann in the middle of the night. She has been awakened by a mouse in her apartment and is sure that the creature is at least three feet tall. Believing there's no other way he'll get any rest, to tame Ann's fears Donald agrees to swap apartments for the night. Lou Marie arrives early the next morning to find Donald at the door in his undershorts and Ann sweeping in with the fixings for a "thank you for last night" breakfast. The enraged Mr. Marie insists they go to Baltimore for a quickie marriage ceremony! Now Ann must locate this three-foot mouse so her father will believe their story.

Highlights
Lew Parker wins the highlight award again. He is a master of farcical facial expressions.

Notes
This installment, despite the usual formula, reflects how much Don loves Ann. He is quite willing to marry her to save her honor.

Who Gets to Say "That Girl!"
Ted Bessell as Don says it as he is bragging about his special United Nations interview: "Need someone for a special interview? Let's assign Hollinger, he's the boyfriend of *that girl!*"

EPISODE 85: BAD DAY AT MARVIN GARDENS
ORIGINAL AIR DATE: MARCH 20, 1969
Writer: Carl Kleinschmidt; Director: Danny Arnold; Guest Cast: Lew Parker (Lou Marie), Rosemary DeCamp (Helen Marie)

Ann's parents come to the city to attend a baseball game and the theater with Ann and Donald, but when the game is rained out the foursome opt to play a game of Monopoly. In no time, the women are out of the contest and Lou and Donald are competing once again. When Donald doesn't want to sell his "Marvin Gardens" property, the game heats up. The competitive ill-feeling continues and when Ann's mother (Helen) agrees with Donald, Lou is enraged. Nonetheless, he comes to his senses in the morning.

Highlights
Lew Parker as Lou Marie plays the game of Monopoly as if his life is at stake!

Notes
It is clear in this episode that Lou and Don are slowly developing a rapport. We also find out that Lou belongs to the American Legion. This is the last *That Girl* episode directed by Danny Arnold.

Who Gets to Say "That Girl!"
Lew Parker as Lou Marie observes his daughter pulling in pots of rainwater from the windowsill: "You raise a girl right and hope for the best and she turns into a rainwater-saver. Sometimes I don't know about *that girl!*"

EPISODE 86: SUE ME, SUE ME, WHAT CAN YOU DO ME?
ORIGINAL AIR DATE: MARCH 27, 1969
Writers: Milt Rosen, Ruth Brooks Flippen and Danny Arnold; Director: Russ Mayberry; Guest Cast: Lew Parker (Lou Marie), Bernie Kopell (Jerry

Bauman), Ned Glass (Dr. Heindorf), Alan Oppenheimer (Stuart Hurley), David Lewis (Robert "Big Bob" Prentice), David Astor (Charles Lindstrom), Byron Keith (Dr. Wheeler), Ceil Cabot (Cleaning Woman), John Harmon (Porter)

While visiting *Newsview* to meet Don and Ann, Lou Marie slips in water on the floor of the building where Donald works. Even though he appears unhurt, Ann calls Dr. Heindorf from Brewster to examine him. In the meantime, Donald is visited by Stuart Hurly from *Newsview*'s claims department who wants Mr. Marie to sign a waiver of responsibility. An angry Donald visits the offices of publisher Robert (Big Bob) Prentice only to discover the man is totally unaware of Hollinger's work. Frustrated, Donald quits his job, but his managing editor, Charlie Lindstrom, is able to talks him out of it.

Highlights
Ned Glass as hometown Dr. Heindorf is positively charming. What a shame he didn't appear with Lew Parker on other *That Girl* episodes.

Notes
The credits list David Lewis as Mr. "Prentiss," but the office doorplate where Donald enters the publisher's office in the episode clearly reads "Robert L. Prentice." This is the last script credited to Danny Arnold. Alan Oppenheimer also will appear in episodes #101: "Ten Percent of Nothing Is Nothing," #109: "Gone-A-Courtin'," and #117: "Rattle of a Single Girl" as Mr. Katz, Morgan Jerome, and Dr. Globe, respectively.

Who Gets to Say "That Girl!"
Bernie Kopell as Jerry Bauman tells everyone who the man who slipped and fell is: "He's the father of *that girl!*"

Awards and Honors for Season Three

There were no major awards or honors given to the series for this season.

SEASON FOUR
SEPTEMBER 1969–MARCH 1970

Season Four Overview

The departure of Danny Arnold necessitated bringing in first-time producers Bernie Orenstein and Saul Turteltaub (they also became the script consultants). Luckily, having written for the show, they were already very familiar with *That Girl* and the continuity was maintained for the new episodes.

While Ann and Donald's relationship stays on an even keel, Ann continues to pursue her acting career. She supplements it with such oddball jobs as becoming an industrial spy for a pajama company, directing her father's annual country club show, and doing personal appearances as a dancing chicken. Her legitimate acting jobs include playing Doris the Ding-a-ling on a TV soap opera, doing a commercial for No-Freeze Antifreeze, taking a lead role in a Las Vegas show called *Funny Man*, doing a standup comedy act with her agent, Sandy, and appearing in her first original role in a Broadway production.

Production Team for Season Four
Executive Producers and Series Creators: Bill Persky and Sam Denoff; Producers and Story Consultants: Bernie Orenstein and Saul Turteltaub; Associate Producer: Lew Gallo; Director of Photography: Leonard J. South, A.S.C.; Art Director: Lewis E. Hurst Jr.; Film Editor: Homer Powell; Music: Earle Hagen; Miss Thomas's wardrobe by Cardinelli, Inc.; Hair: Lynn Masters; Makeup: Tom Case; Casting: Fred Roos; Set Decorator: John D. W. Lamphear; Production Manager: John Banse; Supervising Production Manager: Dan A. Baer; Executive in Charge of Production: Ronald Jacobs; Origination: Filmed at Cinema General Studios and on location in New York City and elsewhere by Daisy Productions; Sponsors: Bristol-Myers Company, Noxell Corporation, and Lever Brothers

**EPISODE 87: MISSION IMPROBABLE
(PART ONE)**
ORIGINAL AIR DATE: SEPTEMBER 18, 1969
Writer: Rick Mittleman; Director: John Rich; Guest Cast: Lew Parker (Lou

Marie), Lou Jacobi (Leo Schneider), Avery Schreiber (Al Taylor), Naomi Stevens (Sophie), Paul Bryar (Mort), Danny Goldman (Waiter), Sandy Kenyon (Mr. Becker)

While modeling pajamas at Unifit, Ann is hired to spy on a competitor (Sleeptite) who is suspected of stealing Unifit's designs. When Ann gets hired by Sleeptite as a seamstress, the Unifit people give her a camera disguised as a banana with which to photograph Sleeptite's new product line.

Highlights
Ann's handling of the banana/camera is the comic highlight of this not-too-hot season opener.

Notes
We find out that Ann is a bad seamstress, despite the fact that in episode #4: "I'll Be Suing You" she claimed that she sewed all her own clothes.

Who Gets to Say "That Girl!"
Lou Jacobi as Leo Schneider the Pajama King has some plans of his own "for *that girl!*"

EPISODE 88: MISSION IMPROBABLE
(PART TWO)
ORIGINAL AIR DATE: SEPTEMBER 25, 1969
Writer: Rick Mittleman; Director: John Rich; Guest Cast: Lou Jacobi (Leo Schneider), Avery Schreiber (Al Taylor), Naomi Stevens (Sophie), Sandy Kenyon (Mr. Becker)

Unaware that her cover has been blown, Ann is tricked into photographing reject designs. When Ann is confronted by Becker, and then offered a job as a counterspy, she quits her job completely. She then finds out that Schneider and Taylor are feuding brothers and she brings them back together.

Highlights
The sweetness of Ann getting the two brothers back together helps raise this episode above the ordinary.

Notes

Ann's undercover spy name is Ina Albert. Schneider means "tailor" in German.

Who Gets to Say "That Girl!"

Avery Schreiber as Al Taylor, as he looks at Ann photographing his fashions with a banana: "Ever see a spy? We got one now. *That girl!*"

EPISODE 89: MY PART BELONGS TO DADDY

ORIGINAL AIR DATE: OCTOBER 2, 1969

Writers: Saul Turteltaub and Bernie Orenstein; Director: Richard Kinon; Guest Cast: Lew Parker (Lou Marie), Rosemary DeCamp (Helen Marie), Dave Ketchum (Harry), Carole Cooke (Dorothy), Ned Wertimer (Bob Brooks)

Against Donald's warnings, Ann is roped into directing the annual Brewster town play, in which her father will perform his usual stage number. Conflict arises when she must inform her dad that he doesn't have the starring role this year.

Highlights

The unquestionable highlight is Lew Parker as Lou Marie knockin' 'em dead as he sings his rendition of the Cab Calloway classic "Minnie the Moocher." It is obvious that Parker has stage experience as a musical comedy star and he is a delight.

Notes

This installment marks the first time that Lou Marie comes to think of his daughter, Ann, as a professional theater person.

Who Gets to Say "That Girl!"

Ted Bessell as Don says it as a question, referring to Ann becoming a director.

EPISODE 90: NOBODY HERE BUT US CHICKENS

ORIGINAL AIR DATE: OCTOBER 9, 1969

Writer: Arnold Horwitt; Director: Richard Kinon; Guest Cast: Lew Parker (Lou Marie), Rosemary DeCamp (Helen Marie), Slim Pickens (Major Culpepper), Ed Peck (Walter Clark), Don Eitner (Young Man), Mari Oliver

(Girl #1), Doris Lorenz (Girl #2), Linda Sue Rusk (Little Girl), Harry Basch (Driver), H. B. Barnum III (Little Boy)

Ann is hired to do personal appearances for a fried chicken chain as "Miss Chicken Big." When the owner makes a pass at her after a day's work, she gets out of the car and has to fend for herself as she struggles to get to her father's award banquet—dressed in a yellow chicken suit!

Highlights
The unquestionable high point is the montage that shows Ann doing the "courtship dance of the chicken" as a record player grinds out "Turkey in the Straw."

Notes
Oddly enough, Ann's audition for the role of the chicken seems to emphasize her clucking ability, but the job itself is a dancing one. In this episode, Lou Marie receives (offscreen) the Golden Knife and Fork Award as Restaurateur of the Year. Writer Arnold Horwitt may be best remembered as the lyricist of the 1955 Broadway musical *Plain and Fancy*, which contained the hit song "Young and Foolish."

Who Gets to Say "That Girl!"
Ted Bessell as Donald says it while watching Ann rehearse her clucking for the audition. He calls her "the biggest cuckoo bird that ever lived . . . *that girl!*"

EPISODE 91: AT THE DROP OF A BUDGET
ORIGINAL AIR DATE: OCTOBER 16, 1969
Writers: Ed Scharlach and Warren Murray; Director: Russ Mayberry; Guest Cast: Monte Hall (Dr. Pellman), Gino Conforti (Nino), Will Mackenzie (Fiancé), Walter Mathews (Jeweler), Sam Denoff (Dudley Moss, the director of the soap opera), Mari Oliver (Ticket Seller), Abigail Kanter (Salesperson)

After she gets a recurring role on a soap opera (as Ding-a-ling Doris, a girl with sixteen psychological hang-ups), Ann asks Donald to help her create a budget that she can stick to so that she can save some money. He reluctantly agrees. Meanwhile, Ann goes to a dentist who uses hypnotic suggestion to help patients avoid pain. In the middle of the procedure, the dentist gets a call from his wife and he yells, "At the drop of a hat, you will buy anything!" Ann picks up the hypnotic suggestion and goes on a buying spree every time a hat is dropped. Don finally figures it out, but not before Ann loses her job on the daytime drama.

Highlights

The scene on the live soap opera, where Ann and her fellow actors are in a jewelry shop and a hat drops, is very funny. It is hilarious watching Sam Denoff practically pulling out his hair as Ann buys everything in the store.

Notes

It is *That Girl* co-creator/co-executive producer Sam Denoff who appears as the director of the soap opera.

Who Gets to Say "That Girl!"

Gino Conforti asks the famous question after Don says that Ann can't have any wine because she is a girl with many psychological hang-ups.

How Many *That Girl*s Did They Write?

The largest number of scripts for *That Girl* were written by producers Saul Turteltaub and Bernie Orenstein. They hold the record with nineteen aired episodes. Script consultant for the years 1967 to 1969, Ruth Brooks Flippen, follows with fourteen aired segments. Richard Baer wrote ten installments, while the team of Peggy Elliot and Ed Scharlach tie with the team of Tom and Helen August, each with six entries to their credit. Broadway writers Milton Pascal and Arnold Horwitt each wrote five offerings, as did the team of Martin Donavan and Stan Cutler. The creators, Sam Denoff and Bill Persky, wrote three installments (four counting the unaired pilot).

EPISODE 92: HEARING TODAY, GONE TOMORROW
ORIGINAL AIR DATE: OCTOBER 23, 1969
Writers: Bernie Orenstein and Saul Turteltaub; Director: Hal Cooper; Guest
Cast: Richard Stahl (Director), Roy Applegate (Actor), Andre Phillip (Dino),
Bill Quinn (Doctor)

Donald works at Ann's apartment so that he can be with her as she
tries to recover from a bad cold in time to do a TV commercial. As
the cold worsens, Ann loses her hearing and totally ruins the commercial.

Highlights
The scene in which Ann gets dopey on cold medicine, and then goes
deaf, is the installment's funniest point.

Notes
This episode shows us how far Ann and Donald's relationship has
progressed over the three seasons. With Donald typing at the table
and Ann sick on the couch, they seem like a married couple. When
Ann tries out for the antifreeze commercial, she even sings the jingle
in her nasal, cold-ridden voice, "Put No-Freeze in your car . . ."
Although we never see her agent, we hear several phone conversations with him and it is clear that he is still Seymour. But, oddly
enough, instead of his last name being Schwimmer, Donald calls him
Seymour Stone. Her next agent's name is Sandy Stone.

Who Gets to Say "That Girl!"
Ted Bessell as Donald, frustrated by Ann's insistence on doing a commercial in the snow despite her bad cold, tells Dino, the waiter at
Nino's, that he has no need for a dish that is unusual with a funny
noodle: "I've already got it. *That girl!*"

EPISODE 93: THE SNOW MUST GO ON (PART ONE)
ORIGINAL AIR DATE: OCTOBER 30, 1969
Writer: Arnold Horwitt; Director: Russ Mayberry; Guest Cast: Lew Parker
(Lou Marie), Rosemary DeCamp (Helen Marie), Milton Parsons (Mr. Bailey),
John Stephenson (Howard Samroce), Larry McCormick (Walsh), Jeff
Whipple (Jud Bailey), Danny Goldman (Counterman), Burt Brandon (Pilot),
Steven Benson (Porter), Rodolfo Hoyos Jr. (Announcer)

Ann and Donald see Ann's parents off at Kennedy Airport and become stranded in a blizzard. Ann is due at a Broadway audition and is determined to get there despite the bad weather. Meanwhile, her father, fearing they will run out of food, hoards sandwiches in an airport locker. And then he forgets which locker he hid them in. In the end, Ann gets to audition on live TV and the sandwiches are distributed to the hungry.

Highlights

There are several highlights in this entry, including the scene where Ann must audition over the phone and uses her mother, a non-pro, as an acting partner. Then there's the scene where Lou sniffs lockers in an effort to track his hidden sandwiches.

Notes

Looking for a low fare, Lou and Helen book an economy package on Manana Airlines. It just happens to be for a morticians' convention. Don mentions that he has never written a story about Ann, which is not actually true. He should review episode #13: "All About Ann."

Who Gets to Say "That Girl!"

Ted Bessell as Donald when he realizes who will be the most upset of all about being snowed in: "You wanna see panic, keep your eye on *that girl!*"

EPISODE 94: WRITE IS WRONG (PART TWO)

ORIGINAL AIR DATE: NOVEMBER 6, 1969
Writer: Ruth Brooks Flippen; Director: John Rich; Guest Cast: Lew Parker (Lou Marie), William Schallert (Harry Cook), Tom Kennedy (Barry Forbes), Alice Borden (Ruth Bauman), Arthur Julian (Milton East), Forrest Compton (Jonathan Adams), Dick Curtis (Drunk)

At a party, Ann and Don meet a TV producer who wants Don to write a segment for his show, about being snowed in at the airport. Don agrees to do it only if Ann gets the lead role. After signing the contract and writing the script, everyone wants to give Don input. Lou doesn't want him to mention the sandwich hoarding and Don agrees. Who would guess that the whole script eventually would be totally rewritten anyway? Ann tries to prevent everyone from watching the results on TV and, luckily for her, the show is preempted.

Highlights
As usual, Lew Parker's performance sparkles. Where was his well-deserved Emmy?

Notes
This is the second part of "The Snow Must Go On" installment and the first time we see Alice Borden as Ruth Bauman. Forrest Compton plays Jonathan Adams, Don's publisher, but in all later *That Girl* episodes he is played by James Gregory. The TV show Ann appears on is called *The Barry Forbes Show* and the character she is to play is named Cindy. William Schallert is recognizable as Patty Duke's dad on *The Patty Duke Show* (1963–66).

Who Gets to Say "That Girl!"
William Schallert as TV producer Harry Cook is wondering where the new TV writers are coming from. He is told, "I think we just got one from *that girl!*"

EPISODE 95: SHAKE HANDS AND COME OUT ACTING
ORIGINAL AIR DATE: NOVEMBER 13, 1969
Writers: Bernie Orenstein and Saul Turteltaub; Director: John Rich; Guest Cast: Billy DeWolfe (Jules Benedict), Scoey Mitchell (Tony Harris), Gino Conforti (Nino), Allan Jaffe (Jake), James McCallion (Max), John Pare (Frank), Frankie Van (Mel), Harry Basch (Charlie), Dick Dial (Fighter), Melvin Stewart (Dal)

Don is researching a story on fighter Tony Harris and learns that the fighter really wants to become an actor. Ann convinces Jules Benedict to allow Tony to audition for Benedict's workshop in exchange for the promise of a mention in Don's article. However, the men who own Tony's career don't want him to abandon boxing. They offer Ann $1,000 to make Tony look bad in the audition. But Tony needs no help on that score, as he is no actor. But he does show some flair at being a standup comedian.

Highlights

The prime moments here include Billy DeWolfe changing his mind about letting Tony audition and Ann being taken for "a ride" by the boys who want her to fix the acting tryout.

Notes

This is the last appearance of Billy DeWolfe as Ann's acting coach on the series.

Who Gets to Say "That Girl!"

Don is in the ring with Tony and, when Ann walks by, he looks at her and takes a punch. He tells Tony, "It wasn't that fist, it was *that girl!*"

EPISODE 96: FIX MY SCREEN AND BUG OUT

ORIGINAL AIR DATE: NOVEMBER 20, 1969

Writers: Bernie Orenstein and Saul Turteltaub; Director: Saul Turteltaub; Guest Cast: Michael Callan (Bobby Miller), Alice Borden (Ruth Bauman), Lillian Adams (Mrs. Stern), Don Lorbett (Supervisor), Penny Marshall (Joan, the receptionist), Andre Phillipe (Dino)

Ann's apartment building is sold to a corporation run by an ex-boyfriend, Bobby Miller. The other tenants want Ann to head the complaint committee and Bobby wants to rekindle Ann's flame. Donald is not at all happy. In the end, Ann once again realizes that it is only Donald whom she loves.

Highlights

This is a typical episode, but the warmth between Don and Ann at the end of this segment once again saves the day.

Notes

It is apparent that we will never see the Brentanos again and, oddly enough, we never see Bobby, the new landlord again either! Michael Callan was the star of *Occasional Wife* (1966–67) and is best remembered as the original Riff in the Broadway cast of *West Side Story* (1957). Don's secretary is now Nancy.

Who Gets to Say "That Girl!"

Lillian Adams as Mrs. Stern, one of Ann's disgruntled neighbors, realizes that Ann would be a good tool to getting their apartments fixed: "Better than a lawyer, I think we'll use *that girl!*"

EPISODE 97: KISS THAT GIRL GOODBYE
ORIGINAL AIR DATE: NOVEMBER 27, 1969
Writers: Fai Harris and Lynn Farr; Director: John Rich; Guest Cast: Lew Parker (Lou Marie), Mark Miller (Robert Harrison), Bernie Kopell (Jerry Bauman), Alice Borden (Ruth Bauman), Elaine Princi (Elaine)

Donald gets a job offer that would mean moving to Paris for at least eighteen months. Before Donald can discuss the offer with Ann, neighbor Ruth Bauman tells her that Donald is positively going to Paris. Ann is devastated when Don's secretary calls and says that he is definitely getting a new job. But all ends well when *Newsview* offers him a comparable promotion and raise.

Highlights
It is lovely once again to see how much Ann loves Don and how she would miss him if he were gone.

Notes
Don's new promotion makes him an associate editor. And his secretary, who was Nancy just a week ago, is now Elaine.

Who Gets to Say "That Girl!"
Mark Miller as Robert Henry Harrison, the rival publisher, tells Don that he knows all about "*that girl!*"

EPISODE 98: SHE DIDN'T HAVE THE VEGAS NOTION (PART ONE)
ORIGINAL AIR DATE: DECEMBER 11, 1969
Writers: Saul Turteltaub and Bernie Orenstein; Director: Richard Kinon; Guest Cast: Jack Cassidy (Marty Haines), Hope Holiday (Joanne Ferrar), Pat Boone (as Himself), Carl Reiner (as Himself), Morty Gunty (as Himself), Allen Davis (Desk Clerk), Bill McLean (Waiter), Keith Rogers (Flight Attendant), Brad Trumbull (Reporter)

Ann gets a role in a Las Vegas show starring egomaniacal Marty Haines. Don accompanies her to Nevada where they hope to have a wonderful time, but Marty becomes jealous of Don and makes trouble. Meanwhile, Don, not having had anything to eat on the trip, drinks too much and is pulled into Marty's scheme. At the finale, Don is wed to a starlet he hardly knows.

Highlights

This episode contains another famous *That Girl* montage. This time, the famous sights of Las Vegas are explored by Ann and Don.

Notes

The name of the show within the episode is *Funny Man*, with Marty Haines, Joanne Ferrar, and Ann Marie. It is playing at the Celebrity Theatre at the Sands Hotel. Also playing at the Sands are Steve Lawrence and Eydie Gorme, and Morty Gunty. Gunty, Carl Reiner, and Pat Boone all do cameos on this entry. The next time we see Morty Gunty he will be Ann's new agent, Sandy Stone (episode #101: "Ten Percent of Nothing Is Nothing").

Who Gets to Say "That Girl!"

Jack Cassidy as the womanizing Marty Haines, after being told that he will have to find another victim in his show, points at Ann and says, "This trip, *that girl!*"

EPISODE 99: SHE DIDN'T HAVE THE VEGAS NOTION (PART TWO)

ORIGINAL AIR DATE: DECEMBER 18, 1969

Writers: Saul Turteltaub and Bernie Orenstein; Director: Richard Kinon; Guest Cast: Lew Parker (Lou Marie), Jack Cassidy (Marty Haines), Hope Holiday (Joanne Ferrar), Allen Davis (Desk Clerk), Bill McLean (Waiter), Lillian Field (Gertrude), Sam Edwards (Harold)

Both Ann and Don think that Don is married to Joanne, until Joanne reveals that it is all a practical joke perpetrated by Marty. Ann and Don decide to turn the tables on Marty. Donald leaves a note that he is on his way to the Hoover Dam—to jump. Meanwhile, Ann's father is on his way to Las Vegas after hearing of the "marriage."

Highlights

As usual, the high point is the look on Lew Parker's face when he thinks his little girl has been wronged. He never fails to amuse.

Notes

This is the second part of episode #98 and uses real Las Vegas locations, including the Sands Hotel.

Who Gets to Say "That Girl!"
Sam Edwards, as Harold, watches as Don and Ann fight over what they think is his quickie marriage. His wife, Gert, says Don has no morals. Harold points to Ann and adds that he has "no taste either. I'd have married *that girl!*"

EPISODE 100: I AM A CURIOUS LEMON
ORIGINAL AIR DATE: DECEMBER 25, 1969
Writer: Alex Barris; Director: Russ Mayberry; Guest Cast: Cindy Eilbacher (Caroline), Gino Conforti (Nino), Corrine Conley (Trudy), Susan Quick (Heather), William Christopher (Chippy)

Ann's cousin Trudy asks Ann to babysit her small daughter. When the child arrives she brings her lemon tree, which needs constant and bizarre care. Meanwhile, Don invites his college buddy and his wife for dinner at Ann's, forgetting to mention that his friend's spouse is an ex-girlfriend of his. All of Ann's attempts to impress fail, as the guests arrive an hour early, her hair falls, her refrigerator becomes unplugged, and she blows the kitchen fuse.

Highlights
Seeing Ann fall apart from nerves and situations beyond her control is very revealing, as it shows her vulnerable side. This show resembles the later *Mary Tyler Moore Show* episode in which Mary's perfect persona goes to hell.

Notes
William Christopher later achieved fame as Father Mulcahy in *M*A*S*H* (1972–83). We find out that Don's nickname in college was "old skunk."

Who Gets to Say "That Girl!"
Gino Conforti as Nino says it when Ann and her cousin fool him into thinking that Ann is going to have a child: "Oh no! Not *that girl!*"

EPISODE 101: TEN PERCENT OF NOTHING IS NOTHING
ORIGINAL AIR DATE: JANUARY 1, 1970
Writers: Bernie Orenstein and Saul Turteltaub (story by Ron Clark, Bernie Orenstein, and Saul Turteltaub); Director: John Rich; Guest Cast: Morty

Gunty (Sandy Stone), Alan Oppenheimer (Mr. Katz, owner of Havenhurst Manor in the Catskills), Bob Ross (Party Guest), Lew Gallow (Man at Table), Sam Denoff (Big Guy), Olan Soule (President), Diana Herbert (Secretary), Lew Gallo (Another Man at Party)

Against her better judgment, but encouraged by the response at a party, Ann joins her agent's comedy act. When he doesn't show up for a gig in the Catskills, Ann replaces him and Donald does her part of the routine—with disastrous results.

Highlights

The highlights are the scenes at the Massapequa Gold and Country Club, the Eastern Retail Association, and the Drapers Reunion where Ann and her agent Sandy Stone perform their act. It is understandable that Morty Gunty as Sandy is a good standup, but Marlo Thomas's delivery of the comedic zingers is a delightful surprise. The scene where Donald plays Ann's part and heckles her from the audience is interesting for its nonfeminist psychology. It is seemingly all right for a woman to heckle a man, but not the reverse.

Notes

Co-creator and co-executive producer Sam Denoff appears in one of the nightclub scenes. Lew Gallo, associate producer, appears in another. We learn that Ann would rather be an actress than a comic, despite lucrative bookings. It is interesting to note that one of the telephone routines Sandy and Ann do resembles a classic Mike Nichols and Elaine May sketch of the period. Alan Oppenheimer also appears in episodes #85: "Bad Day at Marvin Gardens," #109: "Gone-A-Courtin'," and #117: "Rattle of a Single Girl."

Who Gets to Say "That Girl!"

Ann, herself, says it when trying to find a comedy partner for her agent. "How about *that girl?* This girl?"

EPISODE 102: OPENING NIGHT

ORIGINAL AIR DATE: JANUARY 8, 1970

Writer: Arnold Horwitt; Director: Russ Mayberry; Guest Cast: Lew Parker (Lou Marie), Bobo Lewis (Gloria), Gino Conforti (Nino), Sam Weston (Plumber), Evelyn King (Actress), Patty Regan (Phone Operator), Army Archerd (as Himself), Vernon Scott (as Himself), Joyce Haber (as Herself)

It is the day of Ann's opening night on Broadway and she is very nervous. Donald advises her to take a nap, but when she does she has nightmares of bad reviews. To add to her anxiety, her father arrives to keep her company. She sends both Don and Daddy away and tries to relax. Then she gets her finger stuck in the kitchen faucet. Luckily Don, Lou, and a plumber arrive in time to get Ann to her opening. After the show, she and Don await the reviews, which are worse than the ones in her dreams.

Highlights
The unquestioned apex is Ann trying to dial her telephone with her toe because her finger is stuck in the faucet.

Notes
This episode is reminiscent of the one (episode #28: "This Little Piggy Had a Ball") where Ann got her toe stuck in a bowling ball. However, this excursion is more imaginative directorially. The dream and fantasy sequences are very well executed. Army Archerd, Vernon Scott, and Joyce Haber appear as themselves in the critics' dream. Ann refers to this show, entitled *North of Larchmont,* as her first Broadway production. Since she did appear in *The Revolutionary Heart* with Barry Sullivan in episode # 61: "Sock It to Me," we assume she means this is her first show in which she is to originate a role (she was a replacement in the Barry Sullivan play).

Who Gets to Say "That Girl!"
Marlo Thomas as Ann says it as she is put on hold by her answering service: "Hold? *That girl?*"

EPISODE 103: THAT METER MAID
ORIGINAL AIR DATE: JANUARY 22, 1970
Writers: Jerry Ross and William Lynn; Director: Ted Bessell; Guest Cast: Lew Parker (Lou Marie), Dennis Weaver (Lewis Franks), Tol Avery (Mayor), Judson Pratt (Sergeant Melvin), Dennis Turner (Harvey Murchison), Claudia Gryar (Mona), Fritzi Burr (Laura, the Maries' maid), Billy Beck (Diggs), Diana Hale (Millie)

When Ann meets Donald's new editor, Lewis Franks, she recalls knowing him back in the summer of 1964 when she was a meter maid in her old hometown and had tried to ticket the mayor's illegally parked car. For this Ann was fired. Upholding her principles—that no one should have special privileges—she wrote a letter of protest to the publication, which they printed, leading the corrupt regime to put the newspaper out of business and forced her father to close his restaurant and move the family to a new town. Donald's new boss is the same newspaper editor who had printed Ann's letter of protest.

Highlights
The high point of this episode is the change in Ann's hairdo. Until the fifth season, this is the only time we see her looking different. This, of course, is because the episode is a flashback (although when we saw her as a teacher she had her usual hairdo!).

Notes
Ann explains very clearly that this incident did *not* take place in Brewster, New York, but in Fenwick, New York, the town in which the Marie family lived before moving to Brewster. This, of course, makes no sense in the context of all the other past episodes, which tell of Ann's childhood and youth in Brewster. As stated earlier, the fictional town of Fenwick was probably used because no one wanted to offend the real town of Brewster with charges of corruption. However, this change does play havoc with the sense of continuity on the series. This was the second entry directed by Ted Bessell, the first being episode #76: "Dark on Top of Everything Else."

Who Gets to Say "That Girl!"
Marlo Thomas as Ann tells Don that he "will be spending time having lunch with [she then reveals a stick-drawing of herself as a meter maid] *that girl!*"

EPISODE 104: FLY BY NIGHT (PART ONE)
ORIGINAL AIR DATE: JANUARY 29, 1970
Writers: Bernie Orenstein and Saul Turteltaub; Director: Saul Turteltaub; Guest Cast: Lew Parker (Lou Marie), Russell Johnson (Jon), Rosemary DeCamp (Helen Marie)

In this first section of a two-part installment (even though given different titles), Ann and Donald plan a trip to her father's cabin in Vermont. Don gets his friend Jon to fly them there in a small plane,

but the craft encounters a storm and has to make an emergency landing when it runs out of gas. The frightened Ann sees her life flash
before her eyes.

Highlights
The very real display of fear by Ann in the small plane brings a start-
ling reality to this episode.

Notes
Russell Johnson played the Professor on *Gilligan's Island* (1964–67).
Ann's extreme fear of flying is a new occurrence. It must have
stemmed from episode #83: "Fly Me to the Moon" when she was traveling all over the world in a fighter plane. Don's secretary is still Elaine.

Who Gets to Say "That Girl!"
Ann (almost) says it when Don wants her to fly to Vermont: "Not
this girl!"

EPISODE 105: UGH WILDERNESS
(PART TWO)
ORIGINAL AIR DATE: FEBRUARY 5, 1970
Writer: Joe Bonaduce; Director: John Rich; Guest Cast: Lew Parker (Lou
Marie), Russell Johnson (Jon), Hal Baylor (Cop #1), Douglas Mitchell (Cop
#2), Bruce Lorange (Bellhop)

After determining that Donald and Ann are okay following the rocky
emergency landing of the plane, Jon goes for help. Ann and Donald
start walking to keep warm. Ann's father gets nervous when they
don't arrive on time and calls out a search party. Don and Ann spend
the night (breaking up all the furniture for heat) in a cabin that turns
out to be right next door to the one they were supposed to stay at.

Highlights
The sweetness between Ann and Donald, when they think that they
are stranded for the night in the middle of nowhere, is a beautiful
moment.

Notes
The nice resolution, to what was potentially a hazardous situation,
provides a good opportunity for the lead characters of this series to
underline the romantic nature of their relationship.

Who Gets to Say "That Girl!"

Russell Johnson, as Jon, to Donald when the plane is about to go down and Ann seems to know it: "You'd be smarter to listen to *that girl!*"

EPISODE 106: STOCKS AND THE SINGLE GIRL
ORIGINAL AIR DATE: FEBRUARY 12, 1970
Writer: Bruce Howard; Director: Bill Persky; Guest Cast: Lew Parker (Lou Marie), Harry Townes (Arnold Lindsey), Jim Connell (Jonas), Pitt Herbert (Ben), William Lantaeu (Eddie), Lieux Dressler (Secretary)

When a wealthy stockbroker spills wine on Ann at a restaurant, he gives her his card and tells her to bill him. On the back of the card she finds a list written under the word "buy." Ann convinces Don and her father to buy the stocks that are listed. When the stocks turn out to be the items the broker was planning to buy at the supermarket, Ann is embarrassed. Luckily, though, the stocks go up in value.

Highlights
Again, the relief reflected on Lew Parker's face, when the stocks increase in value, is a preciously funny moment.

Notes
This is the only *That Girl* episode directed by co-creator and co-executive producer Bill Persky, who would go on to a notable directing career with *Kate & Allie* (1984–89). This segment is reminiscent of the *I Love Lucy* offering in which Ricky finds notes about buying things at the market and also mistakenly buys stocks. Jim Connell appeared in episode #37: "The Philadelphia Story" as Harvey Miller, the actor smitten with Ann.

Who Gets to Say "That Girl!"
Harry Townes as Arnold Lindsey, after he has spilled wine on Ann: "Everyone survived. Everyone but *that girl!*"

EPISODE 107: THE NIGHT THEY RAIDED DADDY'S
ORIGINAL AIR DATE: FEBRUARY 19, 1970
Writer: Coslough Johnson; Director: Hal Cooper; Guest Cast: Lew Parker (Lou Marie), Rosemary DeCamp (Helen Marie), Gene Baylos (Agent), Tom Pedi (Tony), Bill Quinn (Harry), Robert Gibbons (Reverend), Lennie Bremen

(Sheriff), Rayburn Wallace (Blue Boy #1), Jeff Brock (Blue Boy #2), Joe Duckett (Blue Boy #3)

Ann's father is depressed because business is bad at the restaurant. When Ann visits a competing eatery and notices that the rock music is drawing the crowds, she convinces her father that the way to fill his restaurant is to have a rock group perform. After auditions, Lou Marie selects a clean-cut pop group, the Little Blue Boys. But when they perform for the first time, their finale is very revealing: they take off all their clothes!

Highlights
The scene where Ann and Lou are backstage at the restaurant, working the lights and watching the band strip, is very funny. Also amusing is the band that Lou employs before and after the Blue Boys—the Thorndyke Sisters, Ada and Maud, two little old ladies who play the accordion and the sax.

Notes
This is the last appearance of Rosemary DeCamp as Helen Marie. She will be spoken of, but not seen again. Lou and Don's relationship takes a step forward in this episode when Lou admits to liking Don. Marlo Thomas makes a very rare mistake (one wonders why they didn't do a retake on this) when she erroneously calls her dad Mr. Hollinger. She corrects herself and goes on with the introduction for the band, but it is her only obvious onscreen flub of the entire series.

Who Gets to Say "That Girl!"
Lew Parker as Lou Marie is in a very bad mood and doesn't like Ann telling him about the weather. "Who needs Walter Cronkite when we've got *that girl!*"

EPISODE 108: THE REUNION
ORIGINAL AIR DATE: FEBRUARY 26, 1970
Writers: Saul Turteltaub and Bernie Orenstein; Director: Richard Kinon; Guest Cast: Lew Parker (Lou Marie), Iggy Wolfington (Mr. Jensen), Eldon Quick (Melvin), Florence Mercer (Estelle), Oaky Miller (Mike), Anita Alberts (Rusty), Harry Page (Mark), Sandy Brown Wyeth (Joannie), Gene Sheriff (Flip)

It is time for Ann's high school reunion and she is asked to choose the restaurant for the bash. After determining that her father's restaurant is too expensive, Ann books Mr. Jensen's rival diner. However, when the matter of the money to pay for it arises, Ann cannot remember what she did with the $360 she was entrusted with all those years ago. Although Ann suspects three of her classmates of financial hanky-panky, it turns out that it was one of them who had actually been holding the money all along.

Highlights
The scene between Ann and her father in which she must tell him that she has chosen another restaurant for her reunion party is well done and loaded with laughs.

Notes
Interestingly, most of the other former students look older than Ann does.

Who Gets to Say "That Girl!"
Marlo Thomas as Ann points out her picture in the high school yearbook to Don, "Not that girl, *that girl!*"

EPISODE 109: GONE-A-COURTIN'
ORIGINAL AIR DATE: MARCH 5, 1970
Writer: Joe Bonaduce; Director: Russ Mayberry; Guest Cast: Frank Maxwell (Samuels), Alan Oppenheimer (Jerome), Allen Davis (Vernon), William Lally (Judge), Dee Carroll (Lydia), Ellen Clark (Actress), Hal Williams (Court Clerk), Harvey J. Goldenberg (Jones), Sam Denoff (Man #1), Lew Gallo (Man #2)

Ann auditions for a Broadway role, but the producer, Samuels, hires her for a role in court. He is being sued for a shish kebab skewer accident in a restaurant and anticipates that the clumsy Ann's engineered appearance in the courtroom will so unnerve the plaintiff that he will win the case.

Highlights
Ann's performance in court as "the phantom klutz" is the highlight of the show.

Notes
Another appearance for Sam Denoff, co-creator and co-executive producer of the series, and associate producer Lew Gallo. We see Ann at the top of the show in one of her survival jobs, this time as a hatcheck girl. Ann still refers to Seymour as her agent in this episode.

Who Gets to Say "That Girl!"
Ted Bessell as Donald does a play on words when he takes over Ann's hatcheck job so she can pursue her acting assignment: "You want the *hat girl!*"

EPISODE 110: THEY SHOOT PICTURES, DON'T THEY?
ORIGINAL AIR DATE: MARCH 12, 1970
Writers: Saul Turteltaub and Bernie Orenstein; Director: Russ Mayberry; Guest Cast: Bernie Kopell (Jerry Bauman), Alice Borden (Ruth Bauman), Bobo Lewis (Gloria)

After seeing a small independent film, Jerry, Don, and Ann decide to make their own movie. Don brings home a camera to test and he shoots Ann washing her windows. But when the film is developed, Ann sees Ruth Bauman kissing another man across the court. Just as Ann jumps to conclusions and thinks that Ruthie is having an affair, Ruth tells her husband, Jerry, she is pregnant. She also tells him that she has found the perfect new apartment for them across the court, which explains why she was gratefully kissing the realtor!

Highlights
The very touching moment when Ruth tells Jerry she is going to have a baby is the best moment of Alice Borden's portrayal in the series.

Notes
On this episode Jerry has sideburns and a mustache. He loses them next season. Alice Borden was, coincidentally, also pregnant at this time. Borden spoke about it at the 1996 *That Girl* seminar at the Museum of Television and Radio: "My favorite episode is when I got pregnant. I was afraid to tell Saul [Turteltaub] and Bernie [Orenstein] because they wouldn't let me come out [from the East Coast] and do more shows if I was out to here. And they called and said, 'You're

coming out to do a show.' I said, 'Great, what is it?' They said, 'Well, you're going to be pregnant.' I also remember when Claudia was born in New York I got a bunch of daisies from Daisy Productions. I'll never forget it, from Marlo. This big! I had never seen anything quite like it. But there it was, greeting my daughter." This is also Kopell's favorite *That Girl* episode.

Who Gets to Say "That Girl!"

Marlo Thomas as Ann says it this time: "Sure, let the girl make costumes and sandwiches, but when it comes to ten million dollars, whatever happened to *that girl?*"

The *That Girl* Game

"Thrill to the glamour and excitement of Broadway's bright lights. Experience with *That Girl* the heartbreak, disappointment, hard work and setbacks of a star-struck girl in the big city!"

In 1968, Remco Toys licensed the title, logo, and image of Marlo Thomas as Ann Marie and created a *That Girl* board game. The inside of the box makes the proclamation above and apparently not many children played the game at the time, as collectors agree that it is one of the most difficult-to-find board games ever made. Two to four people can play, and the object of the game is to "become a star." Each player gets a game piece (which is designed to look like the logo of the television show) and a hundred dollars. The players then roll the die (there is only one) and move their little Ann Maries around the board. They are given the opportunity to select a card from the Work Card pile, which pays a player money for a job well done, or from the stack of cards that cost the player money—for example, "pay union dues," "rent a TV," "get a massage," "take girlfriend to lunch," "pay for dinner with Don," "subscribe to *Variety*," and so forth. Only when a player obtains all five segments of a cardboard star (which can be bought when landing on the proper spaces) will that player be "a star" and win the game.

EPISODE 111: EASY FALLER

ORIGINAL AIR DATE: MARCH 19, 1970

Writers: Saul Turteltaub and Bernie Orenstein; Director: John Rich; Guest Cast: Lew Parker (Lou Marie), Warren Berlinger (Dr. Goldfisher), Bobo Lewis (Gloria), Albert Carrier (Jean Paul LeMairre)

While demonstrating in Ann's apartment how safe skiing can be, Donald hurts his back. A doctor orders Donald to stay put overnight, but Donald is nervous about missing an important interview. Ann solves the problem by having the interviewee come to her apartment. Of course, her father arrives to complicate matters.

Highlights

As always, Lew Parker as Lou Marie provides the show with its comic highlights. Why this actor was never nominated for an Emmy is a mystery!

Notes

This entry's premise is similar to one later used by Neil Simon as one of the playlets in his Broadway comedy *California Suite* (1976). We find out that Don has great trouble swallowing pills and that Ann was fourth in her high school shorthand class, which is odd since she couldn't take shorthand at all in episode #24: "A Tenor's Loving Care."

Who Gets to Say "That Girl!"

Ann has been imagining Donald and another woman skiing in Stowe, Vermont. When Don tells her that it's starting to snow in Vermont, Marlo Thomas as Ann says, "Fine, for you . . . and *that girl!*"

EPISODE 112: ALL'S WELL THAT ENDS

ORIGINAL AIR DATE: MARCH 26, 1970

Writer: Sydney Zelinka; Director: Saul Turteltaub; Guest Cast: Mary Robin Redd (Janie), Colin Male (Doctor), Vernon Weddle (Murray)

Don wants to surprise Ann with theater tickets on her birthday, but Ann, thinking they have no place to go, decides to babysit for her neighbor to allow the couple some much needed rest. Don and Ann stay home with the infant. Ann convinces herself that her charge has the mumps, and what's scary is that Ann hasn't had them. The doctor arrives and allays her fears.

Highlights

This episode gives us a glimpse of Ann's maternal side. It is very sweet to see.

Notes

Janie and Harry are Ann's new friends and neighbors, but they never show up again. Don, too, has a new co-worker and friend at the office, Murray. Bet that Bernie Kopell was filming a *Get Smart* episode that week and couldn't do his ongoing role for *That Girl*. The play that Ann and Don don't get to see is called *Among the Living*.

Who Gets to Say "That Girl!"

Vernon Weddle as Don's new friend, Murray, asks Don, who is fooling Ann about the tickets, "What are you doing to *that girl?*"

Nominations, Awards, and Honors for Season Four

Marlo Thomas received an Emmy nomination for Outstanding Continued Performance by an Actress in a Leading Role in a Comedy for Season #4. She lost to Hope Lange of *The Ghost and Mrs. Muir.*

SEASON FIVE
SEPTEMBER 1970–MARCH 1971

Season Five Overview

The big surprise of the fifth and last season of *That Girl* is the plotline engagement of Ann Marie to Donald Hollinger. After knowing her for years, Don finally pops the question and Ann accepts. The engagement opens up new story premises. They deal with Don giving Ann a ring, Ann losing the ring in a cake she bakes, the couple looking for an apartment, the duo seeing a pre-marital counselor, Ann going to St. Louis to meet Don's entire family, Don getting cold feet and calling the whole thing off (for a day), Ann's bridal shower, and Don's stag party. In fact, everything occurs but a wedding!

On the professional front, Ann appears in a play called *Queen of Diamonds* in St. Louis, plays "Miss Everything" at the "New York Has Everything" exhibit, quits a Broadway revue because of principles, almost gets to star in the movie version of *A Woman's Story*, plays the Friars Club with Milton Berle and Danny Thomas, and models at the race track.

At the end of the season—also the finale of the series—Don and Ann are still engaged and the fate of their relationship is left to the viewers' imagination.

Production Team for Season Five

Executive Producers and Series Creators: Bill Persky and Sam Denoff; Producers and Story Consultants: Saul Turteltaub and Bernie Orenstein; Associate Producer: Lew Gallo; Director of Photography: Leonard J. South, A.S.C.; Art Director: Peter Wooley; Film Editor: Homer Powell; Music: Earle Hagen with theme by Earle Hagen and Sam Denoff; Miss Thomas's wardrobe by Cardinelli, Inc; Hair: Lynn Masters; Makeup: Tom Case; Casting: Fred Roos; Set Decorator: John D. W. Lamphear; Production Manager: John Banse; Assistant Director: Roger Duchowny; Origination: Filmed at Cinema General Studios and on location in New York City and elsewhere by Daisy Productions; Sponsors: Bristol-Myers Company, Noxell Corporation, and Lever Brothers

EPISODE 113: COUNTER-PROPOSAL
ORIGINAL AIR DATE: SEPTEMBER 25, 1970
Writers: Saul Turteltaub and Bernie Orenstein; Director: Saul Turteltaub; Guest Cast: Ronnie Schell (Bob Howard), Avery Schreiber (Mr. Franklin), Martin Walker (Mr. Steinmetz), Sandy de Bruin (Joan), Reva Rose (Marcy)

After four years of dating, Donald finally asks Ann to marry him and presents her with an engagement ring he has bought from Bob, a coworker. Ann is ecstatic until Bob asks Ann to return the ring. She goes out and buys a new one with the money Bob gives her so that Don won't know the difference. Meanwhile, Don feels guilty for giving her a used ring, and he buys a new one too.

Highlights

The ultimate highlight is the very romantic moment when Don proposes to Ann. Viewers had been waiting for this for a long time. Marlo Thomas's on-camera reaction as Ann is sensational.

Notes

The (used) ring that Don gives Ann has a round diamond, a carat and a half, with four baguettes, and a platinum band. It cost $1,400 retail, but only $950 from Bob. Avery Schreiber appeared in episodes #87 and #88: "Mission Improbable, Parts One and Two," as Al Taylor. Ronnie Schell had been in the first few episodes of *That Girl* as Harvey Peck, Ann's first agent (not counting Don Blue Sky). Although she is billed, Reva Rose (as Marcy) never appears in the final print of the episode. If she had, we might have found out more about this elusive story-line character. As it stands, Marcy is just another next-door neighbor/friend for Ann. This is the first time we see Ann/Marlo's new hairdo, minus the flip and the bangs. And it is the first time we hear the lyrics to the series' established theme song.

Who Gets to Say "That Girl!"

Ted Bessell as Don doesn't quite say it in the story line. What he actually says is that Ann is *"this girl."*

EPISODE 114: DONALD, SANDI AND HARRY AND SNOOPY

Original air date: October 2, 1970

Writer: Peggy Elliot; Director: Earl Bellamy; Guest Cast: Cloris Leachman (Sandi Hollinger), Mark Roberts (Harry), Dave Ketchum (Man in Restaurant), Bob Ross (Waiter)

Donald's sister, Sandi, comes to town to see an actor with whom she is having a serious relationship. Donald enlists Ann's help and asks her to play master spy and check out her fellow actor. After Ann meets him, she is shocked when he makes a play for her. All ends well when he admits that he knew what she was up to and was just teaching her a lesson.

Highlights

Cloris Leachman's underplayed performance as Donald's sister gives an interesting contrast to her neurotic, slightly over-the-top Phyllis Lindstrom on *The Mary Tyler Moore Show* (1970–75).

Notes
Cloris Leachman was appearing simultaneously as Phyllis Lindstrom on *The Mary Tyler Moore Show*. We wonder whatever happened to the brother whom Don mentioned years ago. And we never get to see Hollinger's sister again.

Who Gets to Say "That Girl!"
Marlo Thomas as Ann gets to say it, to a picture of herself, in response to Don's question about who would want a bigoted reporter. She answers, "Not *that girl* . . ."

EPISODE 115: I AIN'T GOT NOBODY
ORIGINAL AIR DATE: OCTOBER 9, 1970
Writers: Ed Scharlach and Warren S. Murray; Director: Richard Kinon; Guest Cast: Lew Parker (Lou Marie), Kenneth Mars (Captain Gooney), Bernie Kopell (Jerry Bauman), Hal Peary (Harvey), Eddie Ryder (Mr. Sadler), Sam Carlson (Model), Bob Ross (Bob, the waiter)

While looking at *Playpen* magazine, Jerry, Donald, and Mr. Marie discover that Ann is the centerfold of the month, much to everyone's surprise—including Ann's. She is pictured wearing nothing more than a staple. Of course, it is a composite picture, with Ann's head placed on another girl's body, but it causes nothing but trouble when she is just about to get a role on a children's TV show.

Highlights
Kenneth Mars is very funny as a children's TV star, Captain Gooney, getting excited over Ann and her nude picture.

Notes
This installment depicts some of the hazards of a life devoted to show business.

Who Gets to Say "That Girl!"
Bernie Kopell as Jerry Bauman shows Don the nude picture of Ann and asks, "Isn't Ann *that girl?*"

EPISODE 116: NO MAN IS A MANHATTAN ISLAND

ORIGINAL AIR DATE: OCTOBER 16, 1970

Writer: Arnold Horwitt; Director: Richard Kinon; Guest Cast: Bernie Kopell (Jerry Bauman), Jerry Fogel (Mr. Hale), William Bakewell (Mr. MacIntosh), Ric Roman (Ferrone), Erin O'Reilly (Jill Johnson), Don Eitner (Cop), Charles Lampkin (Mr. Hansen), Amzie Strickland (Mrs. Tanzy), Alex Rocco (Biff)

Ann appears on a TV game show called *Get Rich Quick*. When she is asked back she is told that she needs to know more about her neighbors. She has one week to learn all she can about them before going back on the air. She uses all her wiles to get her reluctant neighbors to open up, including having a fake birthday party—at which her purse is stolen. After thinking it was one of her guests, she is informed by the police that there is a cat burglar in the area. When she goes on the show with all her newfound knowledge, she is asked about her neighbors . . . in Brewster!

Highlights

Ann's sneaky ways of getting her neighbors together is the key entertainment element of the installment.

Notes

It is interesting that, in multicultural Manhattan, only now does Ann finally have African American neighbors (there was once an attempt to do a whole show about the subject). Jerry Fogel also appears in episode #133: "Stag Party."

Who Gets to Say "That Girl!"

Jerry Fogel as the game show host, as he coaxes the audience to applaud for the winner. "Let's hear it for this good neighbor and *that girl!*"

EPISODE 117: RATTLE OF A SINGLE GIRL

ORIGINAL AIR DATE: OCTOBER 23, 1970

Writer: Bruce Howard; Director: John Rich; Guest Cast: Lew Parker (Lou Marie), Alan Oppenheimer (Dr. Globe), Reva Rose (Marcy), Dick Van Patten (Mr. Morse), Bob Ross (Waiter), Harry Basch (Man in Elevator), Sam Denoff (Man in Booth)

Ann's married friend Marcy convinces her to go to a pre-marital counselor with Don to ensure a happy marriage. At the consultation, neither Ann nor Don have complaints to register, but afterwards the fur flies. This is exactly what the counselor wants to happen. He thinks that now that they have opened up they will indeed have a good union.

Highlights
Dick Van Patten as Mr. Morse, the landlord looking to rent to the future Hollingers, gives a wonderful comic performance.

Notes
Note unbilled appearance of co-executive producer and co-creator Sam Denoff in the scene in the shoemaker's shop. Although Reva Rose was billed in episode #113: "Counter-Proposal," this is her first actual appearance on the series. She was apparently hired to fill the vacancy left by the pregnant Alice Borden as Ruth Bauman.

Who Gets to Say "That Girl!"
Reva Rose as Marcy, to the waiter who is bringing a martini: "You'd better give it to *that girl!*"

EPISODE 118: THERE SURE ARE A BUNCH OF CARDS IN ST. LOUIS (PART ONE)
ORIGINAL AIR DATE: OCTOBER 30, 1970
Writers: Saul Turteltaub and Bernie Orenstein; Director: Richard Kinon; Guest Cast: Mabel Albertson (Mildred Hollinger), Frank Faylen (Bert Hollinger), Jim Dixon (Herb), Art Metrano (Dave), Jack Frey (Cabbie), Catherine McKeown (Janet), Fran Ryan (Mrs. Booth), William Christopher (Chippy), Susan Quick (Heather), Lindsey Workman (Man), Gail Bonney (Lady), Elizabeth Harrower (Mrs. Parker), John Hubbard (Passenger)

Traveling to St. Louis with a two-fold purpose—to appear in a play and to meet Donald's family and friends—Ann is very nervous about passing inspection. When she arrives, Mrs. Hollinger is her usual cold self and Mr. Hollinger is warm as can be. Ann gets jealous when one of Don's old flames comes to a party in Ann's honor.

Highlights

Don's parents are marvelous. Mabel Albertson is her acerbic self and the addition of Frank Faylen as Don's father is inspired. He is warm and funny, and we can glimpse what Don might be like in later life.

Notes

It's nice to see Don's old friend Chippy and his wife, Heather, again. They appeared in episode #100: "I Am a Curious Lemon." One wonders where Don's sister, Sandi, is (not to mention his once-referenced brother) and his best friend, Harry Banner (not seen since episode #35: "The Apartment"). However, it is wonderful to see his mother again. His father is now played by Frank Faylen, best known as the father on *The Many Lives of Dobie Gillis* (1959–63). (Marlo Thomas once guest-starred on this sitcom.) Mr. Hollinger senior is called Bert on this episode. In the past he was called Harold or Ed. Mrs. Hollinger seems to fluctuate between being Lillian and Mildred. The show that Ann is going to do in St. Louis is titled *The Queen of Diamonds* and she is to play Megan, the queen's sister.

Who Gets to Say "That Girl!"

When Don tells her that she is warm, sensual, and beautiful, Marlo Thomas as Ann asks, "Oh, Donald, am I *that girl?*"

EPISODE 119: THERE SURE ARE A BUNCH OF CARDS IN ST. LOUIS (PART TWO)

ORIGINAL AIR DATE: NOVEMBER 6, 1970

Writers: Saul Turteltaub and Bernie Orenstein; Director: Richard Kinon; Guest Cast: Mabel Albertson (Lillian Hollinger), Frank Faylen (Bert Hollinger), Ruth McDevitt (Aunt Belle), Stan Musial (as Himself), Dave Willock (Director), Richard Schaal (Bill), Richard Libertini (John), Ann Johnson (Hostess), Lee Amber (Customer), Penny Kenard (Hostess), Shari Sommers (Jeannie)

In St. Louis to appear on stage and visit with Donald's parents, Ann finds it difficult to get close to Mrs. Hollinger. After turning down the lead in the play, Ann meets baseball great Stan Musial and sees that everyone loves a star. So she takes on the role, but risks missing an important dinner party with Don's snooty Aunt Belle. Ann once again changes her mind, shows up at the dinner, and wins Aunt Belle over to her side, making Don's mother realize how charming Ann really is.

Highlights
The highlight is the scene with Ruth McDevitt as Aunt Belle condescendingly looking over her lorgnette at Ann, and Ann's reversal of the delicate situation.

Notes
Baseball great Stan Musial has a brief cameo. As an ABC press release offered, this was his "television (not World) series debut." His St. Louis restaurant, *Stan Musial's and Biggies*, was recreated on the set from color photos. Musial was quoted as saying that "doing this show is fun and it's great for the restaurant." Marlo said that he was "a darling man and I loved working with him." In this episode we find out that Don can make the tough Mrs. Hollinger weep nostalgically at just the mention of his second-grade play.

Who Gets to Say "That Girl!"
Mabel Albertson, in her last appearance as Mrs. Hollinger, gets to utter the famous words.

EPISODE 120: THAT CAKE
ORIGINAL AIR DATE: NOVEMBER 13, 1970
Writer: Rick Mittleman; Director: Richard Kinon; Guest Cast: Lew Parker (Lou Marie), Regis Philbin (Ron Riser, the producer), Woodrow Parfrey (Magleson), Reva Rose (Marcy), Eric Brotherson (Lazlo), Sheila Rogers (Mrs. Kling), Bob Ross (Tommy, the waiter), Harvey J. Goldenberg (Assistant), Lew Gallo (Commentator)

Ann loses her engagement ring while appearing as "Miss Everything" at the "New York Has Everything" convention at the New York Coliseum. She is frantic, until she realizes that she may have baked it into the cake that will be served to the governor for dessert. She and Don go through the pastry before it is served, but do not find it. She finally realizes that the cake she baked is not the one being served to the governor, and she is able to retrieve the ring.

Highlights

Ann and Don's disruption of the governor's kitchen is definitely the high point.

Notes

Regis Philbin, of course, went on to greater glory as half of TV's famed syndicated talk show in the 1990s, *Regis and Kathie Lee.* Eric Brotherson was well known on Broadway in such musicals as *Gentlemen Prefer Blondes* (1949). When Ann watches herself on TV, we discover that she has a black-and-white television. New York's governor, Nelson Rockefeller, was sought to appear on this episode but, unfortunately, turned down the offer to make his TV acting debut. Don does an imitation of him instead at the end of the show.

Who Gets to Say "That Girl!"

Woodrow Parfrey as the querulous Magleson says, "Who is *that girl?*"

EPISODE 121: THAT GIRL'S DADDY
ORIGINAL AIR DATE: NOVEMBER 20, 1970
Writers: Saul Turteltaub and Bernie Orenstein; Director: John Rich; Guest Cast: Lew Parker (Lou Marie), Ralph Williams (Charlie), Corine Conley (Jeanie), Betty Kean (Mrs. McCarty, a nosy neighbor), Lew Gallo (Policeman #1), Harrison Page (Policeman #2), Don Eitner (Poker Player #1), Bernie Orenstein (Poker Player #2)

When Helen Marie goes to visit her mother, Ann asks her father, Lou, to stay with her. Lou is feeling old, so Don makes a point of including him in his poker game. When Ann brings home an older acquaintance, Jeanie, it seems as if Lou gets younger. He and Jean flirt and soon have a date for the next night. When Lou shows up the next day with his hair dyed, Ann fears the worst, but it turns out that he is interested only in his wife and thinks that coloring his hair will please Helen.

Highlights

The sight of Lou Marie with dyed hair, for what Ann assumes to be all the wrong reasons, is hilarious.

Notes

Producer Bernie Orenstein is seen as one of the poker players. Betty Kean, who appears as a neighbor, was the real-life wife of Lew

Parker, and famous as one of the Kean Sisters (her sister Jane appeared as Trixie on the 1960s *The Honeymooners* segments of *The Jackie Gleason Show*). We find out that Lou Marie is fifty years old.

Who Gets to Say "That Girl!"
Lew Parker as Lou Marie describing his daughter: "She's a little spoiled, pretty as her mother, prettier than her father, and the spittin' image of *that girl!*"

EPISODE 122: STOP THE PRESSES, I WANT TO GET OFF
ORIGINAL AIR DATE: NOVEMBER 27, 1970
Writer: Gordon Farr; Director: Saul Turteltaub; Guest Cast: Bernie Kopell (Jerry Bauman), James Gregory (Mr. Adams), John Aniston (Harvey), Bill Mullikin (George), Michael Stanwood (Pennet), Army Archerd (Reporter #1), Jim Bacon (Reporter #2)

Ann may be hired to be a model for Girl Friday Publications, but when they realize that she is engaged to Don Hollinger they hire her to write stories, knowing that Don will help her. Don ghostwrites several stories for Ann until his boss, Mr. Adams, recognizes Don's style in a rival magazine and orders him to stop assisting Ann. Without Don's aid, Ann, who is no writer, becomes of no use to the publishers.

Highlights
The sly ways in which Don helps Ann rewrite the stories that she supposedly pens shows us just how loving he is.

Notes
This is the first appearance of James Gregory as Mr. Adams, Don's boss. The role was played before by Forrest Compton in episode #94: "Write Is Wrong." John Aniston had been with Marlo Thomas in *Sunday in New York* (1963) and went on to become a soap opera regular. He is the father of actress Jennifer Aniston.

Who Gets to Say "That Girl!"
John Aniston as Harvey, the publisher, as he proclaims Ann his "new star reporter . . . *that girl!*"

Marlo Thomas
Filmography

The Knack and How to Get It (1965) (Uncredited)
That Girl (1966-71) [TV Series]
Jenny (1969)
"That Girl" in Wonderland (1973) [Animated TV Special]
Thieves (1977)
It Happened One Christmas (1977) [TV Film]
The Lost Honor of Kathryn Beck (1984) [TV Film]
Consenting Adult (1985) [TV Film]
Nobody's Child (1986) [TV Film] (Emmy Award as Best Actress)
In the Spirit (1990)
Held Hostage: The Sis and Jerry Levin Story (1991) [TV Film]
Ultimate Betrayal (1994) [TV Film]
A Century of Women (1994) [Miniseries]
Reunion (1994) [TV Film]
The Real Blonde (1997)
Starfucker (1998)
Two Goldsteins on Acid (Forthcoming)

EPISODE 123: SUPER REPORTER
ORIGINAL AIR DATE: DECEMBER 4, 1970
Writers: Saul Turteltaub and Bernie Orenstein; Director: Richard Kinon; Guest Cast: Bernie Kopell (Jerry Bauman), James Gregory (Mr. Adams), Barbara Minkus (Elaine), Roy Roberts (Deputy Mayor), Fred Holliday (Charlie), Brad Trumbull (Cop), Jimmy Cross (Guy), Robert Rothwell (Commentator), Arline Anderson (Secretary), Florence Mercer (Person)

Don is to be presented with the Humanitarian Award for Writing from the deputy mayor of New York City, and Ann and his colleagues give him a gag gift: a "Super-Don" costume that Ann has been sewing for weeks. What Ann doesn't know is that the guys plan to play a practical joke on Don and steal his clothes for a few hours, forcing him to remain in costume. The prank goes awry when someone forgets to give Don back his clothes and he must rush to appear on television to accept his award. Meanwhile, he has written a speech for his boss, Mr. Adams, to deliver on the air that criticizes the deputy mayor.

Highlights
The best sequence of this installment comes early, when Ann hides a man from Don in her living room closet. He is one of Don's coworkers, who has been innocently coming over to her apartment daily to model the Super-Don costume, but Ann's actions make the scene hilarious. Classic Ann line: "I love secrets. They give me something to talk about."

Notes
Don still has Elaine as his secretary, but the role is now played by Barbara Minkus. This episode was inspired by a real-life occurrence. According to the May 26, 1970, issue of the *Hollywood Reporter*, Marlo Thomas gave producer/writer/director Saul Turteltaub a Superman suit and then proceeded to hide his clothes, which meant he had to go to an important meeting dressed in the costume. He and Bernie Orenstein obviously thought this was a funny enough premise upon which to base this entry.

Who Gets to Say "That Girl!"
Marlo Thomas, as Ann, says it while trying to hide the Super-Don costume model in her closet. A flustered Ann grabs Don's coat from him and quickly throws it into the closet, telling him that "every man wants a girl who will do everything for him, and for you I want to be *that girl!*"

EPISODE 124: THAT SENORITA
ORIGINAL AIR DATE: DECEMBER 11, 1970
Writers: Saul Turteltaub and Bernie Orenstein; Director: John Rich; Guest Cast: Alejandro Rey (Felix), Bernie Kopell (Jerry Bauman), Alice Borden (Ruth Bauman), Rodolfo Hoyos Jr. (Felix), Forest Compton (Producer), Dick Yarmy (Director), Sarah B. Fankboner (Miss Barnett, the auditioning actress), Pepe Callahan (Raoul), Army Archerd (Forbes, the TV reviewer)

Ann gets a part in a Broadway revue in which she has to do a sketch with a fake Hispanic accent. She doesn't seem to mind, until the other actor in the routine and his friends convince her that it is offensive to Mexicans and Mexican Americans. The two actors quit the show, forcing the producer to drop the sketch, and he brings them up on charges at Actors Equity, their union. Fortunately, the show gets good reviews and Ann and her fellow actor get paid off so that the producers can take the credit for dropping the offensive sketch.

Highlights
The comic highlight is Jerry Bauman entering Ann's apartment dressed as a comic Mexican doing a hat dance during the serious discussion about offensive accents. Very funny, and very humiliating for Ann, who walks into the closet and closes the door behind her.

Notes
Alejandro Rey was one of the stars of TV's *The Flying Nun* (1967–70). He also appeared in episode #30: "The Mating Game" as Ann's date for the evening. We are told that Ann's residential address in New York is 627 East 54th Street. This location would place her in the East River. This episode derived from real life when actor Ricardo Montalban gave a pro-Mexican, anti-poor-taste talk at the Writers Guild.

Who Gets to Say "That Girl!"
Alejandro Rey watches Ann audition for the part and tells his friends, "This sketch will never be performed by *that girl!*"

EPISODE 125: AN UNCLE HERBERT FOR ALL SEASONS
ORIGINAL AIR DATE : DECEMBER 18, 1970
Writer: Bob Garland; Director John Rich; Guest Cast: Lew Parker (Lou Marie), Joe Flynn (Uncle Herbert), James Gregory (Mr. Adams), Ed Peck (Official #1), Joe Mell (Official #2), Gloria Hill (Girl), Tipp McClure (Lars)

A telegram alerts Ann that her eccentric and flamboyant Uncle Herbert is coming for a visit from Iceland. When he arrives without any money and hasn't even paid for his ticket, there is every indication that Lou Marie is right about his brother and that he is a con man. However, when Herbert's new tuna company proves to be legitimate, everyone—except Ann and Don's boss—must admit they had been wrong in their judgment of Ann's uncle.

Highlights
Joe Flynn's performance as Ann's uncle is masterful, very funny, and ultimately endearing. We can appreciate why Ann has always loved him.

Notes
Joe Flynn was famous for his role as Captain Binghamton ("Old Lead-Bottom") on TV's *McHale's Navy* (1962–66). We find out that Ann was called "Lollipop" as a child and that she had tap danced and played the violin as a youngster.

Who Gets to Say "That Girl!"
Ted Bessell as Don. After Ann says that she was bright and talented and beautiful in high school, Don says, "My luck! I never got to meet *that girl!*"

EPISODE 126: THAT SCRIPT
ORIGINAL AIR DATE: JANUARY 1, 1971
Writers: Saul Turteltaub and Bernie Orenstein; Director: Roger Duchowny; Guest Cast: William Windom (Joseph Nelson), Nina Foch (Frances Nelson), Morty Gunty (Sandy Stone), Bob Ross (Waiter)

Ann wants to buy the film rights to her favorite novel, *A Woman's Story* by Joseph Nelson. Her agent, Sandy, tries to obtain them for her but the author will not sell at any price. Ann and Don trick their way into Nelson's country house and meet the author. When Nelson looks at Ann he sees the image of his dead wife on whom he based the novel and changes his mind. He resolves to write the screenplay himself, in which Ann will star. His new wife is concerned about this turn of events and explains to Ann that her husband can't really write anymore. To spare him the embarrassment, Ann turns down the movie.

Highlights
Nina Foch's moving performance as the author's second wife takes the show to a new level of drama. Very impressive.

Notes
Roger Duchowny, who had been the assistant director on *That Girl* for some time, finally gets to direct his own episode. He will direct two more installments, including the series' finale.

Who Gets to Say "That Girl!"

Ted Bessell as Don once again utters those famous words, in a moment of mixed exasperation and fondness about Ann Marie.

EPISODE 127: THOSE FRIARS

ORIGINAL AIR DATE: JANUARY 8, 1971

Writer: Marvin Walkenstein; Director: Allan Rafkin; Guest Cast: Lew Parker (Lou Marie), Milton Berle (as Himself), Danny Thomas (as Himself), Morty Gunty (Sandy), Alice Borden (Ruth Bauman), Fabian Dean (Moving Man)

Ann's late Uncle Harry Marie (a vaudevillian) wills her an old trunk that has been sitting in the basement of the Duke Hotel. Ann is thrilled to have some show business history. After her agent plants a story in *Variety* about the inheritance which paints Ann as a starving actress, she gets a visit from Milton Berle and Danny Thomas who try to buy the old trunk and its contents. It turns out that they are just trying to help the "starving actress" and that they were very fond of Harry Marie. Instead of giving her money, they star her in a Friars Club benefit and try to give her career a jump-start.

Highlights

The act that Ann, Milton Berle, and Danny Thomas perform at the Friars is wonderful. Ann is a great standup comic, as we have seen in other episodes, and even does a delightful song and dance to "Together Wherever We Go," from *Gypsy* (in which she "appeared" with Ethel Merman in episode #31: "Pass the Potatoes, Ethel Merman"), with her real-life father, Danny Thomas.

Notes

This was the only "billed" appearance on *That Girl* of Marlo Thomas's father, Danny Thomas, as himself. He appeared in episode #79: "My Sister's Keeper" in a cameo.

Who Gets to Say "That Girl!"

Fabian Dean as a moving man as he is lugging the vaudeville trunk to the basement: "I could be in Tahiti and I wouldn't be talking to *that girl!*"

EPISODE 128: A LIMITED ENGAGEMENT
Original air date: January 15, 1971
Writers: Saul Turteltaub and Bernie Orenstein; Director: Richard Kinon;
Guest Cast: Lew Parker (Lou Marie), Bernie Kopell (Jerry Bauman), Alice
Borden (Ruth Bauman), Buddy Lester (Man)

As Ann has her bridal shower at Ruthie's apartment, Donald gets cold
feet and realizes that he's not prepared for marriage. He and Ann
break their engagement. After a day of being unengaged, Don comes
to his senses and decides that, after all, he really does want Ann to
be his wife.

Highlights
As is often the case, the scenes between Ann and her father are
incredibly touching. Very few other sitcoms touched the heart as
much as this series constantly did. Despite all his yelling, Lou is the
most loving father a girl could wish for.

Notes
This is a very sad entry and has a feeling of reality about it that few
others do. The actors get to really experience their characters' feelings on this installment. Well done.

Who Gets to Say "That Girl!"
Ted Bessell as Donald says what is perhaps the most poignant version
of the line yet, to Jerry as Ann (unaware of Don's feelings) gathers her
gifts: "Jerry, I don't think I can marry *that girl.*"

EPISODE 129: THE RUSSIANS ARE STAYING
Original air date: January 29, 1971
Writers: Saul Turteltaub and Bernie Orenstein; Director: Homer Powell;
Guest Cast: Lew Parker (Lou Marie), Bob Dishy (Nicholai), Richard Erdman
(Milton), Gino Conforti (Nino), Jack DeLeon (Demitri), Paul Camen (Ivan)

Ann befriends a Russian comedian, Nicholai, who decides to defect
and hides in Ann's apartment. Ann and Don, and even Lou, are only
too happy to help him "become" an American. The only problem is
that he's a con man who's just using them to get free meals and
new clothes.

Highlights

The performance of Bob Dishy as Nicholai is warm, funny, and delightful. What a shame he is a fake and could not really defect and become a regular on *That Girl*, or have a spin-off.

Notes

Ann goes to a new acting teacher, named Milton. Mr. Benedict must have retired.

Who Gets to Say "That Girl!"

Jack DeLeon utters the words with an appropriate Russian accent: "Bad enough we have to watch him, now better keep an eye on *that girl!*"

EPISODE 130: THAT SHOPLIFTER

ORIGINAL AIR DATE: FEBRUARY 5, 1971

Writer: Arnold Horwitt; Director: Richard Kinon; Guest Cast: Jerry Hausner (Harrison, aka Baxter), Stafford Repp (Jim), Matt Reitz (Baxter), Bobo Lewis (Shopper), Judy Cassmore (Secretary), Pat Weidler (Clerk), George Ives (Dawson)

While working temporarily in a department store, Ann is conned into becoming a shoplifter. She thinks she is helping the store, when in reality she is the innocent dupe of a criminal.

Highlights

Ann's expert shoplifting makes the show entertaining.

Notes

Jerry Hausner is well known for his many appearances as Ricky Ricardo's agent (1951–54) on *I Love Lucy*. We see Ann in another of her survival jobs, this time as a sales announcer at Dawson's department store.

Who Gets to Say "That Girl!"

Jerry Hausner, looking Ann over: "If there was ever the perfect shoplifter, it's *that girl!*"

Marlo Thomas's Guest Appearances on TV Series

Dick Powell's Zane Grey Theater (1959) ["A Thread
   of Respect"]
The Many Loves of Dobie Gillis (1960) ["The Hunger Strike"]
77 Sunset Strip (1960) ["The Fanatics"]
Dick Powell's Zane Grey Theater (1961) ["Honor Bright"]
Thriller (1961) ["The Ordeal of Dr. Cordell"]
The Danny Thomas Show (1961) ["Everything Happens
   to Me"]
Insight (1963) ["The Sophomore"]
Arrest and Trial (1964) ["Tigers Are for Jungles"]
Bonanza (1964) ["A Pink Cloud Comes from Old Cathay"]
My Favorite Martian (1964) [Miss Jekyll and Hyde"]
Wendy and Me (1964) ["Wendy's Anniversary Fun?"]
McHale's Navy (1964) [The Missing Link"]
Valentine's Day (1965) ["Follow the Broken Pretzel"]
The Donna Reed Show (1965) ["Guests Guests, Who
   Needs Guests?"]
Ben Casey (1965) ["Three Li'l Lambs"]
The Practice (1976) ["Judy Sinclair"]
Friends (1994) ["On with the Wedding"]

EPISODE 131: CHEF'S NIGHT OUT

ORIGINAL AIR DATE: FEBRUARY 12, 1971
Writer: Bud Grossman; Director: Richard Kinon; Guest Cast: Tom D'Andrea
(Frankie), Jane Connell (Laura), Leon Belasco (Andre), Al Molinaro (Marv),
Louis de Farra (Pierre), Shirley O'Hara (Mrs. Sloan), Pat Marlow (Mrs.
Jones), Peter Bruni (Herman), Steve Benson (Chicken Boy), Tom Pace (Pizza
Boy), Albert Popwell (Morris)

Ann's parents go to Miami Beach for their first vacation in two years.
The minute they leave, the maitre d', and then the cook, at Mr. Marie's
restaurant come down with a virus. There is nothing for Ann and Don
to do but try to run the establishment until her father returns home.

After trying to rehire a former chef, they come up with the idea of sending out for food and having a very limited menu at the restaurant.

Highlights

Most amusing is when Don, who has never made a Caesar salad before, finds himself having to prepare one at a customer's table.

Notes

Jane Connell appears as Laura, the Maries' maid. When last we saw Laura, she was played by Fritzi Burr in a flashback (episode #103: "That Meter Maid"). In between, we saw Amanda Randolph as Harriet the domestic. She appeared only in episode #22: "Paper Hats and Everything." This Laura claims that she has been with the family for twenty years. Jane Connell was a familiar face from her appearances on *Bewitched* (1964–72) and her role as Agnes Gooch in the Broadway (1966) and film (1974) versions of *Mame*. Al Molinaro is better known for his roles in *The Odd Couple* (1970–75) and *Happy Days* (1974–84).

Who Gets to Say "That Girl!"

For a change of pace the title is not said, but a variation is uttered by Ted Bessell as Don when he is told he must run Lou's restaurant: "Not *this* man!"

EPISODE 132: THAT KING
ORIGINAL AIR DATE: FEBRUARY 19, 1971
Writer: Warren S. Murray; Director: Richard Kinon; Guest Cast: Bernie Kopell (Jerry Bauman), Alice Borden (Ruth Bauman), David Doyle (Albert Berg), Brook Fuller (The King), Herbie Faye (Morris Cohen, the Waiter), Tiger Joe Marsh (Bodyguard), Noel De Souza (Ambassador)

The U.S. State Department asks Ann to go on a date with the King of Kowali. Ann agrees, and when the U.S. government–owned jewels she is to wear arrive, she is even more excited. Imagine her surprise when the monarch turns out to be an eleven-year-old brat! Of course, in the end, Ann teaches him good manners.

Highlights

When Ann and the king stop off to get ice cream, he meets his match in the waiter, Morris Cohen, played by Herbie Faye.

Notes
The king has seen Ann in a commercial playing "Duchess Ducky of Diet Soda Land." Classic Ann line: "That darn women's lib! They got me drafted!" Ann would change her thinking very soon. David Doyle is fondly remembered from his years as Bosley on *Charlie's Angels* (1976–81).

Who Gets to Say "That Girl!"
David Doyle as Albert Berg says, "Uncle Sam wants *that girl!*"

EPISODE 133: STAG PARTY
ORIGINAL AIR DATE: FEBRUARY 26, 1971
Writers: Saul Turteltaub and Bernie Orenstein; Director: John Rich; Guest Cast: Lew Parker (Lou Marie), Bernie Kopell (Jerry Bauman), Alice Borden (Ruth Bauman), George Furth (Maury), Jerry Fogel (Frankie), Hal Williams (Herbie)

Donald's friends throw him a stag party, while Ann and Ruthie stay home. Lou Marie is invited, but as Don gets more and more intoxicated, Mr. Marie takes offense and leaves. Don has fantasies about his marriage, including one about his future daughter, named Lou. In the end, it turns out that Mr. Marie was in cahoots with Don's pals and he is the surprise guest who pops out of the cake.

Highlights
The moment when we discover that the anticipated sexy girl coming out of the cake is actually Lou Marie is very special. This is followed by a lovely drunken scene, in which Don tells Ann that she is his best friend. The fantasy sequences are cute too.

Notes
This is the last appearance of Lew Parker as Lou Marie on the series. He goes out in a burst of "glory" dressed as a woman. It is also the final appearances of Bernie Kopell and Alice Borden on *That Girl*.

Who Gets to Say "That Girl!"
Marlo Thomas as Ann is worried about a girl jumping out of a cake. She says she would feel more secure "if I were *that girl!*"

EPISODE 134: TWO FOR THE MONEY
ORIGINAL AIR DATE: MARCH 5, 1971
Writer: Sam Nicholas; Director: Roger Duchowny; Guest Cast: Bunny
Summers (Wardrobe Lady), Louis de Farra (Oscarelli), Joe Ross
(Photographer), Michael Lerner (Charley, the ticket seller), Dick Yarmy
(Cashier), Alex Rocco (Employee), Bernie Orenstein (Bettor), Sam Denoff
(Big Bettor), Hal Williams (John), Vince Eli (Ragged Man), Arthur Abelson
(Harry), Ron Applegate (Bill)

While Ann is modeling at Belmont Race Track, she places a bet for
Donald's friends. The horse wins, but Ann loses the ticket. She writes
them a postdated check to make up for it, but the guys want her to
let the money ($500) ride on another race. Ann and Don decide not
to gamble the money and hope that the horse loses. In the end, the
animal is disqualified and Ann finds the missing ticket.

Highlights
Ann's distress over losing the winning ticket is played brilliantly by
Thomas.

Notes
Both Bernie Orenstein (producer) and Sam Denoff (co-executive
producer and co-creator) play small roles. Louis de Farra was in
episode #131: "Chef's Night Out" as Pierre, the chef in Lou Marie's
restaurant. Hal Williams was at Don's bachelor party as Herbie in
episode #133: "Stag Party." He is now named John, but would later
become famous in *Private Benjamin* (1981–83) and *227* (1985–90).

Who Gets to Say "That Girl!"
Louis de Farra as designer Oscarelli, as Ann runs to place a bet: "Stop
that girl!"

EPISODE 135: SOOT YOURSELF
ORIGINAL AIR DATE: MARCH 12, 1971
Writers: Saul Turteltaub and Bernie Orenstein; Director: Saul Turteltaub;
Guest Cast: James Gregory (Mr. Adams), Gino Conforti (Nino), Phyllis Hill
(Agnes Adams), Reva Rose (Marcy), Peter Brocco (Mr. Stone)

As a member of an ecology-minded group, Ann is assigned to picket
in front of the *Newsview* magazine building where Donald works.

This proves to be very embarrassing when his boss recognizes her. To get *Newsview* removed from the picket list, Ann invites Don, his boss, and the boss's wife to a dinner to prove her point about pollution. In the end, they all agree and Don does a news story about the problem.

Highlights
The dinner party scene in which Ann proves her points about pollution to Don's boss is the highlight of this now-dated episode.

Notes
We find out that Ann's new landlord is named Mr. Dawson.

Who Gets to Say "That Girl!"
Marlo Thomas as Ann points to a picture of herself in a gas mask: "I'm telling you, Marcy, I'm *that girl!*"

EPISODE 136: THE ELEVATED WOMAN
ORIGINAL AIR DATE: MARCH 19, 1971
Writers: Saul Turteltaub and Bernie Orenstein; Director: Roger Duchowny; Guest Cast: Jack Kissel (Bellhop), Howard Storm (Elevator Operator), Tani Phelps (Audrey), Sherry Alberoni, John Cluet (Honeymoon Couple)

When Don writes an article on women's liberation, Ann finds it condescending and she requests that he accompany her to a meeting on the topic. Don, who has tickets to a hockey game, placates Ann by agreeing to go for a short while. On their way to the meeting, Ann and Donald become trapped in a broken elevator and, as they discuss men and women, we see flashbacks to many other episodes. In the end, the elevator starts moving again, but the meeting is now over. No other men showed up for the discussion.

Highlights
All the flashbacks are nostalgic and, although not a neat and clean way to end the series, it is a sweet reminder of the show's five seasons on the air.

Notes
This is the last filmed episode (containing flashbacks selected from the series) and leaves it up in the air as to whether Ann and Donald

might ever marry. According to Marlo Thomas, she did not want the traditional wedding episode that the ABC network and the sponsors craved because she did not wish to send the wrong message to young girls—that every happy ending must entail marriage. In fact, if the proposed reunion film had ever materialized (it was shelved when Ted Bessell died in 1996), it would have become clear that the two never did marry each other but went their separate ways. If the creators had had the courage to show that scenario in the final episode, it would have been a more poignant finale to a daring television series. The flashbacks used were from "A Muggy Day in Central Park" (episode #68), "Anatomy of a Blunder" (episode #5), "Author, Author" (episode #29), "This Little Piggy Had a Ball" (episode #28), "These Boots Weren't Made for Walking" (episode #18), "Gone with the Breeze" (episode #20), "You Have to Know Someone To Be an Unknown" (episode #26), "Little Auction Annie" (episode #8), and "Don't Just Do Something, Stand There" (episode #1).

Who Gets to Say "That Girl!"
The final "that girl" is uttered twice by Ted Bessell as Donald Hollinger, when he wonders if Ann is a liberated woman: "You're certainly not *that girl*. Are you *that girl?*" Marlo Thomas as Ann nods and agrees, she is indeed *that girl!*

Nominations, Awards, and Honors for Fifth Season

Marlo Thomas received an Emmy nomination for Outstanding Continued Performance by an Actress in a Leading Role in a Comedy for Season Five. The winner in this category was Jean Stapleton for *All in the Family.*

Ted Bessell (for the first time) received an Emmy nomination for Outstanding Continued Performance by an Actor in a Leading Role in a Comedy for Season Five. The winner in this category was Jack Klugman for *The Odd Couple.*

ADDENDUM TO SEASONS
ANIMATED SATURDAY MORNING SPECIAL (1973)

"That Girl" in Wonderland
Writers: L. Frank Baum (*The Wizard of Oz* sequence); Jakob Ludwig Carl
Grimm, Wilhelm Carl Grimm (story); Stu Hample, Charles Perrault (stories);
Producers: Rankin-Bass Productions; Directors: Jules Bass, Arthur Rankin
Jr.; Cast: Marlo Thomas (Ann Marie's voice); Patricia Bright, Dick Heymeyer,
Rhoda Mann, Ted Schwartz (other voices)

In this cartoon feature, former actress Ann Marie is an editor for a
children's book publisher. She daydreams while preparing a book of
fairytales and imagines herself as the various heroines of *The Wizard
of Oz, Snow White, Sleeping Beauty, Cinderella,* and *Goldilocks.* All
the stories become mixed up in her mind and everything ends happily.

Episode Guide by Title

This is a listing of all the episodes of *That Girl,* followed by the date of the episode and its number.

Absence Makes the Heart Grow Nervous (Part One of the
    Philadelphia Story) (10/12/67) **36**
All About Ann (12/1/66) **13**
All's Well That Ends (3/26/70) **112**
Among My Souvenirs (1/5/67) **17**
Anatomy of a Blunder (10/6/66) **5**
Ann vs. Secretary (12/5/68) **71**
Apartment, The (10/5/67) **35**
At the Drop of a Budget (10/16/69) **91**
Author, Author (3/30/67) **29**
Bad Day at Marvin Gardens (3/20/69) **85**
Beard, The (4/11/68) **58**
Beware of Actors Bearing Gifts (12/15/66) **15**
Black, White and Read All Over (9/21/67) **33**
Break a Leg (11/10/66) **10**
Call of the Wild (1/25/68) **50**
Chef's Night Out (2/12/71) **131**
Christmas and the Hard Luck Kid (12/22/66) **16**
Collaborators, The (11/2/67) **39**
Counter-Proposal (9/25/70) **113**
Dark on Top of Everything Else (1/16/69) **76**
Decision Before Dawn (12/12/68) **72**
Defiant One, The (2/27/69) **82**
Detective Story, The (3/14/68) **55**

When in Rome (11/9/67) **40**
Write Is Wrong (11/6/69) **94**
You Have to Know Someone to Be Unknown (3/9/67) **26**

Selected Bibliography

In addition to the author's interviews with Marlo Thomas, Sam Denoff, Bill Persky, Ronald Jacobs, Gloria Steinem, and Susan L. Dworkin, the author consulted the author consulted the following articles, transcripts, and books.

Alley, Robert S. and Brown, Irby B. *Love Is All Around—The Making of The Mary Tyler Moore Show*. New York: Delta, 1989.
_____. *Murphy Brown—Anatomy of a Sitcom*. New York: Delta, 1990.
Amory, Cleveland. "Review: 'That Girl.'" *TV Guide*, October 8, 1966.
Andrews, Bart. *The I Love Lucy Book*. New York: Doubleday & Co., 1985.
"Blasts From the Past." *Globe*. March 11, 1997.
Brooks, Tim and Marsh, Earle. *The Complete Directory to Prime Time Network and Cable TV Shows, 1946–Present*. New York: Ballantine Books, 1995.
Butterfield, Alan, Ely, Suzanne, Fitz, Reginald, and Keck, William. "Marlo Thomas: My 'That Girl' Co-star Didn't Have to Die." *National Enquirer*, November 22, 1996.
"Choice Reruns." *Entertainment Weekly*, July 22, 1994.
Efron, Edith. "I Can." *TV Guide*, May 17, 1969.
Givens, Bill. "Make Room for Marlo." *Memphis*, Volume XVII, Number 11, February 1993.
Gordinier, Jeff (with reporting by Poland, David). "That Guy." *Entertainment Weekly* November 18, 1996.
Hall, Carla. "For Women in Sitcoms, It's the Next Generation." *Los Angeles Times*, May 18, 1998.
Hano, Arnold. "The Velvet Steam Roller." *TV Guide*, November 12, 1966.
Harris, Jay S. *TV Guide—The First 25 Years*. New York: Simon and Schuster, 1978.
Harrison, Dan and Habeeb, Bill. *Inside Mayberry*. New York: Harper Perennial, 1994.
Heldenfels, R. D. Jones, *Television's Greatest Year: 1954*. New York: Continuum, 1994.
Hoaglin, Jess. "Where are they Now?: Rosemary DeCamp." *Tolucan/Canyon Crier/Valley Life*, July 28, 1993.

Hobson, Dick. "She Worked with Orson Wells When He was Thin." *TV Guide*, July 5, 1969.

Hunt, Bob. "That Girl Marlo." *Catholic Miss*, December 1966.

Jewel, Dan. "Chatter." *People*, May 6, 1996.

Jones, Gerard. *Honey, I'm Home*. New York: Grove Weidenfeld, 1992.

Kaplan, James. "That Woman." *TV Guide*, December 10, 1994.

Kim, Jae-Ha. *Best of Friends*. New York: HarperPerennial, 1995.

Kuczynski, Alex. "That Girl, All Grown Up." *New York Times*, February 22, 1998.

Mackin, Tom. "That Girl Grows Up." *Newark Evening News*, June 26, 1968.

McCormick, Bernard. "I Know Her—That's What's-His-Name's Daughter." *TV Guide*, October 7, 1967.

McDonald, Stef. "A Classic Turns 25." *TV Guide*, March 14, 1998.

_____. "Classy Reunions: 'That Girl.'" *TV Guide*, August 10, 1996.

McNeil, Alex. *Total Television*. New York: Penguin, 1996.

Michaleson, Judith. "In the Prime of My Craft Now." *Los Angeles Times*, November 7, 1992.

Oliver, Myrna. "Obituary: Ted Bessell; Actor, Director, Co-starred in 'That Girl.'" *Los Angeles Times*, November 9, 1996.

Parish, James Robert and Terrace, Vincent. *The Complete Actors' Television Credits, 1948–1988*. (Two-volume set, second edition). Metuchen, New Jersey: The Scarecrow Press, 1990.

Peer, Kurt. *TV Tie-Ins*. Tucson, AZ: Neptune Publishing, 1997.

Prelutsky, Burt. "I Just Care a Lot." *TV Guide*, December 10, 1977.

Radcliffe, Donnie. "That Girl is Some Girl." *Washington Evening Star*, September 2, 1968.

Raddatz, Leslie. "In Search of Marlo." *TV Guide*, August 8, 1970.

_____. "Mother, Miss Independence Has Ants." *TV Guide*, December 2, 1967.

Ritchie, Michael. *Please Stand By*. Woodstock, New York: The Overlook Press, 1994.

Rollin, Betty. "That Girl is Some Girl." *Look*, October 17, 1967.

Sackett, Susan. *Prime Time Hits*. New York: Billboard Books, 1993.

Sanders, Coyne Steven and Gilbert, Tom. *Desilu*. New York: William Morrow & Co., 1993.

Schindler, Rick. "Ted Bessell." *TV Guide*, November 2, 1996.

"Secret Ted Bessell took to the grave." *Globe*. October 22, 1996.

Seger, Linda. *When Women Call the Shots*. New York: Henry Holt and Company, 1996.

Smith, Ronald L. *Sweethearts of '60s TV*. New York: St. Martin's Press, 1989.

Stein, Joel. "Q&A: Marlo Thomas." *People*, March 9, 1998.

Stone, Judy. "And Now—Make Room for Marlo." *New York Times*, September 4, 1966.

"That Girl and Those Friends." *TV Guide*, June 8, 1996.

"Ted Bessell, Boyfriend in 'That Girl'—Obituary." *Los Angeles Daily News*, November 9, 1996.

Terrace, Vincent. *Television Specials*. Jefferson, North Carolina and London: McFarland & Co., 1995.

Waldron, Vince. *The Official Dick Van Dyke Show Book*. New York: Hyperion, 1994.

Index

About the Author

Stephen Cole is very theatrical. He has written two other books, including *Noël Coward—A Bio-Bibliography*. As a lyricist-librettist, he has written the musicals *Dodsworth* (produced, starring Hal Linden and Dee Hoty), *After the Fair* (produced off-Broadway and around the country), *Grossinger's* (produced, starring Gavin MacLeod and Ruta Lee), and *The Night of the Hunter* (concept CD starring Ron Raines, Sally Mayes, and Dorothy Loudon; songbook available in stores). He has also written songs and special material for Christine Baranski, Dorothy Loudon, JoAnne Worley, Tyne Daly, and Marlo Thomas.

Mr. Cole has won several awards for his musicals, including the prestigious Leon Rabin Award for Best New Play or Musical of 1997 for *After the Fair*. He lives in the Chelsea section of his native New York City with Lulu (a loud dog), and Max (a quiet cat). Mr. Cole attended Brooklyn College and watched *That Girl* whenever he wasn't sleeping. He is also known as "Mr. Broadway" and can be queried on the Internet at www.broadwayarchive.com.